WHOLESOME GOURMET

THE ART OF GLUTEN-FREE CUISINE

WHOLESOME RECIPES ALSO FREE OF MILK, CORN, YEAST & SUGAR

STEVEN WINKLER, R.N.C.

Illustrations by Steven Winkler, RNC

National Library of Canada Cataloguing in Publication

Winkler, Steven, 1961-
    Wholesome gourmet : the art of gluten-free cuisine / Steven Winkler.

Includes index.
ISBN 1-55395-019-4

1. Gluten-free diet--Recipes. 2. Milk-free diet--Recipes.
3. Yeast-free diet--Recipes. 4. Sugar-free diet--Recipes. I. Title.

RM237.86.W55 2002   641.5'631   C2002-904098-1

Printed in Victoria, Canada

This book was published *on-demand* in cooperation with Trafford Publishing.
On-demand publishing is a unique process and service of making a book available for retail sale to the public taking advantage of on-demand manufacturing and Internet marketing. **On-demand publishing** includes promotions, retail sales, manufacturing, order fulfilment, accounting and collecting royalties on behalf of the author.

Suite 6E, 2333 Government St., Victoria, B.C. V8T 4P4, CANADA
Phone   250-383-6864   Toll-free   1-888-232-4444 (Canada & US)
Fax   250-383-6804   E-mail   sales@trafford.com
Web site   www.trafford.com   TRAFFORD PUBLISHING IS A DIVISION OF TRAFFORD HOLDINGS LTD.
Trafford Catalogue #02-0733   www.trafford.com/robots/02-0733.html

10   9   8   7   6   5   4

This book is dedicated to all whose lives are affected by a physical condition where their diet needs to be restricted, and to those who choose wholesome foods and a wholesome way of life.

I would like to thank all the people who were my 'guinea pigs' in taste testing my foods/recipes, and in return, gave me their honest opinion. Thanks also to all who supported and helped me with this book, ...you know who you are.

also

Thanks to Mother Earth for providing us with wholesome foods.

Special thanks to my mother, Elizabeth, and father, Lorne, for their continued love and support, and along with my grand parents for providing me with creative cooking skills.

CONTENTS

Preface   iv

About The Author   vi

Introduction   vii

Measures Table   ix

Tips, Hints & Other Tidbits   1

Nut, Seed & Other Milks   9

Food Glossary   12

Breakfasts, Breads & Baked Goods   19

Soups & Stews   53

Vegetable Salads & Vegetables   93

Salad Dressings, Sauces & Accompaniments   135

Meat, Poultry & Fish   173

Pasta, Grains & Legumes   205

Wraps & Pie Crusts   245

Desserts & Sweets   271

Syrups, Toppings, Puddings & Ice Milks   303

Index   323

Preface

With my own set of health problems, throughout the years of my life, I eventually discovered that I had food sensitivities/allergies. Once finding out what foods, etc. caused adverse reactions within my body and what I needed to avoid, my search began for allowable foods. At first, changing to a gluten-free diet was a little difficult to adapt to. It wasn't easy, and there was very little available in the way of gluten-free foods. And what was, or eventually became available was either too expensive or contained questionable ingredients. I thought, "how could people afford to eat this way, especially, if it were to be for the rest of their lives." I found many of these 'new' foods were also not too palatable. As I always checked for ingredients, I noticed the main ingredient in gluten-free breads and baked goods quite often was corn or potato starch-not that nutritious.

Along with my passion for cooking and for healthy, simple living, I decided to create my own recipes. Foods that were not only wholesome, flavourful and nutritious I could once again enjoy, but foods that all could enjoy. So I spent many hours in the kitchen, creating and conjuring recipes that where specifically gluten-free, and that also provided substitutes for other common allergenic foods.

Trying to create gluten-free breads and other baked goods was probably my biggest task. Without gluten, these foods do not hold together well and the taste can be somewhat bitter. Finding and testing ingredients that were relatively safe (hypo-allergenic) and pleasing to the palate was another task I was confronted with. Once I overcame these obstacles, I was on my way. As I created new recipes, the prepared food(s) where shared with family and friends, and in return I would await their feedback. I would then work on fine-tuning the recipe and where I could, incorporate substitutes for certain ingredients.

I then became more adventurous and started to make complete meals for groups of people. These meals showed how certain foods or ingredients can be combined or incorporated with other foods and/or ingredients to produce a pleasing taste, be wholesome, nutritious and simple to prepare.

This book is a collection of recipes I have created and worked long and hard at, which I now wish to share with you. Enjoy!

Steven Winkler

Note: This book is not intended to replace medical diagnosis and/or medical treatment and does not make any medical claims. The use of this book and its information is to be used as a guide and for support for preparing and cooking wholesome, nutritious dishes (meals) for people with special dietary needs or for those who simply want to improve their diet.

About The Author

Steven Winkler has been a Registered Nutritional Consultant (R.N.C.) since 1994. Through his own adversity, he has become passionate in alternative (complimentary) healing arts and wholesome living. Along with his nutritional training, Steven is also a Certified Herbalist, and certified in Specialized and Nutritional Kinesiology, Touch For Health, and High Touch Acupressure. He has also designed, developed and conducted workshops on Energy Balancing and Meditation. Steven believes the only way to true health is with a balance of body, mind and spirit.

Working in a private practice, Steven has developed dietary programs and supplementation schedules for his clients. He helps to educate them about the consequences of specific food choices, and what the body needs nutritionally in order to do its own normalizing. He also assesses and tests for nutritional weaknesses and helps to support clients by providing them with advice on such topics as: food selection and preparation, detection and management of food sensitivities, evaluation of nutritional deficiencies (or excesses), and the use of food supplements. Above all, he educates his clients to help themselves.

Living a spiritual and wholesome way of life, Steven has shared his passion for healthy foods and wholesome dining since the early 90's with his family, friends, and all who appreciate goodness and health. He prepares wholesome, nutritious and savory recipes and meals for people with special dietary needs and to those whom just want to eat healthier.

Steven currently makes his home in Waterloo, Ontario (Canada), where he continues to teach clients, create new recipes, conduct dinner parties and enjoy life.

Introduction

If you are one of the growing number of people with a sensitivity or allergy to gluten, then this book is for you. If you are someone who just wants to improve your eating habits, then this book is also for you. All recipes in *Wholesome Gourmet* are gluten-free, as well as milk-free (dairy), yeast-free and corn-free. Along with a food glossary and many important tips, this book contains recipes for; milk alternatives (nut and seed milks); cereals and breads; soups and stews; vegetables, salads and dressings; meats, fish and poultry; pasta, grains and legumes; wraps (rice paper and crepes); desserts and sweets; and, syrups, puddings and ice milks.

Besides gluten, the most common food sensitivities, including both allergies and intolerances, are: cow's milk, lactose, wheat, corn, yeast, sucrose (table sugar), caffeine, soy, eggs, shellfish, peanuts, pork, beef, oranges, strawberries, chocolate, foods from the nightshade family (potatoes, eggplant, tomatoes, peppers), and food additives and preservatives. Trying to find prepared foods that doesn't contain any of these in its list of ingredients, are few and far between, and what can be found can be quite expensive or tasteless.

There are many cookbooks available that are geared towards healthy eating and food sensitivities. Some of these books are quite good, but many contain hard to find or questionable ingredients, contain few, if any, substitutes for common food allergens and can be labor intensive. *Wholesome Gourmet* does its best to eliminate these problems. The recipes where created with consideration using wholesome ingredients, nutrition value, simplicity and pleasure of taste.

This book does contain recipes with some common foods people can be sensitive to, but for some people this isn't a concern. Where possible, substitutes are given so most can enjoy them.

Vegetarians can enjoy this book, too. Many meat-based (animal protein) recipes have a vegetarian substitute, usually tofu or beans. Tofu has little taste and is very easy to work with. Tofu takes on the flavours of other foods or ingredients it is prepared or cooked with in any given dish.

Where possible, organic foods and ingredients are used, and if available, always recommended. Organics foods and their sources are growing rapidly, making them much more available and easier to find. When choosing organic foods, you are choosing foods closest to what Mother Nature intended and has provided for us since eternity.

All foods and ingredients used in this book can be purchased in most health or natural food markets and specialty stores. Meats and other animal proteins can also be purchased at farmers markets or butcher shops. If your local store does not carry a certain product, ask them to order it for you. If they say they can't or it is not available, find another store that will because these foods are available to all health markets.

Last of all, you don't have to be gluten sensitive to enjoy this book and its recipes. You don't have to be a 'health-nut' either. *Wholesome Gourmet* contains recipes that are flavourful and nutritionally sound. Try this: Prepare a meal or any of the following recipes for someone who is a health or natural food antagonist, without them knowing before hand what they are eating. I am certain they will be pleasantly surprised. Most people cannot tell the difference in taste, in a dish prepared with an ingredient substitute, e.g. something made with a milk alternative instead of cow's milk, a sweet made with rice flour and sucanat or apple butter instead of wheat and sucrose, chili made with ground turkey or tofu instead of beef, or a pasta dish made with rice noodles instead of durum semolina (wheat).

Measures Table

Abbreviations

tsp. = teaspoon
Tbsp. = tablespoon
oz. = ounce
lb. = pound
ml = millilitre
gm = gram

Standard (Imperial) Measurements

Dash = less than 1/8 tsp.
3 tsp. = 1 Tbsp.
2 Tbsp. = 1/8 cup
4 Tbsp. = ¼ cup
5 Tbsp. + 1 tsp. = 1/3 cup
8 Tbsp. = ½ cup
16 Tbsp. = 1 cup
1 oz. = 2 Tbsp.
4 oz. = ½ cup
8 oz. = 1 cup

Metric Measurements

1 tsp. = 5 ml
1 Tbsp. = 15 ml
1/8 cup = 30 ml
¼ cup = 60 ml
1/3 cup = 80 ml
½ cup = 120 ml
1 cup = 240 ml
1 oz. = 28 gm
4 oz. = 113 gm
8 oz. = 227 gm
16 oz. (1 lb.) = 454 gm

TIPS, HINTS & OTHER TIDBITS

❖ For better quality and nutritional value, use organic ingredients and GMO free foods whenever possible. Purchase foods that are also non-irradiated.

   Note: Foods are irradiated in order to kill of any bacteria, fungus, mold, etc., and to extend shelf life. Although this may seem to make the food safer to eat, the amount of radiation used to treat food is overkill. Food irradiation decreases food value by up to 80%, produces free radicals and other carcinogens including formaldehyde, benzene, etc. In addition, irradiation does not kill all bacteria, so in time resistant strains of bacteria will be produced, making irradiation a futile method of decontamination.

❖ All baking and cooking times are approximate. Ovens and stoves come in different sizes and means of producing heat. This can vary the temperature and heating times, adjust accordingly.

❖ There is a concern with the safety of various materials used in the manufacturing of bake and cookware. For some people, the use of certain materials (metals, plastics, etc.) can have ill or harmful effects. Remember, we live in a 'buyer beware' world. Stainless steel and glass are the best choices for oven and cookware.

   Note: Non-stick cookware is generally safe. But, once the coating, which is usually Teflon, starts to peel or come off, the metal underneath (usually aluminum) leeches out and is absorbed into the food. This can then cause over exposure to aluminum or other toxic metals, making it harmful to those susceptible.

❖ **Salt & Pepper**
1. Always use unbleached, whole or coarse sea or Celtic sea salts and whole peppercorns, and use salt and pepper mills to grind them. Using spice mills ensures that seasonings will always be fresh, tastier and better for the body. Refined table salt contains sugar (dextrose), up to 20 kinds of chemical additives and has no trace minerals, except for the added potassium iodine. It is chemically bleached and then sprayed with an emulsifier, called sodium aluminosilicate, so that the grains don't stick together. Pre-ground pepper can contain formaldehyde from the manufacturing process. This makes these 'products' unfit for human consumption.
2. Kelp, a type of seaweed, can be used as a substitute or combined with sea salts. Kelp contains the biologically active form of iodine along with other minerals and trace elements. Kelp comes in flakes or pre-ground.
3. Sea salt contains little iodine; combining it with kelp makes it a complete smorgasbord of nutrients and trace elements.

❖ **Herbs & Spices**
1. Purchase herbs and spices that are organic or at the least, non-irradiated.
2. Fresh herbs are added to the last 15-20 minutes of cooking time and dried herbs are added at the beginning of cooking.
3. When recipes call for a ground herb, use the whole form of the herb and grind it into a powder. Dried herbs, when purchased pre-ground or powdered, don't ordinarily have a long shelf life. After about 1 year, they start to lose their flavour and potency. Use dried herbs in their whole form, such as; leaf, seed, root or flakes. Rub dried leaf herbs between fingers to bring out flavour and increase potency. Harder herbs, such as: cumin seeds, rosemary, chili flakes, etc., can be ground with a mortar & pestle or a spice mill.

4. A mortar & pestle and/or a spice mill are great tools to have for grinding herbs and spices. Most spice mills have an adjustment for granule size.
5. In recipes, fresh or dried herbs can be replaced with its opposite. A basic rule of thumb is: use approximately 4-6 times, or more, fresh herbs than dried herbs.
6. Unless otherwise stated, most recipes are made with a mild to medium flavoured taste. Add extra spices to make dishes 'hotter' or spicier.

❖ **Butter**
1. Butter is used in many recipes throughout this book. Butter is a much better choice than any margarine or vegetable spread and any vegetable oil, except olive. Margarines and vegetable oils are toxic and unfit for human consumption because they contain high levels of trans fatty acids. And, because they are processed, they offer little, if any, nutritional value. Unlike margarine and vegetable oils, butter is chemically stable which makes it easier for the body to assimilate.
2. Butter contains short and medium chain fatty acids that the body uses for energy, instead of being stored in the adipose (fat) tissue. Butter contains fat-soluble vitamins, is rich in lecithin and trace minerals.
3. Butter also contains butyric and lauric fatty acids. These fatty acids have anti-fungal, anti-bacterial and anti-cancerous properties. Butter is a rich source of conjugated linoleic acid (CLA). Research has shown CLA kills cancer cells and reduces fatty streak formation in the coronary arteries.
4. Always use organic unsalted butter. Commercial butter contains high amounts of synthetic hormones, antibiotic, pesticide and other drug and chemical residues.

❖ Ghee

1. Some recipes call for "ghee" as an oil substitute. Ghee is clarified butter. It is known as an ancient holy food and is valued in Ayurvedic medicine. Ghee is one of the best forms of fat for the body. It is easier to digest than butter and is less mucous forming. Ghee has an array of healing properties. When food is prepared with ghee, the nutrients and flavours are enhanced.

2. To make ghee: using only a glass or stainless steel sauce pan, heat 1 lb. of <u>unsalted</u> butter over medium heat. After butter melts, lower heat to medium-low and let simmer, uncovered. Remove froth as it appears on top. After approximately 30 minutes the butter will start to boil silently, become golden yellow, and have somewhat of a popcorn odor. The ghee is done at this point. Let the ghee cool slightly and then, using a fine strainer, strain it into a <u>glass jar</u>. During this heating process, the water evaporates and the milk solids precipitate out. This removes the components that cause butter to spoil.

3. Ghee can be stored either in the refrigerator or at room temperature, indefinitely.

❖ Fats & Oils

- For sautéing on high settings, the best choices are; ghee, unsalted butter, coconut butter or oil, and macadamia nut oil.
- For light sautéing, the best choices are; all of the above plus, olive oil, almond oil, walnut oil, and sesame oil.
- For baking and cooking in general, the best choices are; ghee, unsalted butter, macadamia nut oil, coconut butter or oil, olive oil, almond oil, and walnut oil.
- For salad dressings, the best choices are; flax seed oil, pumpkin seed oil, hemp seed oil, extra virgin olive oil, and to a little lesser degree; almond oil, walnut oil, macadamia nut oil, and sesame oil.

1. When used in cooking and baking, saturated fats (ghee, butter, coconut butter and oil) and monounsaturated fats (olive oil, almond, walnut, macadamia and sesame oils) are chemically more stable under heat than polyunsaturated fats (vegetable oils).

2. Purchase all oils that are in opaque containers and have preferably been kept under refrigeration, especially flax, pumpkin and hemp seed oils. Make sure all purchased oils have been manufactured by 'cold pressing'. Once opened, all oils require refrigeration. Some oils, like olive, thicken or gel when refrigerated. To liquefy, bring out to room temperature a few minutes before using or keep a small amount-enough that will be used in a week-stored at room temperature. Properly stored oils, preserves the essential fatty acids (EFA's) and prevents them from going rancid, which produces trans fatty acids (free radicals).

3. *Note:* Because it is a saturated fat, there are a lot of misconceptions about coconut butter/oil. This oil is very stable under heat. Coconut butter/oil is very rich in a fatty acid called, lauric acid (same as in butter). Lauric acid is a powerful anti-fungal and anti-bacterial when converted to monolaurin in the intestines. Coconut butter/oil also contains caprylic acid, another powerful anti-fungal.

4. When oiling bakeware and cookware, use olive oil, ghee, unsalted butter, coconut butter/oil macadamia nut oil or an olive oil cooking spray.

5. *Note:* Don't worry about frying foods in olive oil, as in the recipe 'Fried Zucchini Lasagna'. Olive oil needs to be 350 degrees before it burns and medium-high heat will not produce this temperature when there is enough oil in the pan. Sautéing with high temperatures is not recommended with olive oil.

❖ **Sweeteners**

1. Raw sugar, 'sucanat', is the only powdered or granulated dried form of sweetener used in this book. This is a 'true' raw sugar that maintains most of its nutrients after processing. Some sugars that are labeled as 'raw' or 'natural', are actually refined white sugars mixed with molasses and colour additives, and then crystallized.

2. Liquid and other forms of sugar used are; honey (always purchase unpasteurized), brown rice syrup, unsweetened (sugar-free) jams or fruit spreads, apple or fruit butters and unsweetened (sugar-free) fruit juices. (A couple of recipes may use maple syrup or molasses, usually as a substitute.)

3. Other kinds of sweeteners that are not used because of their sweetness, aftertaste or availability, are; amazake, maple sugar, date sugar, fructose, sorghum and malts or barley malt (contains gluten).

4. Another sweetener gaining popularity these days is 'honey leaf', a.k.a. 'stevia'. Honey leaf is a potent herb sweetener that does not affect blood sugar, making it very promising for those with diabetes and other blood sugar handling problems. Honey leaf comes in powdered or liquid form. Approximately 1-3 drops of liquid honey leaf will sweeten 1 cup of liquid. There is a bitter aftertaste when using this form of sweetener. The manufacturing process of certain brands of honey leaf has rectified this problem, although some claim there is still a bitter aftertaste.

Note: At time of this publication, there is controversy over the safety of the use and processing of this herb sweetener.

Therefore, honey leaf was not experimented with in any recipe.

❖ Cheese & Other Dairy Substitutes

1. Rice, soy and almond cheeses can be and are substituted for cow's milk cheese. These types of cheese come in different flavours and make a wonderful substitute for cow's milk cheese. When melted with other foods, most cannot tell the difference between these types of cheese and cow's milk cheese. These cheese substitutes do, however, contain casein, a cow's milk protein. Some brands do not contain casein and will be labeled as 'dairy-free'.

2. Goat's milk cheese is also used in many recipes. Goat's milk cheese is more nutritionally balanced and easier to tolerate than cow's milk cheese.

3. Goat's milk or soy yogurt is also used as a substitute for cow's milk yogurt.

❖ Liquid Aminos

1. Some recipes call for 'liquid aminos'. This is a substitute for soy sauce and/or tamari. Unlike commercial brands of soy sauce, liquid aminos is a pure liquid soy protein that is non-fermented and does not contain alcohol, additives and wheat. Liquid aminos can be purchased in health food stores and grocery stores that have a health/natural food section and will go by the name, 'Bragg, All Purpose Seasoning'.

❖ Extracts

Always use pure extracts, not artificial and extracts that are alcohol-free or contain a grain alcohol. Pure extracts are more expensive than their counterparts but are better quality and worth the price. Pure extracts are tastier and do not have an aftertaste like some commercial artificial extracts do. Artificial or 'not pure' extracts contain propylene glycol, a known toxin, and other additives.

❖ **Dried Fruit**

Use organic and unsulfured dried fruit whenever possible. Non-organic dried fruit can be contaminated with concentrated traces of pesticide residues and also contain preservatives, additives and chemicals. Dried fruit can also carry mold, fungus, and harbour parasites and their eggs. Always wash and rinse dried fruit well and pre-soak in boiling water to kill any bacteria, mold, etc., it may be carrying. Pre-soaking also re-hydrates dried fruit, making it easier for digestion and assimilation. One way to rectify the problem of contaminated dried fruit is to dry your own fruit in a food dehydrator.

Note: There are many kinds of sport and fruit bars on the market these days. These 'convenient' bars are concentrated with lots of 'stuff', so it is important to drinks lots of water when consuming these products, in order to make it easier for digestion and assimilation. Many of these bars also contain a lot of sugar/s.

❖ **Wine**

The purpose of wine [some may say wine is not a wholesome food, although a little alcohol (wine) is fine, when consumed in moderation] in certain recipes is to add, or enhance the flavour of foods. When wine is added to foods during the cooking process, the alcohol burns off leaving only the flavour. As most wines have added additives or preservatives, it is best to find an organic source or wines free of chemicals. Choose good quality wines for cooking. The better quality wine will assure better-flavoured foods; so-called cooking wines are of poor quality and contain additives and/or preservatives. Use dry wines for main dishes and sweeter wines for dessert dishes. Wine, especially red, contains proanthocyanidins (flavonoids), which have antioxidant capabilities.

Nut, Seed & Other Milks

❖ The milks used throughout this book are; almond milk, sesame seed milk, pumpkin seed milk, cashew milk, and coconut milk. They are a substitute for dairy milks.

❖ Nut and seed milks are very nutritious; they are rich in calcium, minerals, essential fatty acids and enzymes.

❖ Nut and seed milks have a creamy texture.

❖ <u>To make nut and seed milks</u>: use 1/3 cup raw nuts or seeds to 2 cups of water. Blend mixture in a blender for 2 or more minutes, on high speed. Milk may then be strained, but is not necessary. Seeds that still contain their hull and nuts that still contain their skins will produce a thicker, 'gritty-like' milk. Straining nut/seed milks makes them smoother and less 'gritty'. If straining: it is best to use a medium type of sieve rather than a fine one. If sieve is too fine, it may take a while to strain milk.

> *Hint:* Nuts can be pre-softened, by soaking them in water for a few hours or overnight before blending. Pre-soaking helps to soften the meat of the nut, making it easier to blend and a smoother milk. Water does not need to be discarded before blending. Seeds do not need pre-soaking.
> Also, nuts can be blanched beforehand. To blanch nuts: place nuts in a skillet and add enough water to cover. Turn heat on high. As soon as water starts to boil, remove from heat and let sit for 1-2 minutes. Skins will then slip off easily.

❖ Store nut and seed milks in the refrigerator for up to 7 days. Store milks, preferably, in glass jars and shake before using.

❖ Nut and seed milks can be sweetened with honey, brown rice syrup, maple syrup or sucanat. Pure vanilla extract or any pure flavoured extract can be added. Carob/cocoa powder or syrup can also be added.

❖ Almost any nut or seed can create wonderful milk. Experiment with different milk combinations.

❖ Purchase only nuts and seeds that are raw and organic, or at the very least, non-irradiated, and that have preferably been stored in the refrigerator, especially peanuts and non-irradiated nuts and seeds. Nuts and seeds can carry dangerous molds (aflatoxin), which are very toxic to the body. When the outer shell or hull of nuts and seeds is removed, exposure to light, oxygen and heat causes them to deteriorate and become rancid.

❖ Nuts and seeds can be pre-ground in a blender, food processor or coffee bean (nut and seed) grinder; do not over process. Store ground nuts and seeds in the refrigerator. Do not purchase pre-ground nuts and seeds that are stored at room temperature or exposed to light or heat, they are rancid and more than likely carrying dangerous molds and toxins.

❖ Use plain nut or seed milks in soups and main dishes, and sweetened milks in desserts, baked goods, fruit smoothies and ices.

❖ Almond milk can be purchased from health food and grocery stores. These milks are sweetened and not recommended for many recipes. (Barley malt, which contains gluten, is one of the sweeteners used in these milks) Store purchased almond milks are generally pasteurized. This kills or alters the vitamins, minerals and enzymes in the milk. Store purchased almond milks may be convenient, but it is better and more economical to make your own nut and seed milks.

❖ Although rice and soy milks are generally not used in this book, they may be substituted in some recipes. Nut and seed milks are nutritionally superior to rice and soy milks. Rice milks tend to be more watery in consistency and sweeter than other milks. Store bought milks are okay in any dessert or 'sweet' recipe; sweetener may need to be adjusted.

❖ Some recipes call for coconut milk. Use good quality canned coconut milk free of preservatives. Coconut milk can also be made by; combining ¼-1/3 cup unsweetened, shredded coconut with 1 cup hot water, blend on high speed, in a blender, for 1-2 minutes; strain if needed. Some grocery stores carry a pure creamed coconut (dry coconut) that is free of preservatives. By adding hot water to it, it makes coconut milk. This product can be found in the international section of the grocery store or in international food marts. Coconut milks keeps for up to 3 days under refrigeration.

Food Glossary

Amaranth: A high protein grain-like food that is rich in calcium, magnesium, iron, folic acid and fibre. Amaranth has a grainy nut-like flavour. Always purchase fresh amaranth flour, preferably kept under refrigeration. If the flour sits at room temperature too long it becomes rancid and has an unpleasant taste.

Almond butter: Lightly roasted almonds, ground until creamy, like peanut butter.

Almond milk: A good dairy substitute that is rich in protein, calcium and essential fatty acids.

Apple cider vinegar: Vinegar made from fermented apples (apple cider). It contains pectins, trace minerals, beneficial bacteria and enzymes. Apple cider vinegar is an acid-alkaline balancer and has many other medicinal uses. It is used in salad dressings, marinades, sauces, etc. Commercial vinegars have little, if any, nutritional value and can be harmful to the body over time.

Arrowroot flour: Starchy flour made from a dried root (tuber) of a tropical plant similar to the cassava plant. The properties and its uses are the same as tapioca flour.

Baking powder: see page 28.

Brown rice syrup: A ground rice with added enzymes cooked to a slurry. This process converts the starches to complex sugars. It is less sweet than honey.

Buckwheat flour: A grain-like food with moderate amounts of protein, fibre and minerals. Comes in dark and light flours, the darker the flour the stronger the flavour.

Butters; nut & seed: Nuts or seeds ground until creamy, like peanut butter.

Carob powder/chips: A seedpod, called St. John's bread that comes from a Mediterranean evergreen tree, ground into a powder. It is a legume that is used as a chocolate substitute. Carob is alkaline and contains a good source of natural sugar. It is also rich in minerals, low in starch and fat. Carob is caffeine-free.

Celtic sea salt: A naturally moist sea salt that has a perfect balance of essential trace minerals (electrolytes) the body requires. Celtic sea salt has many medicinal applications. It comes in fine, medium and coarse grains.

Cheese substitutes; rice, soy & almond: A dairy substitute for cheese but contains casein, a milk protein. Some brands are casein-free and will be labeled as 'dairy-free'. These cheese substitutes come in blocks, slices, spreads and different flavours, and some brands also make cream cheese, sour cream, etc.

Chickpeas & flour: A legume used mainly in Middle Eastern cuisine. Chickpeas, also called garbanzo beans, are easier to digest than most beans. They are rich in protein, calcium, phosphorus, potassium and iron. Chickpea flour is a good thickening agent for soups, stews, sauces, etc.

Cream of tartar: A by-product from grapes during wine making, used as an acidic ingredient in baking powder.

Egg substitutes: Substitutes are shown in selective recipes. The typical one used is: 1 Tbsp. ground flax seeds mixed in 3 Tbsp. of water; this replaces one egg.

Emu, meat: A bird that resembles the ostrich, but slightly smaller. Emu is a very lean red meat rich in protein, iron and nutrients, the flavour resembling that of a good cut of beef. Emu products (meat, oils and cosmetics) are becoming more popular, making them easier to find.

Flakes; rice, quinoa or soy: Pressed and steam-rolled whole raw rice, quinoa or soy that are crushed or chopped after rolling. Flakes cook very quickly.

Flax seeds: A very nutritious seed high in nutrients and fibre. Flax seeds have a nutty flavour and mild laxative effect. Add fresh ground flax seeds to salads, yogurts, cooked cereals, etc. Flax seeds are also used as an egg substitute (see egg substitute). To keep ground flax seeds from spoiling and going rancid keep them refrigerated in an opaque container.

Flax seed oil: Oil pressed from flax seeds, rich in essential fatty acids (omega 3'S). Always purchase flax seed oil that is kept under refrigeration and never heat the oil. Flax seed oil has many medicinal applications.

Garam masala: An Indian spice blend usually containing, black pepper, cardamom, cinnamon, cloves and cumin. It may also contain allspice, cassia, ginger and mace. Garam masala can be purchased in any East Indian market, and some health food and major grocery chain stores. Garam masala can also be home made, see page 164.

Goat's milk; cheese & yogurt: A substitute for cow's milk cheese and yogurt. Goat's milk products are more nutritionally balanced and easier to digest and tolerate than cow's milk products. Those who are sensitive or allergic to cow's milk can usually tolerate goat's milk.

Guar gum: Comes from an East Indian seed. Guar gum is used as a thickener, binder and to help non-gluten baked goods rise and hold moisture. Use guar gum in small amounts.

Hemp; seeds & flour: A very nutritious seed high in plant protein. Weight for weight, hemp seed is higher in protein than animal or fish protein. Add hemp seeds to salads, soups, cereals, baked goods, etc. Unlike flax seed, hemp seed can be made into flour. In recipes, substitute $\frac{1}{4}$ of the amount of flour called for with hemp seed flour. The flour is green in colour and has a nutty earth-like flavour.

Hemp seed oil: An excellent and rich source of essential fatty acids (EFA's), hemp seed oil is called 'nature's most perfectly balanced oil'. Hemp seed oil is the only edible oil that contains both EFA's and GLA (gamma linoleic acid). EFA's and GLA have been touted for its medicinal uses. The oil has a mild nutty flavour, a little milder than flax seed oil. Always purchase hemp seed oil that is kept under refrigeration and never heat the oil.

Kelp: A seaweed, ground into a powder, used with or as a sea salt substitute.

Lentils; brown & green: A legume used mainly in Middle Eastern cuisine. One of the easiest legumes to digest, lentils are an excellent source of folic acid. They are also rich in protein, fibre, iron and other nutrients.

Lecithin granules: A product made from soy used in bread and ice recipes. Lecithin granules acts as a binder, emulsifier and as a natural preservative.

Liquid aminos: A pure liquid soy protein used as a seasoning. It is non-fermented and contains no alcohol.

Macadamia nut; butter & oil: A rich tasting nut high in fat (EFA's) and fibre. Most of the fat in macadamia nuts are monounsaturated, the same as olive oil. This fat is chemically stable and does not break down under heat, making it very good for frying and sautéing.

Milk substitutes: Dairy-free milk substitutes made from nut and/or seeds. See page 9.

Millet: An ancient grain popular in Asia and Africa. Millet is the most alkaline of all grains and in general, an alkalizing whole food. Millet has a mild taste and is beneficial for people with delicate digestive systems. Millet is a good source of protein, is rich in magnesium, silicon and folic acid. Millet flour can have a bitter taste when used on its own. The flour is also good as a thickening agent for soups, stews, sauces, etc.

Miso: A fermented soy paste with various degrees of flavour and saltiness. The darker the colour of miso the stronger the flavour. Some varieties can contain gluten. Miso is used mainly in soups and sauces. Dissolve a small amount of miso into a little liquid and add to the end of cooking time. Never boil miso, it will kill its goodness.

Pasta, rice: Made from ground rice and water. Some contain added rice bran to increase fibre and nutrient count. Choose brown rice pastas over white varieties for its nutritional superiority and blood sugar handling qualities. Rice pastas come in a variety of shapes, such as; spaghetti, lasagna, fettuccini, elbows, penne, shells, spirals, etc. Some brands of rice pasta also contain added vegetable powder and spices.

Pumpkin; seeds & butter: A superior seed and seed butter. When compared to other nuts and seeds, pumpkin seeds have the highest amount of protein. They are rich in fibre, zinc, iron, potassium, magnesium, folic acid and an excellent source of essential fatty acids.

Pumpkin seed oil: An excellent and rich source of essential fatty acids. Pumpkin seed oil is also an anti-bacterial and is known for its ability to fight parasitic infections. It has a mild flavour and its use is the same as flax seed or hemp seed oil.

Quinoa: A grain-like food, quinoa means 'mother grain" and was the main staple for the Inca Indians. It is virtually the best vegetable source of protein because of its ideal balance of amino acids. Quinoa is also a rich source of calcium, iron, potassium, magnesium and folic acid. Rinse quinoa well in order to remove the bitter tasting coating.

Quinoa flakes: See flakes.

Rice; brown, basmati & wild: Rice is the most balanced and easily digested grain. Rice is rich in B-complex and overall good in nutrients. Basmati rice has a distinctive nutty flavour. Wild rice, not a true type of rice but actually a seed of a wild grass, is the tastiest of all rice, having a nutty, chewy texture. Wild rice has more protein and a higher nutrient count than any other rice. Sweet brown rice is excellent used as a breakfast cereal or in rice pudding.

Rice cheese: See cheese substitutes.

Rice flakes: See flakes.

Rice paper or wraps: See page 246.

Rolled rice or soy: Pressed and steam-rolled whole raw rice or soy that cooks quickly.

Safflower threads: North America's version of saffron. Safflower is milder in flavour than true saffron.

Saffron threads: The dried stigmas from the saffron crocus flower. True saffron comes from Spain and is used to colour food and as a spice.

Sea salt: A salt that comes from seawater. True unrefined sea salt is light gray in colour and slightly moist. It is hand harvested and naturally dried by the sun and air. Sea salt contains an abundance of natural minerals and trace elements. Purchase only unbleached, whole or coarse sea salt because fine or white sea salt is usually heavily refined.

Sesame seed milk: A good dairy substitute rich in protein, calcium and other nutrients. Sesame seed milk is good for lubricating the intestinal tract.

Soy cheese: See cheese substitutes.

Soy flakes: See flakes.

Sucanat: One of the only true forms of raw sugar. Sucanat is a natural sweetener derived from dried cane juice and is less sweet than regular sugar. Sucanat is not heavily processed therefore it still contains most of its vitamins and minerals.

Tahini: Sesame seeds that are ground until creamy, like peanut butter.

Tapioca flour: Starchy grain-free flour that comes from the tubers of the cassava plant. Tapioca has a slightly sweet flavour and is used as flour in baked goods and as a thickening agent for liquids, sauces, etc. Tapioca flour is very easily tolerated.

Tofu: A soy product used as a meat or dairy substitute. Tofu is made from pressed, ground and cooked soybeans/flour and water. Tofu is rich in protein, calcium, magnesium, iron and folic acid. Tofu has little flavour, is very versatile in many dishes and easy to digest.

Breakfasts, Breads & Baked Goods

Tips On Cereal Grains 20
Cooked Whole Breakfast Grains 21
Amaranth Banana "Risotto" 22
Cooked Creamy Cereals 23
Creamy Millet with Cherries 24
Tips For Baking Breads 25
Gluten-Free Baking Powder 28
Brown Rice Bread; with eggs 29
Millet Rice Bread; with eggs 30
Tapioca Rice Bread; with eggs 31
Multi Grain Bread; with eggs 32
Small Loaf Brown Rice Bread 33
Brown Rice Bread; with flax seed 34
Tapioca Rice Bread; with flax seed 35
Multi Grain Bread; with flax seed 36
Brown Rice Bread; with gelatin 37
Rice Flatbreads 38
Quinoa Flatbreads 39
Millet Flatbreads 39
Chapattis 39
Rice & Hempseed Flatbreads 40
Millet & Hempseed Flatbreads 40
Quinoa & Hempseed Flatbreads 40
Rice 'Pancake" Flatbreads 41
Pancakes 42
Basic Egg-Free Pancakes 43
Amaranth Pancakes 44
Sweet Potato Pancakes 45
Granola 46
Scones 47
Cheese Scones 48
Tea Biscuits 49
Crust-less Quiche 50
Breakfast Crepes 51

Tips On Cereal Grains

❖ Soaking grains makes them more digestible. Grains contain phytates that bind minerals. Phytates causes a high amount of minerals in the grain to be poorly absorbed by the body. Soaking the grain corrects this problem. Whole or ground grains can be soaked.

❖ For ground grains: purchase whole grains and grind them in a grain mill, nut and seed or coffee bean grinder. Some stores will grind grains, while you wait, using a stone-ground grain mill. Store ground grains in the refrigerator because they spoil and go rancid when stored at room temperature. Grains can be purchased pre-ground providing they are kept under refrigeration.

❖ Check grains for small stones, dirt balls and other foreign objects.

❖ In general, only rice and quinoa need to be pre-washed and rinsed. Although, it is recommended that all grains be pre-washed for health and sanitary reasons. Rinse grains 2-4 times, or until the water runs clear.

❖ To start cooking, it is best to add ground grains to cool water than warm/hot water to avoid lumping together. It doesn't matter when whole grains are added.

❖ For thicker cereals use less liquid and for thinner cereals use more liquid.

Cooked Whole Breakfast Grains

Choose one of the following:
   1) $\frac{1}{4}$ cup whole amaranth
      $\frac{3}{4}$ cup liquid
   2) $\frac{1}{4}$ cup whole millet
      $\frac{3}{4}$-1 cup liquid
   3) $\frac{1}{4}$ cup whole quinoa
      $\frac{3}{4}$ cup liquid

Basic cooking method:
In a saucepan, bring grain and liquid to a boil.
Reduce heat and simmer, covered, for 20-25 minutes; or until liquid is absorbed.

• Serve warm or hot with nut or seed milk.
• Makes 1 generous or 2 small servings.
• For liquid choose: water, nut or seed milk, coconut milk or a combination.
• If grain is pre-soaked: soak overnight in the refrigerator and in the morning, stir once before cooking.

Variations: add any of the following, before or after cooking, (combinations are endless).
❖ *Fresh fruit; whole, sliced, mashed or pureed.*
❖ *Pure extracts; vanilla, almond, lemon, orange, peppermint or maple.*
❖ *Sweeteners; honey, brown rice syrup, sucanat, jams or fruit butters.*
❖ *Carob; powder, chips or syrup.*
❖ *Spices; cinnamon, cardamom, ginger, nutmeg, orange or lemon peel, etc.*

- ❖ *Nuts or seeds; chopped or ground.*
- ❖ *Dried fruit (can be pre-soaked with grain).*
- ❖ *Protein powder; rice, soy, etc.*
- ❖ *After cooking: add ground flax seeds or hemp seeds and/or flax seed, pumpkin seed or hemp seed oil.*

Note: Adding a protein powder, seed oil and ground flax seeds or hemp seeds, makes this a complete healthy breakfast.

Amaranth Banana 'Risotto'

(An example of a cooked whole breakfast grain)

$\frac{3}{4}$ cup almond milk
3 to 4 Tbsp. whole amaranth
1 banana, sliced or mashed
$\frac{1}{2}$ tsp. vanilla or almond extract
1 tsp. carob powder
$\frac{1}{4}$ tsp. cinnamon or cardamom
1 scoop rice protein

In a saucepan, stir together all ingredients and bring to a boil.
Reduce heat and simmer, covered, for 20-25 minutes.

- Serve warm or hot with almond milk, ground flax seeds and flax seed oil.
- Makes 1-2 servings.
- For easier digestion: soak amaranth in the $\frac{3}{4}$ cup almond milk for a few hours or overnight.

Cooked Creamy Cereals

Choose one of the following:
1) ¼ cup ground amaranth
   1 cup liquid
2) ¼ cup ground millet
   1 cup liquid
3) ¼ cup ground quinoa
   7/8 –1 cup liquid
4) ¼ cup ground brown or sweet brown rice
   1 cup liquid
5) ¼ cup rice flakes
   1 cup liquid
6) 1/3 cup rolled rice
   1 cup liquid
7) 1/3 cup quinoa flakes
   1 cup liquid
8) 1/3 cup rolled soy or soy flakes
   1 cup liquid

Basic cooking method:

Add grain and liquid to a saucepan.

Cook over medium-high heat; stirring constantly until it comes to a boil. (If temperature is too hot, grains will burn and stick to bottom of pan.)

Reduce heat and cook for 2-3 minutes; stirring constantly. (This step only applies to ground grains.)

Remove from heat and cover for 5 or more minutes.

- Serve warm or hot with nut or seed milk.
- Makes 1-2 servings.
- For liquid choose: water, nut or seed milk, coconut milk or a combination.

- Although it is not necessary, pre-soaking the grains improves digestibility. Grains, when ground, do not need a long soaking time. Usually ½ to 1 hour is enough, or they can be soaked longer. Flakes do not need pre-soaking.
- Rolled rice or soy can be soaked in hot/boiling water for 10-15 minutes. They usually do not require any further cooking after soaking.
- For thicker cereals use less liquid and for thinner cereals use more liquid.
- For variations: use same as cooked whole breakfast grains on page 20-21.

Creamy Millet with Cherries

(An example of a cooked creamy cereal)

½ cup almond milk or water
½ cup coconut milk
¼ cup ground millet
1/8 cup dried cherries, diced
1-2 tsp. cherry jam (optional)
¼ tsp. almond extract
1 scoop rice protein (optional)

In a saucepan, stir together all ingredients.
Cook over medium-high heat; stirring constantly until it comes to a boil.
Reduce heat and cook for 2-3 minutes; stirring constantly.
Remove from heat and cover for 3-5 minutes.

- Serve warm or hot with almond milk and top with ground almonds, ground flax seeds and flax seed or pumpkin seed oil.
- Makes 1-2 servings.

Tips for Baking Breads

❖ Breads bake better and more evenly when the dry ingredients are mixed together <u>well</u>. Use a flour sifter or food processor to mix dry ingredients.

❖ Breads bake more easily in metal pans than non-stick pans. Non-stick pans tend to cook breads around the outside, while leaving the inside slightly under cooked. Glass pans are not recommended because breads tend to burn easily.
Note: 'Air' bakeware was not tested with these recipes.

❖ When using metal pans, lightly oil the whole inside of the pan. Wipe out any excess oil then sprinkle flour all around the inside. Turn pan upside down and tap lightly to remove excess flour.

❖ Breads tend to bake better in smaller size loaf pans. If the pan is too big, there is a greater possibility the bread will not cook all the way through, cracks will form on top and it will be more crumbly.

❖ When adding dry ingredients to wet mixture, it is best to mix briskly with a large spoon or a good strong wire whisk. Using a hand mixer will not do a good enough job, because the batter will become stiff and somewhat sticky as ingredients are mixed. A food processor can also be used.

❖ Do not let batter sit too long after wet and dry ingredients are mixed together. It is best to bake almost immediately or bread will not rise as good. Make only 1-2 breads at a time.

❖ After scooping or pouring the dough into the pan, always spread the top evenly with a spatula. This helps to lessen the possibility of cracks forming during baking. Cracks can still form occasionally, as this is common with gluten-free baking.

❖ Do not crowd pans in oven. Leave enough space all around pan to allow air and heat to circulate. Use only one rack at slightly lower than middle setting.

❖ To test bread for doneness, insert a small-serrated knife or long tooth pick into the center of the bread. It will come out clean when bread is done. Do not remove bread from oven while testing or it will stop baking and the inside will be under cooked, even if put back into the oven.

❖ After breads are baked, let them cool before removing them from the pan. Turn pan upside down and the bread will fall out quite easily.

❖ Cool breads completely in the refrigerator or at room temperature before slicing. Use a serrated knife to slice bread.
Hint: Gluten-free breads slice much easier when chilled for 4-6 hours.

❖ Gluten-free breads become bitter when refrigerated for more than 2 days. It is best to freeze breads after slicing. Breads also taste better when toasted. If breads are eaten raw (untoasted) they tend to be dough-like.

❖ Any spice or combination of spices can be added to the dry ingredients, such as; a) for spiced breads; cinnamon, nutmeg, ginger, allspice, etc. or b) for herb breads; basil, oregano, parsley, rosemary, etc. c) for cheese bread; add shredded or grated cheese. Add cheese to liquid along with dry ingredients. Add garlic powder with dry ingredients, for garlic cheese bread.

❖ Water is the standard liquid used in all bread recipes. Water can be replaced with nut or seed milks or fruit juices.

❖ Before baking, breads can be topped with sesame seeds, flax seeds, rice flakes, etc. The same toppings can also be added to the flour mixture.

❖ Bread batter can also be put into muffin tins, to make muffins. Bake at 375 degrees for 25-35 minutes.

❖ Ground nuts or seeds can be added to any recipe. Replace 1/3 cup of the main flour with ½ cup ground almonds or nuts/seeds of choice.

❖ Lecithin granules can be added to any bread recipe. Lecithin granules make the bread firmer. If there is no allergy with soy, then lecithin granules are recommended. Use 1½-2 Tbsp. lecithin granules per recipe and add 1/8 cup more water. Blend lecithin granules with water before adding remaining ingredients.

❖ 1 tsp. gelatin can be added to any bread recipe for stronger and firmer bread. Stir gelatin into water and let sit for 1-2 minutes before adding remaining liquids.

❖ Breads made with ground flax seeds tend to be firm and moist, while breads made with eggs tend to be light, dry and somewhat crumbly in texture.

Gluten-Free Baking Powder

❖ Baking powder consists of an acidic ingredient (cream of tartar), an alkaline ingredient (baking soda) and a starch (flour). Most commercial brands of baking powder contain gluten, usually from wheat, and aluminum (alum), a known toxin, or other additives. This baking powder recipe uses tapioca flour as the starch. Guar gum is also added to help make baked goods rise and hold together better.

3 Tbsp. tapioca flour
3 Tbsp. cream of tartar
1½ Tbsp. baking soda
1 Tbsp. guar gum

Put all ingredients into a sifter and sift over a bowl. Repeat 2-3 times.
Or
Put all ingredients in a blender, food processor or coffee bean/seed grinder and blend for 10 seconds.

- To keep baking powder from spoiling or losing its effectiveness, store in a glass jar in a dry, cool place.
- *Note:* It is very important for baking powder to stay dry when stored.
- Store for up to 6 months.

Brown Rice Bread; with eggs

2 eggs, beaten
1 cup water
3 Tbsp. olive or nut oil
1½ cups brown rice flour
1 cup tapioca flour
1 Tbsp. baking powder
1½ tsp. guar gum
½ tsp. sea salt

In a bowl, mix together eggs, water and oil.
In another bowl, sift or mix together remaining ingredients until well combined.
Add dry ingredients to wet mixture; stir until well combined.
Pour or scoop dough into a prepared loaf pan; spread the top to even out.
Bake at 375°F for 60-70 minutes.

Variations
- ❖ *Add 1½ Tbsp. lecithin granules and 1-2 Tbsp. more water for firmer bread. Blend lecithin granules with water before mixing in eggs and oil. Do this with any bread recipe that contains eggs.*
- ❖ *Replace 1/3 cup rice or tapioca flour with ½ cup ground almonds. This can be done with any bread recipe as long as the flour that is substituted contains 1 or more cups at beginning of recipe.*

Millet Rice Bread; with eggs

2 eggs, beaten
1 cup water
3 Tbsp. olive or nut oil
1½ cups millet flour
1 cup brown rice flour
1 Tbsp. baking powder
2 tsp. guar gum
½ tsp. sea salt

In a bowl, mix together eggs, water and oil.
In another bowl, sift or mix together remaining ingredients until well combined.
Add dry ingredients to wet mixture; stir until well combined.
Pour or scoop dough into a prepared loaf pan; spread the top to even out.
Bake at 375°F for 60-70 minutes.

Tapioca Rice Bread; with eggs

2 eggs, beaten
7/8 cup water
3 Tbsp. olive or nut oil
1¼ cups tapioca flour
1 cup brown rice flour
1 tbsp. baking powder
2 tsp. guar gum
½ tsp. sea salt

In a bowl, mix together eggs, water and oil.
In another bowl, sift or mix together remaining ingredients until well combined.
Add dry ingredients to wet mixture; stir until well combined.
Pour or scoop dough into a prepared loaf pan; spread the top to even out.
Bake at 375°F for 60-70 minutes.

Variation
❖ For **Tapioca Millet Bread; with eggs**: *replace rice flour with millet flour.*

Multi Grain Bread; with eggs

1 egg, beaten
1 cup water
2 Tbsp. olive or nut oil
½ cup brown rice flour
½ cup tapioca flour
¼ cup millet flour
¼ cup quinoa flour or hempseed flour
¼ cup buckwheat flour
2 tsp. baking powder
1 tsp. guar gum
¼ tsp. sea salt

In a bowl, mix together eggs, water and oil.
In another bowl, sift or mix together remaining ingredients until well combined.
Add dry ingredients to wet mixture; stir until well combined.
Pour or scoop dough into a small prepared loaf pan; spread the top to even out.
Bake at 375°F for 55-65 minutes.

Small Loaf Brown Rice Bread; with eggs

1 egg, beaten
2/3 cup water
2 Tbsp. olive or nut oil
1 cup brown rice flour
¾ cup tapioca flour
2 tsp. baking powder
1 tsp. guar gum
½ tsp. sea salt

In a bowl, mix together egg, water and oil.
In another bowl, sift or mix together remaining ingredients until well combined.
Add dry ingredients to wet mixture; stir until well combined.
Pour or scoop dough into a small prepared loaf pan; spread the top to even out.
Bake at 375°F for 55-65 minutes.

Brown Rice Bread; with flax seed

7/8 cup water
1 Tbsp. ground flax seeds
2 Tbsp. olive or nut oil
1¼ cups brown rice flour
¾ cup tapioca flour
2 tsp. baking powder
1 tsp. guar gum
½ tsp. sea salt

In a bowl, stir together water and ground flax seeds; let sit for 1-2 minutes.
Stir in oil.
In another bowl, sift or mix together remaining ingredients until well combined.
Add dry ingredients to wet mixture; stir until well combined.
Pour or scoop dough into a small prepared loaf pan; spread the top to even out.
Bake at 375°F for 55-65 minutes.

Variation
❖ *Add 2 Tbsp. lecithin granules and 1/8 cup more water for firmer bread. Blend lecithin granules with water before adding ground flax seed. Do this with any egg-free bread recipe.*

Tapioca Rice Bread; with flax seed

1 cup water
1½ Tbsp. ground flax seeds
2 Tbsp. olive or nut oil
1 cup tapioca flour
¾ cup brown rice flour
2 tsp. cream of tartar
1 tsp. baking soda
1½ tsp. guar gum
¼ tsp. sea salt

In a bowl, stir together water and ground flax seeds; let sit for 1-2 minutes.
Stir in oil.
In another bowl, sift or mix together remaining ingredients until well combined.
Add dry ingredients to wet mixture; stir until well combined.
Pour or scoop dough into a small prepared loaf pan; spread the top to even out.
Bake at 375°F for 55-65 minutes.

Variation
❖ *For **Tapioca Millet Bread; with flax seed**: replace rice flour with millet flour.*

Multi Grain Bread; with flax seed

1¼ cups water
2 Tbsp. ground flax seeds
¼ cup olive or nut oil
¾ cup tapioca flour
½ cup brown rice flour
¼ cup millet flour
¼ cup quinoa flour
¼ cup amaranth flour or hempseed flour
2 tsp. cream of tartar
1 tsp. baking soda
2 tsp. guar gum
½ tsp. sea salt

In a bowl, stir together water and ground flax seeds; let sit for 1-2 minutes.
Stir in oil.
In another bowl, sift or mix together remaining ingredients until well combined.
Add dry ingredients to wet mixture; stir until well combined.
Pour or scoop dough into a prepared loaf pan; spread the top to even out.
Bake at 375°F for 60-70 minutes.

Brown Rice Bread: with gelatin

7/8 cup water
2 tsp. gelatin
2 Tbsp. olive or nut oil
1 cup brown rice flour
$\frac{3}{4}$ cup tapioca flour
1 Tbsp. baking powder
$\frac{1}{2}$ tsp. guar gum
$\frac{1}{2}$ tsp. sea salt

In a bowl, stir together water and gelatin; let sit for 1-2 minutes.
Stir in oil.
In another bowl, sift or mix together remaining ingredients until well combined.
Pour or scoop dough into a small prepared loaf pan; spread the top to even out.
Bake at 375°F for 55-65 minutes.

Rice Flatbreads

(Unleavened bread that has few ingredients and many uses)

1 cup brown rice flour
$\frac{1}{2}$ cup tapioca flour
$\frac{1}{2}$ cup amaranth flour
$\frac{1}{4}$ tsp. sea salt
2/3 cup water
1 Tbsp. olive oil

In a bowl, mix together flours and sea salt.
Add water and oil; stir until dough forms a ball.
Break off balls of dough, about the size of a golf ball.
Roll balls in rice flour and knead a few times.
Roll or flatten with hand on a floured surface; until they are about 6"
round and 1/8" or thinner in thickness.
Heat a skillet over medium-high heat; use no oil.
Place a flatbread in the hot skillet; cook for about 2-3 minutes on
each side. Flatbreads will become lightly brown and appear dry.

- Makes about 10 breads.
- Store in the refrigerator for up to 10 days, or freeze.
- Reheat flatbreads in toaster or oven.
- Use for sandwiches or serve as is with soups, stews, entrées, etc.
- Flatbreads make a good pizza crust. Reheat flatbreads in toaster or
  oven, add your favourite sauce and toppings, and heat in oven.
- Add any type of seasoning(s) to flatbread recipe; add to dry mix.

Quinoa Flatbreads

1½ cups quinoa flour
½ cup buckwheat or tapioca flour
¼ tsp. sea salt
2/3 cup water
1 Tbsp. olive oil
• Follow the directions for rice flatbreads.
• Use quinoa flour for rolling.

Millet Flatbreads

1¼ cups millet flour
½ cup amaranth flour
¼ cup tapioca flour
¼ tsp. sea salt
2/3 cup water
1 Tbsp. olive oil
• Follow the directions for rice flatbreads.
• Use millet flour for rolling.

Chapattis

(Chickpea flour flatbreads)

1½ cups chickpea flour
2 Tbsp. tapioca flour
¼ tsp. sea salt
½ cup water
1½ Tbsp. olive oil
• Follow the directions for rice flatbreads.
• Makes a sticky dough.
• Use chickpea flour for rolling.
• Add curry spices to dry mix; ¼ tsp. cumin, chili powder & coriander.

39

Rice & Hempseed Flatbreads

1 cup brown rice flour
$\frac{1}{2}$ cup hempseed flour
$\frac{1}{2}$ cup tapioca flour
$\frac{1}{4}$ tsp. sea salt
2/3 cup water
4 tsp. olive oil
• Follow the directions for rice flatbreads.
• Use rice flour for rolling.

Millet & Hempseed Flatbreads

1 cup millet flour
$\frac{1}{2}$ cup hempseed flour
$\frac{1}{2}$ cup tapioca flour
$\frac{1}{4}$ tsp. sea salt
2/3 cup water
4 tsp. olive oil
• Follow the directions for rice flatbreads.
• Use millet flour for rolling.

Quinoa & Hempseed Flatbreads

1 cup quinoa flour
$\frac{1}{2}$ cup hempseed flour
$\frac{1}{2}$ cup tapioca flour
$\frac{1}{4}$ tsp. sea salt
2/3 cup water
4 tsp. olive oil
• Follow the directions for rice flatbreads.
• Use quinoa flour for rolling.

Rice 'Pancake' Flatbreads

(A stir & pour flatbread that is somewhat moist & chewy)

¾ cup brown rice flour
¼ cup buckwheat or tapioca flour
¼ tsp. sea salt
1 cup water
1 Tbsp. olive or nut oil

In a bowl, mix together flours and sea salt.
Add water and oil; whisk or stir until well combined.
Let stand for 2 or more minutes.
Heat a skillet over medium heat; no oil is necessary if using a non-stick skillet.
Pour 2-3 Tbsp. of batter on to the hot skillet, enough to make a 4-5" round bread, and cook until the bread appears dry around the edges.
Turn bread over and cook the other side.

- Makes 8 breads 4-5" round.
- Add more or less water, to make a thinner or thicker bread.
- Refrigerate for up to 7 days, or freeze.
- To make them more crisp; reheat in toaster or oven.
- *Note:* If too high of a heat is used when making breads, only the out side will be cooked and the inside will be raw. If this happens, put breads in the oven or toaster to finish cooking or dry out.
- As a pancake: serve with apple berry sauce or any favourite topping.
- Flatbread 'pancakes' can also be used for sandwiches; the same as flatbreads.
- Any seasoning(s) can be added to recipe; add to dry mixture.

Variations
❖ *Replace rice flour with quinoa or millet flour.*
❖ *Replace ½ cup rice flour with ½ cup amaranth flour.*

Pancakes

1 egg
¼ cup sugar-free fruit juice, any flavour
1/3 cup almond milk
2 tsp. nut oil or melted ghee
½ tsp. vanilla extract (optional)
1 cup brown rice flour
1 tsp. baking powder
½ tsp. cinnamon (optional)

In a bowl, beat egg until light and foamy.
Beat in fruit juice, milk, oil or ghee and extract (if using).
Combine flour, baking powder and cinnamon (if using); beat into wet mixture.
Heat a little oil or ghee in a skillet over medium heat.
Spoon about 3 Tbsp. of batter onto hot skillet; cook until bubbles form on surface and underside is golden brown, about 2 minutes.
Turn over pancake(s) and cook until bottom is lightly brown.

• Makes 8-12 pancakes.

Variations
❖ *Replace almond milk with any nut or seed, coconut, rice or soy milk.*
❖ *Replace ¼ cup rice flour with ¼ cup tapioca or buckwheat flour.*
❖ *Stir ¼ cup fresh berries or chopped fruit into batter.*
❖ *Replace 1-2 Tbsp. fruit juice with honey or brown rice syrup.*
❖ *Add more liquid or flour to make a thinner or thicker pancake.*
❖ *Serve with fresh fruit, apple butter, goat's milk or soy yogurt, or any favourite topping.*

Basic Egg-Free Pancakes

(These pancakes can be used for sandwiches or, as breakfast pancake)

2 tsp. nut oil or melted ghee
1 cup plain nut or seed milk
¾ cup brown rice flour
¼ cup tapioca flour
2 tsp. baking powder
pinch of sea salt

In a bowl, mix together oil or ghee and milk.
In another bowl, combine flours, baking powder and sea salt.
Heat a little oil or ghee in a skillet over medium heat.
Add the dry ingredients to the wet mixture; mix well.
Don't let batter sit, make pancakes immediately.
Scoop 2-3 Tbsp. of batter into skillet.
Turn over the pancake(s) when bottom is browned; cook the other side until lightly brown.
Lightly oil the skillet before each new batch.

- Makes about 12 pancakes.
- Use this basic recipe as a bread for sandwiches or with soups etc.
- Add more liquid or flour to make a thinner or thicker pancake.
- They can be eaten cold or reheated in the toaster or oven.

For Breakfast Pancakes:
- Replace plain nut or seed milk with; sweetened nut or seed milk, coconut milk or sugar-free fruit juice.
- Add ½ tsp. vanilla, or other kind of extract to wet ingredients.
- Add ¼ tsp. cinnamon, cardamom or nutmeg to dry ingredients.

Other variations
- ❖ *Replace rice flour with quinoa or millet flour.*
- ❖ *Replace ¼ cup rice flour with ¼ cup ground nuts or seeds.*

Amaranth Pancakes

(A superb grain-free pancake)

1 egg
$\frac{1}{2}$ cup nut or seed milk
2 tsp. nut oil or melted ghee
$\frac{1}{2}$ tsp. vanilla or almond extract (optional)
$\frac{1}{2}$ cup amaranth flour
$\frac{1}{4}$ cup ground nuts or seeds
2 Tbsp. tapioca flour
1 tsp. baking powder
$\frac{1}{4}$ tsp. cinnamon

In a bowl, beat egg until light and foamy.
Beat in milk, oil or ghee and extract (if using) until smooth.
Combine the dry ingredients and add to wet mixture until well combined.
Lightly oil a skillet and bring to medium heat.
Scoop 2-3 Tbsp. of batter into hot skillet and cook until bottom is browned.
Flip pancake(s) over and cook the other side until lightly brown.

- Makes about 8 pancakes.
- Serve with fruit butter, fresh fruit or any favourite topping.

Variations
❖ *Replace 3 Tbsp. amaranth flour with 3 Tbsp. hempseed flour.*

Sweet Potato Pancakes

(Make these delicious pancakes with cooked sweet potato or pumpkin leftovers from the holidays)

1 egg
¼ cup cooked sweet potato, mashed
½ cup almond milk
2 tsp. nut oil or melted ghee
½ tsp. vanilla
½ cup brown rice flour
2 Tbsp. tapioca flour
½ tsp. baking powder
¼ tsp cinnamon
pinch or 2 cloves, ginger & nutmeg

In a bowl beat egg until light and foamy.
Beat in sweet potato, milk, oil or ghee and extract.
Combine the dry ingredients and add to the wet mixture; mix until well combined.
Lightly oil a skillet and bring to medium heat.
Scoop 2-3 Tbsp. of batter into hot skillet and cook until the bottom is browned.
Flip pancake(s) over and cook the other side until lightly brown.

• Makes about 8 pancakes.
• Serve with goat's milk or soy yogurt and fresh fruit or apple butter.

Variation
❖ *For **Pumpkin Pancakes**: replace sweet potato with cooked pumpkin.*
❖ *Replace 2 Tbsp. rice flour with 2 Tbsp. ground nuts or seeds, hempseed flour or amaranth flour.*

Granola

6 cups rolled rice
1½ cups mixed nuts, chopped
¼-½ cup unsweetened shredded coconut (optional)
½ cup sunflower seeds
¼ cup brown rice flour
1½ tsp. cinnamon (optional)
½ tsp. ground ginger (optional)
½ cup almond or walnut oil
½ cup brown rice syrup
1 tsp. vanilla or almond extract
1¼ cups mixed dried fruit, chopped

In a large bowl, mix together rolled rice, nuts, coconut (if using), sunflower seeds, flour and spices (if using).
In a saucepan, combine the oil and rice syrup over medium-low heat until liquefied.
Stir in extract.
Pour liquid mixture over dry mixture and mix well.
Place mixture in an oiled jellyroll or roasting pan and bake at 350°F for 30 minutes; stirring every 5-10 minutes until golden brown.
Remove from oven and stir in fruit.
• Store granola in air tight containers at room temperature.

Variations
❖ *Replace up to 2 cups rolled rice with equal amounts of quinoa flakes or (rolled) soy flakes.*
❖ *Replace sunflower seeds with ½ cup more mixed nuts.*
❖ *Replace cinnamon and ginger with cardamom and nutmeg, or use any combination of spices.*
❖ *For dried fruit choose any combination of the following: raisins, apricots, figs, cherries, cranberries, blueberries, papaya, etc.*

Scones

(Make a few batches of these & store them for snacks)

½ cup plain yogurt, goat's milk or soy
2 Tbsp. plain nut or seed milk
2 Tbsp. melted ghee or butter
1½ Tbsp. honey or brown rice syrup
1¼ cups brown rice flour
¼ cup tapioca flour
2½ tsp. baking powder
1 tsp. guar gum
¼ tsp. sea salt
1 tsp. grated orange peel
¼-1/3 cup dried fruit, finely chopped

In a bowl, mix together yogurt, milk, ghee and sweetener until well combined.
In another bowl, mix together remaining ingredients, except dried fruit, until well combined.
Add ½ flour mixture into yogurt mixture; mix well.
Add dried fruit and remaining flour mixture; mix well until dough becomes stiff.
Turn out dough onto a lightly floured surface and knead about 10 times.
Divide dough into 2 equal parts and press onto a lightly oiled baking sheet, until they are about 5" in diameter.
With a wet knife, cut each circle into quarters and move each quarter apart slightly.
Bake at 400°F for 15-20 minutes, until golden brown.

• Store in a metal tin at room temperature.
• Scones can be reheated or eaten as is.
• For dried fruit, try: cranberries, blueberries or cherries.
• Add ½-1 tsp. of any favourite spice or combination of spices.

Cheese Scones

(A good accompaniment for lunchtime soups)

½ cup plain yogurt, goat's milk or soy
3½ Tbsp. olive oil or melted ghee
2 Tbsp. plain nut or seed milk
1¼ cups brown rice flour
¼ cup tapioca flour
2½ tsp. baking powder
1 tsp. guar gum
¼ tsp. sea salt
1/8 tsp. garlic powder & chili powder
2 oz. shredded cheese, rice or soy

In a bowl, mix together yogurt, oil or ghee and milk until well combined.
In another bowl, mix together remaining ingredients, except cheese, until well combined.
Stir cheese into dry mixture.
Add dry mixture into yogurt mixture and mix until dough is stiff.
Turn out onto a lightly floured surface and knead about 10 times.
Divide dough into 2 equal parts and press onto a lightly oiled baking sheet, until they are about 5" in diameter.
With a wet knife, cut each circle into quarters and move each quarter apart slightly.
Bake at 400°F for 15-20 minutes, until golden brown.

- Store in a metal tin at room temperature.
- Scones can be reheated or eaten as is.
- Add 1-2 slices cooked turkey bacon, diced; add to dry mixture.
- Add ½-1 tsp. dried herbs in any combination; add to dry mixture.

Tea Biscuits

2/3 cup brown rice flour
1/3 cup tapioca flour
2 tsp. baking powder
½ tsp. guar gum
¼ tsp. sea salt
¼ cup unsalted butter or ghee
¼-1/3 cup plain nut or seed milk

In a bowl, combine flours, baking powder, guar gum and sea salt.
With fingers, rub in butter or ghee until crumbly. Add 1 Tbsp. more butter if needed.
Add ¼ cup milk and stir until dough forms a ball. Add remaining milk if needed.
Turn dough onto a lightly floured surface and knead a few times.
Break dough off into 6 equal pieces and press to ½" thickness on a lightly oiled baking sheet.
Bake at 400°F for 15-20 minutes, until golden brown.
• Store in a metal tin at room temperature.
• Generally, tea biscuits are dry when eaten as is. To moisten biscuits, top with jam, fruit butters or any other favourite topping.

Variations
❖ *Brush biscuits with nut or seed milk before baking.*
❖ *For **Cheese Tea Biscuits**: add ½-1 oz. finely shredded or grated cheese-rice, soy or goat's milk, to flour mixture.*
❖ *For **Herb Tea Biscuits**: add ½-1 tsp. dried herbs in any combination to flour mixture.*
❖ *Add 1/8 tsp. garlic powder or 1 minced garlic clove to above variations.*
❖ *For **Cinnamon Tea Biscuits**: before baking, brush biscuits with melted ghee or butter and sprinkle with cinnamon and sucanat.*

Crust-less Quiche

1 Tbsp. olive oil
2 small leeks, chopped
4 cups spinach or dandelion leaves, chopped
¼ cup ground almonds
4-6 oz. cooked turkey or chicken, cubed (optional)
2½ cups broccoli, chopped and steamed
4 oz. shredded cheese, rice or soy
8 eggs
2¾ cups plain nut or seed milk
1 tsp. dried thyme
pinch of nutmeg and cayenne pepper
sea salt & pepper

In a skillet, heat oil over medium heat.
Add leeks and sauté for 3-5 minutes, until softened.
Add spinach or dandelion and sauté just until wilted.
Oil a large baking dish and sprinkle bottom with ground almonds.
Sprinkle in turkey (if using), broccoli, leek mixture and shredded cheese.
In a bowl, beat eggs.
Beat in milk and spices.
Pour egg mixture into prepared baking dish; season to taste.
Bake at 350°F, uncovered, for 25-30 minutes or until egg mixture is set and lightly brown.
• Makes 6-8 servings.
• Use a 9"x13" or 2 small square 8" pans.

Variations
❖ *Replace spinach or dandelion with either swiss chard or collards.*
❖ *For a **Crusted Quiche**: use '2' rice flour pie crusts, potato or sweet potato pie crusts from Wraps & Pie Crusts Section.*

Breakfast Crepes

1 Tbsp. olive oil or ghee
2 shallots or 1 onion, finely chopped
4 eggs
2 Tbsp. plain nut or seed milk
1 tomato, finely chopped
1 tsp. dried marjoram
$\frac{1}{2}$-1 oz. shredded cheese of choice
sea salt & pepper
4 crepes

In a skillet, heat oil or ghee over medium heat.
Add shallots or onion and sauté for 2-3 minutes.
Lightly beat together eggs and milk.
Stir in tomato, marjoram and cheese; season to taste.
Pour mixture into skillet and cook until eggs are almost set.
Turn over egg mixture and finish cooking.
Remove from pan and cut into strips.
Line 4 crepes with equal amounts of strips, roll accordingly and serve.
• Makes 2-4 servings.

Variations
❖ *Replace marjoram with any spice or herb: basil, chives, garlic, etc.*
❖ *Replace tomato with any other vegetable: asparagus, broccoli, etc.*
❖ *Sauté leeks, green peepers, etc. with or in place of shallots.*
❖ *Add a couple strips of cooked turkey bacon or crumbled sausage before rolling crepes.*
❖ *Once filled, crepes can be heated. Sprinkle on shredded cheese and sautéed veggies and broil for 2 minutes or until cheese melts.*
❖ *For **Mexican Breakfast Crepes**: sauté $\frac{1}{2}$ diced green pepper & 1-2 Tbsp. chili pepper with onions. Replace marjoram with 1/8 tsp. garlic powder & $\frac{1}{2}$ tsp. cumin. Top crepes with salsa of choice.*

Soups & Stews

Tips for Soups & Stews   54

Stocks   55

Basic Vegetable Stock   56

Basic Meat Stocks   57

Potassium Broth   58

Just Greens Soup   59

Okra & Tomato Soup   60

Lentil & Broccoli Soup   61

Roasted Garlic & Leek Soup   62

Roasted Garlic & Cauliflower Soup   63

Celery & Leek Soup   64

Celery & Cauliflower Soup   65

Carrot Lemon Soup   66

Pumpkin & Squash Soup   67

Curried Squash & Sweet Potato Soup   68

Tomato Coconut Soup   69

'French' Leek Soup   70

Vegetable Lentil Soup   71

Vegetable Curry Soup   72

Garden Vegetable Soup   73

Vegetable & Wild Rice Soup   74

Hot & Sour Soup   75

Turkey Chowder   76

Coconut Chicken Soup   77

Chicken & Dumpling Soup   78

Turkey Vegetable & Pumpkin Soup   79

Turkey Noodle Soup   80

Roasted Garlic & Turkey Soup   81

Lamb & Vegetable Soup   82

Rabbit Vegetable with Saffron Soup   83

Roasted Duck & Mushroom Soup   84

Winter Vegetable Stew   85

Chicken Curry Stew   86

Turkey Saffron Stew   87

Spiced Turkey & Vegetable Stew   88

Turkey Meatball & Vegetable Stew   89

Venison Stew   90

Tips For Soups & Stews

❖ Most recipes are very versatile. If a certain vegetable or spice that is called for in a given recipe is not on hand or available, replace it with another one that is similar.

❖ The stocks and milks used in all recipes are the ones that have been tested for that particular soup or stew. Unless otherwise stated, the type of stock or milk can be replaced with a different one. Although the flavour may be altered with certain milks.

❖ It is not recommended to use pre-cooked or leftover vegetables, unless called for, in soup or stew recipes. Some or most of the flavour and nutritional value can be lost with over cooking. Always use fresh ingredients.

❖ Save leftover water from steamed or cooked vegetables and add it to any stock, soup or stew recipe.

❖ Unless otherwise stated, most recipes will make 8 or more servings. Most recipes can be reduced in size.

❖ Unless otherwise stated, all soup and stew recipes freeze well. It is best to freeze them in glass jars.

❖ To puree soups: use a blender or food processor, and puree in batches, or puree in the stock pot with a hand held blender.

❖ Soups or stews can be made thinner or thicker, by adding more or less stock, water or milk.

❖ Miso can be added to soups to boost their flavour. Dissolve 2 Tbsp. to $\frac{1}{4}$ cup miso in a little liquid (water or broth from soup) and stir into soup at end of cooking time.

Stocks

❖ Use quality vegetables, spices and chicken, turkey, lamb, etc., meat and bones. Don't use pre-cooked vegetables or meat and bones; they have little flavour or nutritional value left.

❖ Use cold, pure water for stocks. Hot water, if used, will lock the flavour in soup bones.

❖ When adding water to stockpot, just cover all the ingredients plus 2 inches. This makes a stronger stock that can always be diluted later.

❖ Bring the water to a boil and remove any froth that forms on top; there will be no froth with a straight vegetable stock.

❖ Add vegetables, herbs and spices after all the froth is removed.

❖ Reduce heat and let simmer, covered, for 2-4 hours. Stocks have a stronger flavour and more nutritional value the longer they are simmered.

❖ When simmering is complete, let cool and then strain. Remove any meat from bones, which then can be used in soup, stew or any other recipe. Throw away the vegetables; they have done their job.

❖ Let the stock cool in the refrigerator, preferably overnight. Once cooled, skim off any fat that has accumulated on top; stock is now ready.

❖ Stocks will last for up to 5 days under refrigeration or put into the freezer for up to 6 months.

❖ Stocks can also be frozen into ice cube trays. This is good for when a cube or two is needed for stir-frying, sautéing, etc.

❖ Any stock can be 'spiced', by adding 1-2 tsp. crushed peppercorns, 1-2 tsp. whole cloves, 4-6 whole star anise and 2 cinnamon sticks.

Basic Vegetable Stock

3-4 carrots
3-4 celery stalks
2 potatoes
1 leek
1-2 onions
2-3 garlic cloves
2-3 dried bay leaves
1-2 tsp. mixed peppercorns
6-8 fresh basil leaves
$\frac{1}{4}$ cup fresh parsley
fresh water

Chop all vegetables into chunks.
Add all ingredients to a stockpot and add enough water to cover ingredients by 2 inches.
Cover and simmer for 2-4 hours.
Let cool, and then strain.

- This is a basic stock. To this add any type of vegetable, herb or spice.
- Dried herbs can be used instead of fresh herbs; adjust accordingly
- For stocks, it's okay to add fresh herbs at the beginning of cooking time.

Basic Meat Stock

2-3 lbs. meat parts with bones
1-2 carrots
1-2 celery stalks
1 onion
1-2 garlic cloves
2 dried bay leaves
3 fresh basil leaves
2 Tbsp. fresh parsley
fresh water

Chop all vegetables into chunks.
In a stockpot, add meat parts with bones and enough water to cover ingredients by 2 inches.
Bring to a boil and remove froth as it appears.
When froth is no longer present, add remaining ingredients; add more water if needed.
Cover and simmer for 2-4 hours.
Let cool, and then strain.
Place stock in the refrigerator and let cool for a few hours or overnight.
Once stock is cooled, skim off any fat from the top.

- For meat with bones, use: chicken, turkey, lamb or venison.
- Add any other vegetable, herb or spice.
- Chicken and turkey stocks are similar in taste; one can be substituted for the other in any given recipe.

Potassium Broth

(A healing, alkalinizing broth)

3 garlic cloves
2-3 carrots
1-2 celery stalks
1 large onion
1-2 turnips
2 potatoes (use only the outer layer)
½-1 cup cabbage
1 cup spinach
1 cup dandelion greens (optional)
2-3 large kale leaves (optional)
1 zucchini
½ Tbsp. celery seeds
½ cup fresh basil
½ cup fresh sage
½ cup fresh parsley
fresh water

Chop all vegetables into chunks. (when a potato is cut in half there will be a noticeable membrane about ½" from the skin. Use only the part from skin to membrane and throw the rest away)
Add all ingredients to a stockpot and add enough water to cover all ingredients by 2 inches.
Cover and simmer for a minimum of 2 hours.
Let cool, and then strain.

• Drink broth cool or warm.
• This is a very good broth to help alkalinize the body, during or after an illness. This broth is also good to use in addition to any cleansing program.
• Use only fresh herbs in this recipe.
• Broth will last for up to 7 days under refrigeration; can be frozen.

Just Greens Soup

(A healing soup rich in nutrients)

2 Tbsp. ghee or olive oil
2 cloves garlic, chopped
1 onion, chopped
2 leeks, chopped
1 bunch broccoli (leaves included), chopped
6-8 celery stalks (leaves included), chopped
2 cups chopped green beans or asparagus
1 bunch spinach
1 bunch dandelion greens
1 bunch Swiss chard, collards or kale, chopped
6-8 cups vegetable or chicken stock
1 tsp. dried basil & oregano
$\frac{1}{2}$ tsp. dried parsley, marjoram, rosemary & thyme
sea salt & pepper

In a stockpot, heat ghee or oil over medium-low heat.
Add garlic, onion and leeks and sauté for 5 minutes,
Add remaining ingredients and bring to a light boil. (The pot will be quite full but will be reduced as the spinach, dandelion and Swiss chard, collards or kale cooks; stir occasionally to incorporate)
Reduce heat and simmer, covered, for 25-30 minutes.
Cool slightly and puree.
Season to taste.

Variation
❖ *Replace any vegetable green with green cabbage.*

Okra & Tomato Soup

(An excellent tasting soup that is good for the digestive system)

2 Tbsp. olive oil
10-12 oz. fresh okra
1 Tbsp. each olive oil & ghee
2 garlic cloves, chopped
1 red onion, chopped
1 leek (white part only), chopped
3 cups chicken or vegetable stock
1-28 oz. can chopped tomatoes (or fresh)
3 oz. tomato paste
1 tsp. dried parsley
$\frac{1}{2}$ tsp. dried sage, savory & tarragon
sea salt & pepper

Remove ends of okra and cut into $\frac{1}{2}$" rounds.
In a sauté pan, heat 2 Tbsp. olive oil over medium-low heat.
Add $\frac{3}{4}$ of the okra and sauté for 10-15 minutes, until browned. Set aside until the end.
In a stockpot, heat oil and ghee over medium-low heat.
Add garlic, onion and leek and sauté for 5 minutes.
Add remaining ingredients and bring to a light boil.
Reduce heat and simmer, covered, for 30 minutes.
Cool slightly and puree.
Add sautéed okra and season to taste.

Lentil & Broccoli Soup

1 Tbsp. olive oil or ghee
3-5 cloves garlic, chopped
1 shallot, chopped
1 medium onion, chopped
2 celery stalks, chopped
2 cups chopped cauliflower
1 large broccoli, chopped (4-5 cups)
1-1$\frac{1}{4}$ cups lentils, washed & rinsed
6 cups chicken or vegetable stock
1 tsp. cumin & parsley
$\frac{1}{2}$ tsp. coriander
sea salt & pepper

In a stockpot, heat oil or ghee over medium heat.
Add garlic, shallot and onion and sauté for 3-5 minutes.
Add remaining ingredients and bring to a light boil.
Reduce heat and simmer, covered, for 30-40 minutes.
Cool slightly and puree.
Season to taste.

Variation
❖ *Add any of the following spices: $\frac{1}{2}$ tsp. chili powder, $\frac{1}{2}$ tsp. turmeric and 1 tsp. garam masala.*

Roasted Garlic & Leek Soup

(A 'light' soup that packs a lot of flavour)

1 Tbsp. each olive oil & ghee
1 shallot, chopped
6-8 small leeks, chopped
5 whole garlic bulbs, roasted (see page 167)
4 cups vegetable stock
1 cup plain sesame seed milk
2 Tbsp. liquid aminos
$\frac{1}{4}$ cup white wine
1 tsp. dried thyme
$\frac{1}{2}$ tsp. dried rosemary
1 Tbsp. fresh chives, finely chopped
sea salt & pepper

In a stockpot, heat oil and ghee over medium-low heat.
Add shallot and leeks, and sauté until softened, about 7-10 minutes.
Add remaining ingredients, except chives, and bring to a light boil.
Reduce heat and simmer, covered, for 20 minutes.
Cool slightly and puree.
Add chives and season to taste.

Roasted Garlic & Cauliflower Soup

(A wonderful taste experience)

1-2 Tbsp. olive oil or ghee
1 white onion, chopped
3 leeks (white part only), chopped
3 whole garlic bulbs, roasted (see page 167)
1 medium-sized head cauliflower, chopped
3 cups chicken or vegetable stock
1 cup plain almond milk
1 tsp. dried parsley & rosemary
$\frac{1}{2}$ tsp. dried marjoram
sea salt & pepper

In a stockpot, heat oil or ghee over medium heat.
Add onion and leeks, and sauté for 5 minutes.
Add remaining ingredients and bring to a light boil.
Reduce heat and simmer, covered, for 30 minutes.
Cool slightly and puree.
Season to taste.

Variation
❖ *Replace $\frac{1}{2}$-1 cup stock with same amount of red wine.*

Celery & Leek Soup

2 Tbsp. olive oil
2-3 cloves garlic, chopped
1 shallot, chopped
3 leeks, chopped
2 cups chopped celery
1½ cups vegetable stock
2 cups plain almond milk
1 tsp. dried dill
½ tsp. dried marjoram
pinch or 2 of cayenne pepper
¼ cup fresh parsley, chopped
sea salt & pepper

In a stockpot, heat oil over medium-low heat.
Add garlic, shallot and leeks, and sauté until softened, about 7-10 minutes.
Add remaining ingredients, except parsley, and bring to a light boil.
Reduce heat and simmer, covered, for 15 minutes.
Add parsley and simmer for 15 more minutes.
Cool slightly and puree.
Season to taste.

• Serve hot or chilled.

Celery & Cauliflower Soup

(Good for a cold winter's or hot summer's day)

2 Tbsp. ghee
1 red onion, chopped
2 cloves garlic, chopped
2 cups chopped celery
2 cups chopped cauliflower
1-2 broccoli stems, chopped
1½-2 cups chicken or vegetable stock
1¼ cups plain nut or seed milk
1 tsp. dried rosemary & thyme
½ tsp. dried parsley
sea salt & pepper

In a stockpot, heat ghee over medium-low heat.
Add onion and sauté until caramelized, approximately 15-20 minutes.
Add remaining ingredients and bring to a light boil.
Reduce heat and simmer, covered, for 20-25 minutes.
Cool slightly and puree.
Season to taste.

• Serve hot or chilled.

Carrot Lemon Soup

(A refreshing summertime soup)

1 Tbsp. olive oil or ghee
1 white onion, chopped
3 cloves garlic, chopped
2 lbs. carrots, chopped
2 cups vegetable stock
2 cups plain almond milk
1 cinnamon stick
1 tsp. dried basil
$\frac{1}{2}$ tsp. each dried marjoram & savory
juice of 1 lemon
sea salt & pepper

In a stockpot, heat oil or ghee over medium heat.
Add onion and sauté for 5 minutes.
Add garlic and sauté another 2 minutes.
Add remaining ingredients, except lemon juice, and bring to a light boil.
Reduce heat and simmer, covered, for 30-40 minutes.
Remove cinnamon stick.
Cool slightly and puree.
Stir in lemon juice.
Season to taste.

• Serve hot or chilled.

Variation
❖ *Add $\frac{1}{2}$-1 cup almonds to last 10 minutes of simmering time.*

Pumpkin & Squash Soup

(The variation for this soup must also be tried)

1-2 Tbsp. olive oil or ghee
3-4 cloves garlic, chopped
½ Tbsp. fresh ginger, finely chopped (optional)
2 shallots, chopped
1 leek, chopped
4 cups pumpkin, chopped into chunks
2 cups butternut squash, chopped into chunks
3 cups vegetable stock
2 cups plain sesame seed milk or 1 cup sesame seed & coconut milk
1½ tsp. dried parsley & cumin
1 tsp. coriander
½ tsp. cardamom & turmeric
2 Tbsp. fresh lemon juice (optional)
sea salt & pepper

In a stockpot, heat oil or ghee over medium-low heat.
Add garlic, ginger (if using), shallots and leek, and sauté for 5-7 minutes.
Add remaining ingredients, except lemon juice, and bring to a light boil.
Reduce heat and simmer, covered, for 35-45 minutes.
Cool slightly and puree.
Stir in lemon juice (if using).
Season to taste.

• Serve hot or chilled.

Variation
❖ *For* **Pumpkin & Squash Soup with Sage & Apples or Pears***:*
   replace cumin, coriander, cardamom and turmeric with 3-4 tsp.
   dried sage (or 1 cup fresh) and garnish with sliced apples or pears.

Curried Squash & Sweet Potato Soup

2 Tbsp. olive oil or ghee
1 large red onion, chopped
4-6 cloves garlic, chopped
1-2 Tbsp. fresh ginger, finely chopped
1¼-1½ lbs. butternut squash, chopped into chunks
2 sweet potatoes, chopped into chinks
2 cups chicken or vegetable stock
2 cups plain sesame seed or cashew milk
1½ tsp. cumin
1 tsp. each chili powder, coriander & turmeric
½ tsp. garam masala & paprika
¼ tsp. cayenne pepper (optional)
¼ cup fresh parsley, chopped
sea salt & pepper

In a stockpot, heat oil or ghee over medium-low heat.
Add onion and sauté until caramelized, approximately 15-20 minutes.
Add garlic and ginger, and sauté another 2-3 minutes.
Add remaining ingredients, except parsley, and bring to a light boil.
Reduce heat and simmer, covered, for 30 minutes.
Add parsley and simmer for 15 more minutes.
Cool slightly and puree.
Season to taste.

• Serve hot or chilled.

Variations
❖ *Replace squash with any other type of squash or pumpkin.*
❖ *Replace 1 cup of sesame seed or cashew milk with 1 cup coconut milk.*

Tomato Coconut Soup

(A unique combination that tastes wonderful)

1 Tbsp. olive oil or ghee
2 cloves garlic, chopped
1 leek, chopped
1 cup vegetable stock
2 cups coconut milk
1-28 oz. can chopped tomatoes (or fresh)
1 tsp. dried basil & marjoram
sea salt & pepper

In a stockpot, heat oil or ghee over medium-low heat.
Add garlic and leeks, and sauté for 5-7 minutes.
Add remaining ingredients and bring to a light boil.
Reduce heat and simmer, covered, for 20 minutes.
Cool slightly and puree.
Season to taste.

• Serve hot or chilled.

'French' Leek Soup

(A new twist on traditional French Onion Soup)

1 Tbsp. each olive oil & ghee
6 large leeks, finely chopped
2 cloves garlic, minced
3 cups chicken or vegetable stock
1 cup white wine
1 Tbsp. apple cider vinegar
1 Tbsp. liquid aminos
1 tsp. paprika
½ tsp. chili powder
sea salt & pepper

In a stockpot, heat oil and ghee over medium-low heat.
Add leeks and sauté until softened, about 7-10 minutes.
Add remaining ingredients and bring to a light boil.
Reduce heat and simmer, covered, for 20 minutes.
Cool slightly.
Remove ½ of the soup and puree.
Return to pot.
Season to taste.

• Add toasted rice bread and/or shredded cheese of choice to each serving bowl.

Vegetable Lentil Soup

1-2 Tbsp. olive oil or ghee
3 cloves garlic, minced
1 onion, finely chopped
1 cup finely chopped carrots
1 cup finely chopped celery
1 cup finely chopped cauliflower
2 red potatoes, cubed
6 cups vegetable stock
1 lb. tomatoes, pureed
1½ cup lentils, washed & rinsed
1 tsp. dried savory & thyme
sea salt & pepper

In a stockpot, heat oil over medium-low heat.
Add garlic and onion, and sauté 2-3 minutes.
Add remaining ingredients and bring to a light boil.
Reduce heat and simmer, covered, for 40-45 minutes.
Cool slightly.
Remove 2 cups of vegetables/lentils and a little stock, and puree.
Return to pot.
Season to taste.

• If lentils are pre-soaked, only simmer for 30 minutes.

Vegetable Curry Soup

(With added nut butter, this soup tastes awesome)

1-1½ Tbsp. each olive oil & ghee
1 large red or Spanish onion, finely chopped
3-4 cloves garlic, minced
1-2 Tbsp. fresh ginger, minced
3 tsp. cumin
2 tsp. chili powder
1 tsp. each coriander, garam masala, paprika & turmeric
¼ tsp. cayenne pepper
3 carrots, finely chopped
2 celery stalks, finely chopped
2 red potatoes, finely chopped
2½ cups chopped cauliflower
2 cups chopped broccoli
½ cup almond or peanut butter
1-14 oz. can chickpeas, rinsed & drained
10 cups vegetable stock
sea salt & pepper

In a stockpot, heat oil and ghee over medium-low heat.
Add onion and sauté until caramelized, approximately 15-20 minutes.
Add garlic, ginger and spices, and sauté another 2-3 minutes.
Add carrots, celery, potatoes & cauliflower, and bring to a light boil.
Reduce heat and simmer, covered, for 20 minutes.
Add remaining ingredients and simmer for 15 more minutes.
Cool slightly.
Remove ½ of the soup and puree.
Return to pot
Season to taste.

Garden Vegetable Soup

1-2 Tbsp. olive oil
4-6 cloves garlic, minced
4 shallots, minced
2 cups finely chopped carrots
1 cup finely chopped celery
2 potatoes, cubed
2 cups finely chopped cauliflower
1 cup finely chopped green beans
2-3 tomatoes, diced
1-6 oz. can tomato paste
9 cups vegetable stock
1 tsp. each dried basil, oregano & parsley
$\frac{1}{2}$ tsp. each dried marjoram, sage & thyme
pinch or 2 of cayenne pepper & nutmeg
2 cups chopped broccoli
1 zucchini, finely chopped
6-8 oz. dry brown rice noodles (elbows), cooked
sea salt & pepper

In a stockpot, heat oil over medium heat.
Add garlic and shallots, and sauté for 2-3 minutes.
Add remaining ingredients, except broccoli, zucchini and rice noodles, and bring to a light boil.
Reduce heat and simmer, covered, for 20 minutes.
Add broccoli and zucchini, and simmer for 15 more minutes.
Stir in rice noodles.
Season to taste.

Vegetable & Wild Rice Soup

1 Tbsp. olive oil & ghee
2-3 cloves garlic, minced
1 shallot, minced
1 onion, finely chopped
2 Tbsp. flour (brown rice, millet or chickpea)
4 cups vegetable stock
2 cups plain almond milk
1½ cups finely chopped carrots
¾ cup finely chopped celery
¾ cup finely chopped cauliflower
1 cup finely chopped green beans
1 tsp. dried basil
½ tsp. each dried marjoram, oregano & parsley
1 cup chopped spinach
2 cups cooked wild rice
sea salt & pepper

In a stockpot, heat oil and ghee over medium-low heat.
Add garlic, shallot and onion, and sauté for 3 minutes.
Add flour and cook for 1-2 minutes, while stirring.
Slowly stir in stock and milk.
Add remaining ingredients, except spinach and rice, and bring to a light boil.
Reduce heat and simmer, covered, for 25 minutes.
Add spinach and rice, and simmer for 10 more minutes.
Season to taste.

Variations
❖ *Replace green beans with green peas.*
❖ *For a tomato based soup: replace milk and flour with 2 cups diced tomatoes and 2 Tbsp. tomato paste.*

Hot & Sour Soup

(Adapted from traditional Asian cuisine)

1 Tbsp. olive & sesame oil
2 cloves garlic, minced
1 onion, finely chopped
2 strands of lemon grass cut into 3" chunks
$\frac{1}{2}$ cup finely chopped carrots
$\frac{1}{2}$ cup finely chopped celery
2 small daikon, finely chopped
1 cup shredded green cabbage
$\frac{1}{2}$ cup liquid aminos
$\frac{1}{4}$ cup apple cider vinegar
1 tsp. hot chili sauce or 1-2 chili peppers, minced
6 cups vegetable stock
1 head baby bok choy, chopped
2 Tbsp. fresh basil & parsley, finely chopped
$\frac{1}{4}$ cup tapioca flour mixed in $\frac{1}{4}$ cup water
3 oz. dry brown rice spaghetti noodles, broken & cooked
sea salt & pepper

In a stockpot, heat oils over medium-low heat.
Add garlic and onion, and sauté for 3 minutes.
Add remaining ingredients, except bok choy, herbs, tapioca mixture
and rice noodles, and bring to a light boil.
Reduce heat and simmer, covered, for 25 minutes.
Add bok choy and herbs, and simmer for 10 more minutes.
Turn off heat.
Remove lemon grass and discard.
Add tapioca mixture and stir until thickened.
Stir in noodles.
Season to taste.

Turkey Chowder

(A delicious cream-like turkey & vegetable soup)

1 Tbsp. olive oil & ghee
2-3 cloves garlic, minced
1 leek, finely chopped
3 Tbsp. flour (brown rice, millet or chickpea)
3 cups turkey stock
4 cups almond or cashew milk
1 cup finely chopped carrots
$\frac{3}{4}$ cup finely chopped celery
3 red potatoes, cubed
1 cup finely chopped parsnips
2 tsp. dried savory
2 cups chopped broccoli
2 cups cooked turkey, cubed
$\frac{1}{4}$ cup fresh parsley, finely chopped
4 oz. dry brown rice noodles (elbows), cooked
sea salt & pepper

In a stockpot, heat oil and ghee over medium-low heat.
Add garlic and leek, and sauté for 3-5 minutes.
Add flour and cook for 1-2 minutes, while stirring.
Slowly stir in stock and milk, until slightly thickened.
Add remaining ingredients, except broccoli, turkey, parsley and rice noodles, and bring to a light boil.
Reduce heat and simmer, covered, for 20 minutes.
Add broccoli, turkey and parsley, and simmer for 15 more minutes.
Stir in rice noodles.
Season to taste.

Coconut Chicken Soup

(A Tandoori style soup)

1 Tbsp. olive oil
3-4 cloves garlic, minced
2 onions, finely chopped
3 cups finely chopped cauliflower
5 cups chicken stock
2 cups coconut milk
1½ tsp. cumin
1 tsp. each dried basil, coriander & turmeric
½ tsp. cardamom
3 cups chopped broccoli
1 cup cooked chicken, cubed
2 Tbsp. fresh lime juice
sea salt & pepper

In a stockpot, heat oil over medium-low heat.
Add garlic and onions, and sauté for 3 minutes.
Add remaining ingredients, except broccoli, chicken and lime juice, and bring to a light boil.
Reduce heat and simmer, covered, for 15 minutes.
Add broccoli and chicken, and simmer for 10-15 more minutes.
Stir in lime juice.
Season to taste.

Chicken & Dumpling Soup

(Easy to prepare dumplings makes this quick to cook soup good anytime)

1 Tbsp. olive oil or ghee
2-3 cloves garlic, minced
1 onion or 2 shallots, finely chopped
2 cups chopped broccoli
5-6 cups chicken or vegetable stock
6-8 oz. cooked chicken, cubed
$\frac{1}{2}$-1 tsp. dried rosemary
1 recipe Rosemary Dumplings (see page 133)
sea salt & pepper

In a stockpot or Dutch oven, heat oil or ghee over medium heat.
Add garlic and onion or shallots, and sauté for 2-3 minutes.
Add broccoli, stock, chicken and rosemary, and bring to a light boil.
Reduce heat to a simmer and add dumplings.
Cover and let simmer for 15 minutes.
Note: Do not lift the cover during simmering time.
Season to taste.

• Makes 4-6 servings.

Variation
❖ For **Vegetable & Dumpling Soup**: *replace chicken with 1-2 cups chopped vegetables of choice.*

Turkey Vegetable & Pumpkin Soup

(A soup that is good for the fall harvest)

2 Tbsp. olive oil
3 cloves garlic, minced
1 shallot, minced
1 onion, finely chopped
2 carrots, chopped
2 celery stalks, chopped
2 turnips, cubed
2 sweet potatoes, cubed
1 lb. pumpkin, cooked & mashed
6-7 cups turkey stock
1 tsp. dried basil & cumin
$\frac{1}{2}$ tsp. each chili powder, dried thyme & turmeric
1$\frac{1}{2}$ cups cooked turkey, cubed
sea salt & pepper

In a stockpot, heat oil over medium-low heat.
Add garlic, shallot and onion, and sauté for 3 minutes.
Add remaining ingredients, except turkey, and bring to a light boil;
stir to incorporate pumpkin.
Reduce heat and simmer, covered, for 25 minutes.
Add turkey and simmer 10-15 more minutes.
Season to taste.

Variation
❖ *Replace turnips with 1-2 finely chopped parsnips.*

Turkey Noodle Soup

2 Tbsp. olive oil
2 cloves garlic, minced
1 shallot, minced
1 leek, finely chopped
3-4 carrots, finely chopped
2 celery stalks, finely chopped
2 red potatoes, cubed
2 turnips, cubed
7-8 cups turkey stock
1 tsp. dried oregano
$\frac{1}{2}$ tsp. dried thyme
pinch or 2 of cayenne pepper
2 cups chopped broccoli
$1\frac{1}{2}$-2 cups cooked turkey, cubed
$\frac{1}{4}$ cup each fresh basil, parsley & sage, finely chopped
6 oz. dry brown rice spaghetti noodles, broken & cooked
sea salt & pepper

In a stockpot, heat oil over medium-low heat.
Add garlic, shallot and leek, and sauté for 3-5 minutes.
Add remaining ingredients, except broccoli, turkey, fresh herbs and rice noodles, and bring to a light boil.
Reduce heat and simmer, covered, for 25 minutes.
Add broccoli, turkey and fresh herbs, and simmer for 15 more minutes.
Stir in rice noodles.
Season to taste.

Variation
❖ *Add 1 cup finely chopped spinach, kale or Swiss chard to last 15 minutes of cooking time.*

Roasted Garlic & Turkey Soup

(Roasted garlic gives this turkey & vegetable soup a unique taste experience)

5 whole garlic bulbs, roasted (see page 167)
2 cups plain almond or cashew milk
2 Tbsp. olive oil
2 shallots, minced
2 carrots, finely chopped
2 celery stalks, finely chopped
2 sweet potatoes, cubed
3 cups shredded cabbage
4 cups turkey stock
½ cup white wine (optional)
1 tsp. each chili powder, cumin & dried parsley
1-1½ cups cooked turkey, cubed
2 Tbsp. tapioca flour mixed in ¼ cup water
sea salt & pepper

Blend together roasted garlic and almond or cashew milk until smooth.
In a stockpot, heat oil over medium-low heat.
Add shallots and sauté for 2 minutes.
Add remaining ingredients, except turkey and tapioca mixture, and bring to a light boil.
Reduce heat and simmer, covered, for 25 minutes.
Add turkey and simmer for 10-15 more minutes.
Turn off heat.
Add tapioca mixture and stir until thickened.
Season to taste.

Lamb & Vegetable Soup

1-2 Tbsp. olive oil
3 cloves garlic, minced
1 shallot, minced
1 onion, finely chopped
2 cups finely chopped carrots
1 cup finely chopped celery
2 cups chopped cauliflower
2 cups shredded green cabbage
2 turnips, cubed
1 cup squash or 1 sweet potato, cubed
10 cups lamb or vegetable stock
2 tsp. dried oregano
1 tsp. dried rosemary & sage
1 tsp. dried mint (optional)
2 cups chopped broccoli
1½-2 cups cooked lamb, cubed
sea salt & pepper

In a stockpot, heat oil over medium-low heat.
Add garlic, shallot and onion, and sauté for 3 minutes.
Add remaining ingredients, except broccoli and lamb, and bring to a light boil.
Reduce heat and simmer, covered, for 25 minutes.
Add broccoli and lamb, and simmer for 10-15 more minutes.
Season to taste.

Variation
❖ *Replace lamb with venison, emu or red meat of choice.*

Rabbit Vegetable with Saffron Soup

(Saffron adds wonderful flavour to the light taste of rabbit)

1-2 tbsp. olive oil
3 cloves garlic, minced
1 shallot, minced
1 onion, finely chopped
1 leek, finely chopped
4-5 carrots, finely chopped
3-4 celery stalks, finely chopped
2 turnips, cubed
7-8 cups vegetable stock
1 tsp. saffron threads
1 tsp, dried marjoram & parsley
pinch or 2 of cayenne pepper
4 Swiss chard leaves, finely chopped
1½-2 cups cooked rabbit, cubed
sea salt & pepper

In a stockpot, heat oil over medium-low heat.
Add garlic, shallot, onion and leek, and sauté for 5-7 minutes.
Add remaining ingredients, except Swiss chard and rabbit, and bring to a light boil.
Reduce heat and simmer, covered, for 25 minutes.
Add Swiss chard and rabbit, and simmer for 15 more minutes.
Season to taste.

• If saffron is unavailable use 1-2 tsp. safflower.

Variation
❖ *Rabbit stock can be used instead of vegetable stock. Make as a meat stock, using ½ or whole rabbit cut into pieces.*

Roasted Duck & Mushroom Soup

(A combination of duck, shitake mushrooms & coconut makes this a
wonderful flavoured soup)

2 Tbsp. ghee
10 oz. shitake mushrooms, sliced
1 Tbsp. olive oil
3-4 cloves garlic, minced
1 Tbsp. fresh ginger, minced
6 cups vegetable, chicken or duck stock
2-3 cups coconut milk
1½-2 cups roasted duck, cubed
1 Tbsp. paprika
½ Tbsp. cumin
1 tsp. coriander
3 Tbsp. tapioca flour mixed in ¼ cup water
2 tbsp. fresh lime juice
sea salt & pepper

In a stockpot, heat ghee over medium-low heat.
Add mushrooms and sauté until lightly browned; remove and set aside.
Add olive oil, garlic and ginger, and sauté for 2 minutes.
Add remaining ingredients, except mushrooms, tapioca mixture and
lime juice, and bring to a light boil.
Reduce heat and simmer, covered, for 15 minutes.
Add mushrooms and simmer for 5 more minutes.
Turn off heat.
Add tapioca mixture and lime juice; stir until thickened.
Season to taste.

Variations
❖ *Cooked wild rice or brown rice noodles can be added at end of
  cooking time.*
❖ *Replace duck with any other roasted bird.*

Winter Vegetable Stew

(Don't let the name fool you; this stew can be enjoyed year-round)

1-2 tbsp. olive oil
1 shallot, finely chopped
1 leek, chopped
2 carrots, cut into bite-sized pieces
2 celery stalks, cut into bite-sized pieces
2 parsnips, cut into bite-sized pieces
2 red or purple potatoes, cut into bite-sized pieces
1 sweet potato, cut into bite-sized pieces
2 turnips or 1 rutabaga, cut into bite-sized pieces
2 cups cooked squash or pumpkin, mashed
about 4 cups vegetable stock
2 Tbsp. liquid aminos (optional)
3-5 dried bay leaves
1 tsp. dried savory & tarragon
$\frac{1}{4}$ cup fresh basil, finely chopped
sea salt & pepper

In a stockpot, heat oil over medium-low heat.
Add shallot and leek, and sauté for 3-5 minutes.
Add remaining ingredients, except basil, and bring to a light boil. (Use only enough stock to just cover the vegetables)
Reduce heat and simmer, covered, for 20 minutes.
Add basil and simmer for 10-15 more minutes, until vegetables are tender.
Season to taste.

• To make a thicker stew: combine 2 Tbsp. tapioca flour with $\frac{1}{4}$ cup water and stir in at the end of cooking time until thickened.

Chicken Curry Stew

1-2 Tbsp. olive oil
3 cloves garlic, minced
1 onion, finely chopped
2 carrots, chopped
2 celery stalks, chopped
2 sweet potatoes, chopped
1 cup shredded green cabbage
1 tsp. coriander & cumin seeds, ground
$\frac{1}{2}$-1 tsp. chili flakes, ground
$\frac{1}{2}$ tsp. garam masala, paprika & turmeric
$3\frac{1}{2}$ cups chicken or vegetable stock
1 cup white wine or water
2 Tbsp. liquid aminos
1 small zucchini or 2 small tomatoes, chopped
$1\frac{1}{2}$ cups spinach, chopped
12-16 oz. cooked chicken, cubed
$\frac{1}{4}$ cup fresh parsley, finely chopped
2-3 Tbsp. tapioca flour mixed in $\frac{1}{2}$ cup water
sea salt & pepper

In a stockpot, heat oil over medium heat.
Add garlic, onion, carrots and celery, and sauté for 5 minutes.
Add sweet potatoes, cabbage, spices, stock, wine or water and liquid aminos, and bring to a light boil.
Reduce heat and simmer, covered, for 20 minutes.
Add zucchini or tomatoes, spinach, chicken, parsley, and simmer for 10-15 more minutes, until vegetables are tender.
Add tapioca mixture and stir until thickened. Season to taste.
Variations
❖ *Replace chicken with curried meatballs or lamb.*
❖ *For **Vegetable Curry Stew**: replace chicken with 1-14 oz. can chickpeas.*

Turkey Saffron Stew

(This stew has some Caribbean flare)

2 Tbsp. olive oil
1½ lb. boneless & skinless turkey, cut into bite-sized pieces
1 onion, finely chopped
½ Tbsp. fresh ginger, minced
1 tsp. cinnamon & turmeric
½-1 tsp. saffron threads
3½ cups vegetable or turkey stock
3-4 Tbsp. tomato paste
3 carrots, cut into bite-sized pieces
2 celery stalks, cut into bite-sized pieces
1 turnip, cut into bite-sized pieces
1 tsp. dried parsley
1 cup frozen peas
3 cups chopped spinach
1 Tbsp. fresh lemon juice
sea salt & pepper

In a stockpot or Dutch oven, heat oil over medium heat.
Add turkey and brown all sides.
Add onion, ginger, turmeric, cinnamon and saffron, and sauté for 3 minutes.
Add stock, tomato paste, carrots, celery, turnip and parsley, and bring to a light boil.
Reduce heat and simmer, covered, for 25 minutes.
Stir in peas and spinach, and simmer for 7-10 more minutes.
Stir in lemon juice.
Season to taste.

• Makes 6 servings.

Spiced Turkey & Vegetable Stew

2-3 cinnamon sticks, broken into pieces
3 Tbsp. whole star anise
1 Tbsp. whole cloves
1 Tbsp. fennel seeds (optional)
2 Tbsp. olive oil
1 lb. boneless and skinless turkey, cut into bite-sized pieces
2 cloves garlic, minced
2-3 tsp. fresh ginger, minced
1 leek, chopped
2 carrots, cut into bite-sized pieces
2 sweet potatoes, cut into bite-sized pieces
1 rutabaga, cut into bite-sized pieces
2 parsnips, cut into bite-sized pieces
$1\frac{1}{2}$-2 cups chopped fennel
4 cups turkey or vegetable stock
1 cup white wine
$\frac{1}{4}$ cup tapioca flour mixed in $\frac{1}{2}$ cup water
sea salt & pepper

Place cinnamon, star anise, cloves and fennel seeds (if using) in the center of a cloth or a piece of cheese cloth and tie into a ball. (spices can also be put into a tea/spice ball)
In a Dutch oven or stockpot, heat oil over medium heat.
Add turkey and brown all sides.
Add garlic, ginger and leek, and sauté for 3 minutes.
Add remaining ingredients, except tapioca mixture, and bring to a light boil.
Reduce heat and simmer, covered, for 25-35 minutes, until vegetables are tender.
Remove spice ball.
Add tapioca mixture and stir until thickened. Season to taste.

Turkey Meatball & Vegetable Stew

1-2 Tbsp. olive oil
2-3 cloves garlic, minced
1 onion or white part of a leek, chopped
2 carrots, cut into bite-sized pieces
2 celery stalks, cut into bite-sized pieces
1 sweet potato, cut into bite-sized pieces
2 turnips, cut into bite-sized pieces
$4\frac{1}{2}$ cups turkey stock
1 tsp. dried basil & rosemary
2 cups shredded cabbage
2 cups chopped Swiss chard
1 recipe Herb Meatballs, cooked (see page 187)
3 Tbsp. tapioca flour mixed in $\frac{1}{4}$ cup water
sea salt & pepper

In a Dutch oven or stockpot, heat oil over medium heat.
Add garlic and onion or leek, and sauté for 3-5 minutes.
Add carrots, celery, sweet potato, turnips, stock and dried herbs, and bring to a light boil.
Reduce heat and simmer, covered, for 15 minutes.
Add cabbage, Swiss chard and meat balls, and simmer for 15-20 more minutes, until vegetables are tender.
Add tapioca mixture and stir until thickened.
Season to taste.
• Makes 4-6 servings.

Variations
❖ *For tomato base stew: replace $1\frac{1}{2}$ cups stock and tapioca mixture with 2 cups diced tomatoes and 3 oz. tomato paste; add both ingredients with stock.*
❖ *Replace Swiss chard with kale, collards or spinach.*

Venison Stew

(This stew has a little zing)

2 Tbsp. ghee
12-16 okra, tips removed and cut into $\frac{1}{2}$" rounds (optional)
1 Tbsp. olive oil
1 lb. stewing venison
1 Tbsp. fresh ginger, minced
3 cloves garlic, minced
1 shallot, minced
1 leek (white part only), chopped
2 tsp. cumin seeds, crushed
1 tsp. each coriander seeds, chili flakes & fennel seeds, crushed
1 tsp. garam masala & dried parsley
$\frac{1}{2}$ tsp. dried oregano & turmeric
2 carrots, cut into bite-sized pieces
2 celery stalks, cut into bite-sized pieces
4 cups vegetable stock
1 cup red wine
$\frac{1}{4}$ cup liquid aminos
2 sweet potatoes, cut into bite-sized pieces
2 cups chopped cauliflower
2 cups chopped spinach or Swiss chard
$\frac{1}{4}$ cup tapioca flour mixed in $\frac{1}{4}$ cup water
sea salt & pepper

In a Dutch oven, heat ghee over medium-low heat.
Add okra (if using) and sauté for 10-15 minutes, until browned. Remove and set aside.
Add oil and bring to medium heat.
Add venison and brown all sides.
Add ginger, garlic, shallot, leek, herbs and spices, and sauté for 2 minutes.

Add carrots, celery, stock, wine and liquid aminos, and bring to a light boil.

Reduce heat and simmer, covered, for 45 minutes.

Add sweet potatoes and simmer for 10 minutes.

Add cauliflower and spinach or Swiss chard, and simmer for 15-20 more minutes or until meat and vegetables are tender.

Stir in okra (if using).

Add tapioca mixture and stir until thickened.

Season to taste.

Variations

❖ *If okra is not used: add 1½ cups shredded green cabbage with sweet potatoes.*

❖ *Replace venison with lamb or red meat of choice.*

❖ *For a tomato base stew: replace 2 cups stock and tapioca mixture with 2 cups pureed tomatoes and 1 small can tomato paste.*

Vegetable Salads & Vegetables

Tips for Salads & Vegetables   94
Lemon Broccoli Salad   95
Broccoli & English Cucumber Salad   96
Mango & English Cucumber Salad   97
Cucumber & Tomato Salad   98
Carrot & Tahini Salad   99
Radicchio & Pear Salad   100
Belgium Endive Salad   101
Spinach Salad with Raspberries   102
Beet Salad Plus   103
Sweet Potato Salad   104
Mixed Vegetable & Pesto Salad with Mint   105
Coleslaw 106
Grilled Vegetable Salad   107
Green Beans & Toasted Almonds   109
Sweet & Sour Leeks   110
Sour Broccoli Sauté   111
Butternut Squash & Sweet Potato Fries   112
Roasted Pesto Potatoes   113
Roasted Root Vegetables   114
Lemon Garlic Spaghetti Squash   115
Vegetable Pakora   116
Scalloped Sweet & Red Potatoes, with Saffron   117
Broccoli & Cauliflower Bake   118
Sweet Potato & Rutabaga Bake   119
Mixed Vegetable Bake   120
Roasted Garlic Squash Gratin   121
Roasted Fennel with Tomato Sauce   122
Vegetable Gratin   123
Grilled Vegetable Lasagna   124
Fried Zucchini Lasagna   126
Broccoli & Cauliflower Pie   127
Cauliflower & Leek Pie with Saffron   128
Spinach Pie   129
Vegetable Curry Pie   130
Spinach Dumplings   132
Rosemary Dumplings   133

Tips for Salads & Vegetables

❖ Always purchase and use fresh crisp vegetables. Frozen vegetables can be used occasionally.

❖ Always wash and rinse all vegetables well with a vegetable cleaner or food grade hydrogen peroxide. Even hard skinned vegetables, like squash, etc., need to be cleaned, because if there is any kind of bacteria or disease on it, the knife used in cutting the vegetable can transport the bacteria to the flesh. Organic vegetables need to be washed as well.

❖ If a certain kind of vegetable is unavailable, replace it with one similar or use frozen. Canned vegetables are the least recommended.

❖ Leave skins on vegetables when possible. Skins carry a lot of fibre and nutrients. Certain vegetables, like potatoes, have more nutrients on the outer part than they do in the middle.

❖ The darker in colour the vegetable the more nutrients.

❖ If there is any mold or spoilage to any area of a vegetable, it is safer to throw it away than it is to cut it off and use the rest. Mold is a sign the whole vegetable is spoiled or rotten and can be harmful if consumed, especially to those who are susceptible to mold, fungus, etc.

❖ These tips apply to fruit as well.

Lemon Broccoli Salad

(A refreshing summer salad)

4 cups broccoli, chopped
1 cup red or orange sweet pepper, finely chopped
3 green onions or ¼ cup red onion, finely chopped
¼ cup sugar toasted almonds (see page 169)
2 Tbsp. flax seed oil
3 Tbsp. fresh lemon juice
1 tsp. liquid aminos
½ tsp. dried thyme (or 1 Tbsp. fresh)
sea salt & pepper

In a bowl, toss together broccoli, red or orange pepper, onions and almonds.
Drizzle on oil, lemon juice and liquid aminos.
Sprinkle on thyme and season to taste.
Toss salad to coat; chill

- Makes 4-6 servings.
- Cover and refrigerate for up to 4 days.

Broccoli & English Cucumber Salad

(An easy to prepare salad with lots of flavour)

1 large head broccoli florets
1 English cucumber, sliced
1 small red onion, sliced thin
$\frac{1}{4}$ cup pumpkin or sunflower seeds
  Dressing:
    $\frac{1}{2}$ cup plain goat's milk or soy yogurt
    3 Tbsp. apple cider vinegar
    3 Tbsp. fresh lemon juice
    1 Tbsp. flax or hemp seed oil
    1-2 Tbsp. fresh herbs; basil, oregano, parsley & thyme, finely chopped
    1 clove garlic, minced
    sea salt & pepper

In a bowl, mix together broccoli, cucumber, onion and pumpkin or sunflower seeds.
In another bowl, stir together ingredients for dressing until well combined.
Season to taste.
Pour dressing over salad and toss to coat; chill.

- Makes minimum 6 servings.
- Cover and refrigerate for up to 3 days.

Mango & English Cucumber Salad

(An awesome tasting hot summer's day salad)

1 mango, sliced into strips
1 small English cucumber, sliced
1 roasted red pepper, finely chopped (see page 167)
   Dressing:
      2 Tbsp. fresh lime juice
      1 Tbsp. olive or flax seed oil
      1 Tbsp. liquid aminos
      $\frac{1}{2}$ -1 tsp. chili powder
      1 tsp. dried mint
      $\frac{1}{4}$ tsp. cumin (optional)
      1/8 tsp. sea salt
$\frac{1}{4}$ cup sugar toasted almonds (see page 169)
         or
$\frac{1}{2}$ cup crispy rice noodles (see page 169)

In a bowl, toss together mango, cucumber and red pepper.
In a small bowl, whisk or stir together ingredients for dressing until well combined.
Pour dressing over mango mixture and toss to coat.
Sprinkle with sugar toasted almonds or crispy rice noodles.
Chill.

• Makes 4-6 servings.
• Refrigerate for up to 3 days.

Cucumber & Tomato Salad

(A simple salad with a salsa feel)

1 field cucumber, sliced
2 large tomatoes, chopped
1 small red or white onion, sliced thin
2-3 Tbsp. fresh parsley or mint, finely chopped
  Dressing:
    3 Tbsp. olive oil
    2 Tbsp. apple cider vinegar
    1 Tbsp. fresh lemon or lime juice
    2 cloves garlic, minced
    $\frac{1}{2}$ tsp. grain or Dijon mustard
    $\frac{1}{4}$ tsp. each chili powder, cumin and sea salt

In a bowl, toss together cucumber, tomatoes, onion and parsley or mint.
In a small bowl, whisk or stir together ingredients for dressing until well combined.
Pour dressing over salad mix and toss to coat; chill.

• Makes 4 servings.
• Cover and refrigerate for up to 5 days.

Carrot & Tahini Salad

(With the added options this salad is...well...just try it & see)

6-8 large carrots, coarsely shredded
  Dressing:
    3 Tbsp. tahini
    $2\frac{1}{2}$ Tbsp. flax seed oil
    $2\frac{1}{2}$ Tbsp. fresh lemon juice
    2 Tbsp. water or apple cider vinegar
    $\frac{1}{2}$ Tbsp. honey
    1 clove garlic, minced
    1 tsp. fresh ginger, minced
    $\frac{1}{2}$ tsp. cinnamon
$\frac{1}{2}$ cup sunflower seeds
$\frac{1}{2}$ cup crunchy sprouts of choice (optional)
$\frac{1}{4}$ cup soaked raisins (optional)

Place carrots in a salad bowl.
In another bowl or blender, mix together ingredients for dressing until smooth.
Pour dressing over carrots and toss to coat.
Top with sunflower seeds, sprouts and raisins (if using); chill.

• Makes 4-8 servings.
• Cover and refrigerate for up to 5 days.

Variations
❖ *Replace tahini with almond, pumpkin seed or sunflower seed butter.*
❖ *For **Carrot Salad with Orange Ginger Dressing**: replace tahini dressing with orange ginger dressing on page 143.*

Radicchio & Pear Salad

(The bitterness of radicchio is balanced with the sweetness of pear)

1 large head radicchio, torn into bite-sized pieces
  Dressing:
    2 Tbsp. olive oil
    2 Tbsp. flax seed oil
    1 Tbsp. apple cider vinegar
    1 Tbsp. liquid aminos
    1 clove garlic, minced
    sea salt & pepper
1 pear, cored and sliced
$\frac{1}{4}$ cup sugar toasted almonds (see page 169)
2 oz. goat's milk feta, crumbled

Place radicchio into a salad bowl.
In a small bowl, whisk or stir together ingredients for dressing until well combined.
Season to taste.
Pour dressing over radicchio and toss to coat.
Top with pear, almonds and feta; chill.
Toss before serving.

• Makes 4 servings.

Belgium Endive Salad

(A light salad with a mild taste that is quick to prepare any day of the year)

2 Belgium endive, chopped
  Dressing:
    1 Tbsp. almond, walnut or flax seed oil
    $\frac{1}{2}$ tsp. sesame oil
    2 Tbsp. fresh lemon juice
    1 tsp. liquid aminos
    1 clove garlic, minced or 1/8 tsp. garlic powder
    $\frac{1}{4}$ tsp. dried marjoram
$\frac{1}{4}$ cup sugar toasted almonds (see page 169)
$\frac{1}{4}$ to $\frac{1}{2}$ cup crispy rice noodles (see page 169)
2 oz. goat's feta, crumbled

Place endive into a salad bowl.
In a small bowl, whisk or stir together ingredients for dressing until well combined.
Pour dressing over endive and toss to coat.
Top with almonds, crispy rice noodles and feta; chill.
Toss before serving.

• Makes 2-4 servings.

Variation
❖ *Add $\frac{1}{4}$ cup sliced olives.*

Spinach & Arugula Salad with Raspberries

(A refreshing, excellent summer-time salad)

3-4 cups spinach
3-4 cups arugula
¼ cup diced green onions
¾ cup fresh raspberries
1½ Tbsp. pumpkin seed or hemp seed oil
1 Tbsp. almond or walnut oil
1½ Tbsp. fresh lemon or lime juice
1 Tbsp. apple cider vinegar
1 Tbsp. water
½ tsp. dried or 1 Tbsp, fresh, finely chopped mint (optional)
1/3 cup sugar toasted almonds (see page 169)
3 oz. goat's milk feta, crumbled

Remove stems from spinach and arugula, and tear leaves into bite-sized pieces.
Place spinach, arugula and onions into a salad bowl.
In a blender, process together ¼ cup raspberries, oils, lemon juice, vinegar and water until smooth.
Mix in mint (if using).
Pour dressing over spinach mix and toss to coat.
Top with remaining raspberries, almonds and feta; chill.
Toss before serving.

• Makes 4-6 servings.
• Mesculin mix may also be used.

Beet Salad Plus

(A salad that is excellent for the liver and gallbladder)

3 large beets, peeled and coarsely shredded
½ fennel bulb, coarsely shredded
1 kohlrabi, coarsely shredded
4-6 radishes, coarsely shredded
2 Tbsp. fresh parsley, finely chopped
   Dressing:
      1½-2 Tbsp. olive or flax seed oil
      3 Tbsp. fresh lemon juice
      1 tsp. grain or Dijon mustard (optional)
      1 tsp. dried herb of choice: dill, oregano, rosemary or tarragon
      sea salt & pepper

Place beets, fennel, kohlrabi, radishes and parsley into a salad bowl.
In a small bowl, whisk or stir together ingredients for dressing until well combined.
Season to taste.
Pour dressing over salad mix and toss to coat.

- Makes 4-6 servings.
- Cover and refrigerate for up to 3 days.

Variations
❖ *Add 1-2 minced garlic cloves.*
❖ *For **Creamy Beet Salad**: add ¼ cup plain goat's milk yogurt to dressing.*
❖ *Add 1 diced apple to salad.*

Sweet Potato Salad

(A different twist on regular potato salad, with a brighter summer colour)

1½ lbs. sweet potatoes, peeled and cut into bite-sized pieces
4-6 green onions, finely chopped
2 Tbsp. fresh parsley, finely chopped
  Dressing:
    1/3 cup plain goat's milk yogurt
    1½ Tbsp. mayonnaise
    1½ Tbsp. olive or flax seed oil
    1½ Tbsp. fresh lemon juice
    ½ tsp. paprika
    sea salt & pepper

Steam or boil sweet potatoes until tender, about 12-15 minutes. Drain and cool slightly.
In a salad bowl, stir together yogurt, mayonnaise, oil, lemon juice and paprika.
Season to taste.
Add potatoes, onions and parsley; stir gently to coat.

• Makes 4-8 servings.
• Cover and refrigerate for up to 3 days.

Variation
❖ For **Sweet Potato Salad with Tarragon Vinaigrette**: *replace dressing with; 1½ Tbsp. olive and flaxseed oil, 3 Tbsp. apple cider vinegar, 1¼ Tbsp. fresh lime juice, ½ Tbsp. Dijon or grain mustard and ½-1 tsp dried or 2 Tbsp. fresh tarragon, finely chopped.*

Mixed Vegetable & Pesto Salad with Mint

(The hint of mint makes this a great summer salad)

1 English cucumber, sliced
6-8 radishes, sliced
1 small red onion, sliced
1 kohlrabi, julienne
  Pesto:
    $1\frac{1}{2}$ cups fresh basil, unpacked
    $\frac{3}{4}$ cup fresh mint, unpacked
    $\frac{1}{4}$ cup pecans
    2 cloves garlic
    2 Tbsp. flax or hemp seed oil
    1 Tbsp. olive oil
    1 Tbsp. fresh lemon juice
    2 Tbsp. water
    sea salt & pepper
$\frac{1}{4}$ cup crumbled goat's milk feta

In a salad bowl, toss together cucumber, radishes, onions and kohlrabi.
In a food processor, combine basil, mint, pecans, and garlic; process until finely chopped.
With machine running, add oils, lemon juice and water; blend until smooth.
Season to taste.
Pour dressing over salad mix and toss to coat.
Top with cheese; chill.

• Makes about 6 servings.
• Cover and refrigerate for up to 3 days.

Coleslaw

(Caraway adds a sharp delightful taste to this coleslaw, but also try the optional dressing)

$3\frac{1}{2}$-4 cups cabbage, shredded

1 large carrot, shredded

$\frac{1}{2}$ fennel bulb, shredded

1 onion, diced

$\frac{1}{2}$ green or red sweet pepper, diced

  Dressing:

    1/3 cup plain goat's milk or soy yogurt

    $\frac{1}{4}$ cup apple cider vinegar

    3 tbsp. fresh lemon juice

    3 Tbsp. mayonnaise

    1 Tbsp. honey or brown rice syrup

    1 tsp. caraway seeds, crushed or ground

    $\frac{1}{2}$ tsp. sea salt

    1/8 tsp. pepper

In a bowl, mix together cabbage, carrot, fennel, onion and pepper.
In another bowl, stir together ingredients for dressing until well combined.
Pour dressing over cabbage mix and toss to coat; chill.

- Makes 8 or more servings.
- Cover and refrigerate for up to 3 days.

Variation

❖ *For **Tangy Orange Cabbage Salad**: replace dressing with orange ginger dressing on page 143 and add, optional, orange segments.*

Grilled Vegetable Salad

(A salad for the barbecue season)

1 zucchini, cut into $\frac{1}{2}$" chunks
1 red, orange or yellow sweet pepper, cut into 1" chunks
8 shitake mushrooms (optional)
2 small onions, cut into $\frac{1}{4}$" slices
3 plum tomatoes, cut into $\frac{1}{2}$" slices or 8-12 whole cherry tomatoes
6 asparagus spears, cut into 2" pieces
  Dressing:
    2 Tbsp. olive oil
    2 Tbsp. fresh lemon juice
    2 Tbsp. apple cider vinegar
    2 Tbsp. water
    1 Tbsp. liquid aminos
    1 clove garlic, minced
    $\frac{1}{2}$ tsp. dried oregano or thyme
    pinch of cayenne pepper
    sea salt & pepper
3 cups mixed chopped salad greens
2 cups mixed chopped salad 'bitters'
3-4 oz. goat's milk feta, crumbled

In a bowl, add zucchini, pepper, mushrooms (if using), onions,
tomatoes and asparagus.
In another bowl, stir together ingredients for dressing until well
combined.
Season to taste.
Pour dressing over vegetables and toss to coat.
Let vegetables marinate for about 30 minutes; toss every 10 minutes.
Grill vegetables, either in a grilling pan, under the broiler or on the
barbecue, until tender, about 10-15 minutes.
Place salad greens and bitters into a salad bowl.

Add grilled vegetables and add any remaining dressing left over from marinade.

Toss to coat.

Top with cheese.

- Makes 4-6 servings.
- Serve warm or chilled.
- For salad greens: choose a mix from any of the following, romaine lettuce, leaf lettuce, butter lettuce, spinach or arugula.
- For salad bitters: choose a mix from any of the following, radicchio, endive, Belgium endive, chicory or escarole.

Green Beans & Toasted Almonds

(A simple dish that is sure to please)

1 cup green beans, chopped into 1" pieces
1 Tbsp. ghee or unsalted butter
$\frac{1}{4}$ sliced or slivered almonds
1-2 cloves garlic, minced
1 tsp. fresh lemon juice
$\frac{1}{2}$ Tbsp. rice or soy Parmesan cheese
sea salt

Steam beans until tender, about 7 minutes.
In a skillet, heat ghee or butter over medium heat.
Add almonds and garlic, and sauté until almonds turn lightly brown, about 3 minutes. Stir occasionally.
Add beans and cook until heated through.
Stir in lemon juice.
Sprinkle on cheese.
Season to taste.

• Makes 2 servings.

Variations
❖ *Add 1 finely chopped tomato. Add with beans.*
❖ *Replace $\frac{1}{2}$ or all of green beans with asparagus.*

Sweet & Sour Leeks

(The delicate flavour of leek is enhanced in this fast & easy to prepare dish)

2 Tbsp. ghee
3-4 leeks (white part only), chopped
2 cloves garlic, minced
$\frac{1}{4}$ cup liquid aminos
$\frac{1}{2}$ Tbsp. honey or brown rice syrup
2 Tbsp. tomato paste
$\frac{1}{2}$ Tbsp. apple cider vinegar
$\frac{1}{2}$ tsp. chili powder
sea salt & pepper

In a skillet, heat ghee over medium-low heat.
Add leeks and sauté for 5 minutes.
In a small bowl, stir together remaining ingredients until well combined.
Add liquid mixture to skillet; reduce heat and let simmer, covered, for 10-15 minutes.
Season to taste.

• Makes 4 or more servings.
• Add onions or shallots with leeks.

Sour Broccoli Sauté

(A simple to prepare dish that adds oomph to a wonderful vegetable)

1 small head broccoli, chopped
1 Tbsp. ghee or olive oil
2-3 cloves garlic, minced
1 shallot, finely chopped
½ tsp. chili powder & cumin
1 Tbsp. liquid aminos
1 Tbsp. apple cider vinegar
sea salt & pepper

Steam broccoli until tender and refresh under cold water.
In a skillet, heat ghee or oil over medium-low heat
Add garlic, shallots, chili powder and cumin, and sauté for 3-5 minutes.
Add broccoli, liquid aminos and apple cider vinegar, and cook until heated through.
Season to taste.

• Make 2-4 servings.

Variation
❖ *Add 1-2 tsp. fresh minced ginger; add with garlic.*

Butternut Squash & Sweet Potato Fries

(The classy French fry)

1 small butternut squash, peeled & pulp removed
   or
2 sweet potatoes, peeled
2-3 Tbsp. olive oil
spice combinations, choose 1:
   1) ½-1 tsp. each chili powder, cumin & garlic salt
   2) ½ tsp. each dried basil, oregano & parsley + 2 Tbsp. ground
      almonds and 1 Tbsp. rice Parmesan cheese.
   3) ½ tsp. garlic powder & sea salt + 1 tsp. dried parsley.
   4) ¼-½ tsp. each saffron threads, ground; garlic salt & chili powder.

Cut squash or sweet potatoes into 3/8-1/2" square slices, and place
into a mixing bowl.
Add 2 Tbsp. olive oil and stir to coat; add 1 more Tbsp. oil if needed.
Stir in spice combination of choice; mix to coat well.
Transfer ingredients to a baking pan and spread out in a single layer.
Bake at 400°F for 30-40 minutes; turn once halfway through.

• Makes 2-4 servings.
• Use squash and sweet potato together.

Roasted Pesto Potatoes

(Pesto gives this potato dish pizzazz)

4 medium red potatoes
1-2 Tbsp. olive oil or melted ghee
3 Tbsp. pesto
2 tsp. Parmesan cheese, rice, soy or goat's milk

Cut potatoes into wedges; can be peeled if desired.
Place potatoes into a mixing bowl.
Add 1 Tbsp. oil or ghee and pesto and stir to coat; add 1 more Tbsp. oil
or ghee if needed.
Transfer to a baking pan.
Sprinkle on Parmesan cheese.
Roast at 400°F for 30-35 minutes; turning once.

• Makes 2-4 servings.
• Make sure pesto is made with olive oil and not flax or hemp seed oil.

Roasted Root Vegetables

(Roasting vegetables gives them a more robust flavour; be sure to add the lemon juice for added zing)

6-8 cups mixed root vegetables: sweet potato, carrots, beets, parsnips, turnip, rutabaga, shallots, pearl onions, etc., cut into bite-sized chunks
3 Tbsp. olive oil
1 tsp. cumin & chili pepper
$\frac{1}{2}$ tsp. coriander, paprika & turmeric (optional)
$\frac{1}{4}$ tsp. garlic powder
sea salt & pepper

Place vegetables into a mixing bowl.
Add oil and spices; toss to coat. Add 1 more Tbsp. oil if needed.
Transfer to a baking pan.
Season to taste.
Roast at 400°F for 30-40 minutes; turning once.
When finished roasting, squeeze fresh lemon juice over top.

• Makes 4 or more servings.
• Sprinkle with rice Parmesan.

Lemon Garlic Spaghetti Squash

(The powerful punch of garlic & the zest of lemon juice gives this mild tasting winter squash some class)

1 spaghetti squash
2 Tbsp. ghee or unsalted butter, melted
2 Tbsp. olive oil
1½ Tbsp. fresh lemon juice
3 cloves garlic, minced
½ tsp. dried basil, oregano & parsley
2 Tbsp. ground almonds
1-2 Tbsp rice Parmesan cheese
sea salt & pepper

To bake squash (any kind):
1) Cut squash in half and scoop out center pulp and seeds.
2) Place cut side down on baking sheet and add water to cover bottom of pan.
3) Bake at 350°F for 45 minutes or until flesh is tender.

Remove spaghetti-like strands of flesh with a fork and place into an oiled baking dish.
Combine ghee or butter, olive oil, lemon juice, garlic and herbs; drizzle over squash.
Sprinkle on ground almonds and Parmesan.
Season to taste.
Bake at 375°F, uncovered, for 15 minutes.

• Makes 4 or more servings.

Vegetable Pakora

(A 'deep-fried' mild curry vegetable dish)

2 cups mixed vegetables, shredded
1/3 cup chickpea flour
1½ tsp. baking powder
½ tsp. chili flakes or 1 tsp. chili powder
¼ tsp. cumin, turmeric & sea salt
¼ tsp. dried oregano (optional)
water
olive oil

In a bowl, stir together vegetables, flour, baking powder and spices.
While stirring; add water, a little at a time, until the ingredients bind together.
In a skillet or saucepan, add enough oil so it comes up about ½" or more from the bottom, and bring to medium-high heat.
When oil is hot, add a spoonful of vegetable mix and cook until golden brown, turning once to cook the other side.
Remove with a slotted spoon and drain on a paper towel.

- Makes 12-16 pakora.
- Serve with Tandoori Sauce.
- For vegetables, choose any of the following: zucchini, carrots, onions, turnips, sweet potatoes or potatoes.

Note: Do not heat oil above medium-high, because if oil is too hot, only the outside will cook and the inside will be raw. If this happens, heat pakora in the oven to finish cooking.

Scalloped Sweet & Red Potatoes, with Saffron

(The sweetness of the potatoes is lightly balanced with the soft bitterness of saffron)

1 large sweet potato (about 14 oz.), sliced thin
2-3 red potatoes, sliced thin
1 large onion, sliced thin
1 Tbsp. ghee
2 cloves garlic, minced
1½ cups plain nut or seed milk
½ cup vegetable stock
½ tsp. saffron threads
1 Tbsp. tapioca flour
sea salt & pepper

In a saucepan, heat ghee over medium heat.
Add garlic and sauté 1-2 minutes.
Stir in 1 cup milk and stock.
Add saffron and infuse for 5 minutes.
In a small bowl, combine remaining milk and tapioca and add to sauce pan; stir until thickened. Set aside.
In an oiled baking dish, arrange 1/3 of the sweet potatoes over bottom.
Add ½ of the red potatoes and then ½ of the onions.
Repeat layers, finishing off with remaining sweet potatoes.
Pour sauce over top.
Season to taste.
Bake at 375°F, uncovered, for 60 minutes, until potatoes are tender.

• Makes 4-6 servings.
• If saffron is unavailable use 1 tsp. safflower.

Variation
❖ *Replace red potatoes with 3 turnips or 2 rutabagas.*

Broccoli & Cauliflower Casserole

2 cups broccoli, chopped
2 cups cauliflower, chopped
1 cup sesame seed milk
½ Tbsp. tapioca flour
1 Tbsp. ghee
2 cloves garlic, minced
1 shallot, finely chopped
½ tsp. dried parsley, rosemary & thyme
¼ tsp. sea salt
1/8 tsp. pepper
2 oz. shredded cheese, rice or soy
¼ cup ground sesame seeds or almonds

Steam broccoli and cauliflower until tender; refresh under cold water.
Transfer to a baking dish.
In a bowl, combine milk and tapioca flour.
In a saucepan, heat ghee over medium heat.
Add garlic and shallot, and sauté for 1-2 minutes.
Add milk mix and spices, and stir until thickened.
Remove from heat and stir in cheese.
Pour sauce over vegetables.
Sprinkle on ground sesame seeds or almonds.
Bake at 375°F, uncovered, for 15 minutes.

Sweet Potato & Rutabaga Bake

2-3 Tbsp. olive oil
2 cloves garlic, minced
1 small onion, finely chopped
2 sweet potatoes, peeled & shredded
2 rutabagas, peeled & shredded
2 oz. shredded cheese, rice soy or goat's milk
½ tsp. dried basil, oregano & parsley
¼ tsp. sea salt
1/8 tsp. pepper

In a bowl, stir together all ingredients.
Transfer mixture to an oiled baking dish.
Bake at 350°F, covered, for 45 minutes; uncovering for last 15 minutes of baking time.

• Makes 4 or more servings.

Variations
❖ *Replace basil, oregano and parsley with: ½ tsp. cumin, chili powder and coriander or with 1 tsp. dried sage and ½ tsp. dried savory.*
❖ *Replace rutabaga with 3 turnips.*

Mixed Vegetable Bake

(A simple to prepare dish that is full of flavour)

1 bulb fennel, sliced
3 cups cauliflower florets
2 carrots, chopped into chunks
10 red pearl onions
4-6 shallots
4-6 cloves garlic, chopped
3 Tbsp. olive oil
$\frac{1}{2}$ cup vegetable stock
1 cup red wine
1-2 tsp. dried herb(s) of choice
sea salt & pepper

Place all vegetables into an oiled baking dish.
Drizzle oil over top of vegetables.
Add stock and wine, and sprinkle with dried herb of choice.
Season to taste.
Cover with parchment paper and then tinfoil.
Bake at 350°F for 50-60 minutes, until vegetables are tender.

• Makes 4 or more servings.

Roasted Garlic Squash Gratin

(The squash comes alive in this dish)

3 whole garlic bulbs, roasted (see page 167)
1 large butternut squash
3 Tbsp. ghee
2 leeks (white part only), chopped
½-1 tsp. chili powder (optional)
1 cup sesame seed milk
¼ cup ground sesame seeds
3 Tbsp. rice Parmesan cheese (optional)
sea salt & pepper

Cook squash accordingly.
Scoop out flesh and transfer to a bowl with 2 Tbsp. ghee.
In a skillet, heat remaining ghee over medium-low heat.
Add leeks and chili powder (if using), and sauté for 7-10 minutes.
In a blender, combine leek mixture, garlic and sesame milk until smooth.
Add milk mixture to squash and stir until well combined.
Transfer to an oiled baking dish.
Sprinkle on ground sesame seeds and Parmesan (if using).
Bake at 375°F, uncovered, for 20-25 minutes, until golden brown.

• Makes 4 or more servings.

Variations
❖ *Replace sesame seed milk and ground seeds with almond milk and ground almonds.*
❖ *Replace squash with any other kind of squash, pumpkin or sweet potatoes.*

Roasted Fennel with Tomato Sauce

1 Tbsp, olive oil or ghee
3 cloves garlic, minced
1 large onion, chopped
1 large fennel bulb, sliced & roasted (see page 167)
1½ cups tomato sauce of choice
½ cup shredded cheese, any kind

In a skillet, heat oil or ghee over medium heat.
Add garlic and onion, and sauté for 3-5 minutes.
In a bowl, stir together garlic mixture, fennel and tomato sauce.
Transfer to a baking dish.
Sprinkle on cheese.
Bake at 375°F for 15-20 minutes, until bubbly and cheese is melted.

• Makes 4 servings.

Vegetable Gratin

1 Tbsp. olive oil
1 leek, chopped
1 zucchini, chopped
3 cups cauliflower, chopped
1-2 oz. shredded cheese, rice or soy
2 cloves garlic or $\frac{1}{4}$ tsp. garlic powder
$\frac{1}{2}$ cup plain nut or seed milk
$\frac{1}{4}$ cup plain soy or goat's milk yogurt
2 eggs
$\frac{1}{4}$ tsp. each dried rosemary, thyme & sea salt
1/8 tsp. pepper
3 Tbsp. ground nuts or seeds

In a skillet, heat oil over medium heat.
Add leek and zucchini, and sauté for 5-7 minutes.
Steam cauliflower until tender.
Transfer leek, zucchini and cauliflower to a baking dish.
Sprinkle cheese over vegetables.
In a bowl or blender, mix together garlic, milk, yogurt, eggs and spices until smooth.
Pour liquid mixture over vegetable mix.
Sprinkle on ground nuts or seeds.
Bake at 375°F, uncovered, for 25-30 minutes until set.

• Makes 4-6 servings.

Variations
❖ *Replace rosemary and thyme with sage and savory.*
❖ *Replace zucchini with green, red or orange peppers.*
❖ *Replace 1$\frac{1}{2}$ cups of cauliflower with broccoli, asparagus or green beans.*

Grilled Vegetable Lasagna

(A grain-free lasagna using zucchini as the noodles)

Marinade for grilled vegetables:
  1 Tbsp. olive oil
  2 Tbsp. fresh lemon juice
  2 Tbsp. apple cider vinegar
  1 Tbsp. liquid aminos
  $\frac{1}{2}$ tsp. chili powder
  $\frac{1}{4}$ tsp. dried oregano & sea salt
  1 clove garlic, minced

Lasagna:
  3-4 zucchini, sliced length-wise $\frac{1}{4}$" thick
  8 oz. portabella mushrooms, sliced $\frac{1}{4}$" thick
  2 green, red or orange peppers, sliced into quarters
  1 Tbsp. ghee or olive oil
  2 leeks, chopped
  1 bunch spinach or Swiss chard, chopped
  $2\frac{1}{2}$ cups tomato sauce
  4 oz. shredded cheese of choice

In a bowl, stir together all ingredients for marinade until well combined.

Add zucchini, mushrooms and peppers, and stir to coat; let marinate for 20-30 minutes.

Grill vegetables in a grilling pan or under the broiler until tender; 10-15 minutes.

In a skillet, heat ghee over medium-low heat.

Add leeks and sauté until softened, about 5-7 minutes.

Add spinach or Swiss chard and sauté until just wilted.

In a 9" square baking dish, cover bottom with $\frac{1}{2}$ cup tomato sauce.

Line bottom of baking dish with $\frac{1}{2}$ of the zucchini.

Add leek and spinach or Swiss chard mixture.

Spread on 1 cup tomato sauce.

Arrange mushrooms and peppers over top.

Line top with remaining zucchini.

Spread on remaining tomato sauce.

Sprinkle on cheese.

Bake at 350°F, uncovered, for 25-30 minutes, until bubbly and cheese is melted.

• Makes 4 or more servings.

Variation
❖ *Add 8 oz. of crumbled tofu with leeks and sauté until browned.*

Fried Zucchini Lasagna

3-4 zucchini, cut into $\frac{1}{4}$" thick round slices (about 3-3$\frac{1}{2}$ cups)
about $\frac{3}{4}$ cup chickpea flour
olive oil
1 bunch spinach leaves (2 cups packed)
2 cups tomato sauce of choice
6 oz. shredded rice cheese

Salt and rinse zucchini; pat dry.
In a bowl, add chickpea flour and zucchini slices; toss to coat.
In a skillet, add enough olive oil so it comes up about 3/8" from the bottom and bring to medium-high heat.
When oil is hot, add zucchini slices (shake off excess flour) and fry until golden brown (only add a few at a time and without overlapping). Remove zucchini with a slotted spoon and drain on paper towels; continue with remaining zucchini. Set aside.
Steam spinach until just wilted.
In a 9" square baking dish, spread $\frac{1}{2}$ cup tomato sauce over bottom.
Line bottom with 1/3 of the zucchini.
Add $\frac{1}{2}$ of the spinach, then $\frac{1}{2}$ cup tomato sauce and 1/3 of the cheese.
Starting with zucchini, repeat layers until complete.
Bake at 375°F, uncovered, for 20-30 minutes, until bubbly.
• Makes 4 or more servings.

Variations
❖ *Replace 1 cup tomato sauce with 1 cup thickened nut or seed milk. To make: in a sauce pan, heat 1 Tbsp. ghee over medium heat. Add 1 Tbsp. chick pea flour and cook, while stirring, for 1 minute. Slowly, stir in 1 cup plain nut or seed milk. Stir until thickened. Add 1 cup tomato sauce and stir until combined.*
❖ *Replace spinach with same amount of Swiss chard, or grilled mushrooms or peppers.*

Broccoli & Cauliflower Pie

(Two powerhouse veggies cooked together in a potato crust)

$1\frac{1}{2}$ cups broccoli, chopped
$1\frac{1}{2}$ cups cauliflower, chopped
$1\frac{1}{2}$ Tbsp. ghee
$2\frac{1}{2}$ Tbsp. brown rice flour
$\frac{1}{2}$ cup vegetable stock
1 cup plain nut or seed milk
$\frac{1}{2}$ tsp. dried rosemary & thyme
1/4-1/3 cup shredded cheese of choice
sea salt & pepper
1 sweet potato or potato pie crust (see page 266)

Steam broccoli and cauliflower until tender; refresh under cold water and set aside.
In a saucepan, melt ghee over medium heat.
Add flour and cook, while stirring, for 1 minute.
While stirring, slowly add stock, milk and spices; stir until thickened.
Add cheese and stir until melted.
Hint: If milk and stock are pre-heated before it's added to sauce pan, sauce will thicken more quickly.
Stir in broccoli and cauliflower.
Season to taste.
Pour or scoop into prepared pie crust of choice.
Bake at 375°F, uncovered, for 20-25 minutes.

• Makes 4-6 servings.

Variations
❖ *Replace broccoli with asparagus.*
❖ *Rice Flour Pie Crust can also be used.*

Cauliflower & Leek Pie with Saffron

(A light delicate flavoured vegetable pie)

1 Tbsp. ghee
3 small leeks (white part only), chopped
2½ cups cauliflower, chopped
½ cup vegetable stock
½ cup white wine or water
½ tsp. saffron threads
½ tsp. sea salt
3 Tbsp. tapioca flour
½ cup plain nut or seed milk
1 potato or sweet potato pie crust (see page 266)

In a saucepan, heat ghee over medium heat.
Add leeks and sauté for 2-3 minutes.
Add cauliflower, stock, wine or water, saffron and sea salt, and bring to a boil.
Reduce heat and simmer, covered, for 10-15 minutes or until cauliflower is tender.
Combine tapioca flour and milk, and add to sauce pan; stir until thickened.
Pour or scoop into prepared pie crust of choice.
Bake at 375°F, uncovered, for 20-25 minutes.

• Makes 4-6 servings.
• If saffron is unavailable, use 1 tsp. safflower or paprika.
• Rice Flour Pie Crust can also be used.

Spinach Pie

(This is a way to get them to eat their spinach)

$\frac{1}{2}$ Tbsp. olive oil
1 onion, finely chopped
5-6 cups spinach, packed
1$\frac{1}{2}$ Tbsp. ghee
3 Tbsp. brown rice flour
1$\frac{1}{2}$ cups plain nut or seed milk
$\frac{1}{2}$ tsp. dried savory & tarragon
sea salt & pepper
2 oz. shredded cheese of choice
1 potato or sweet potato pie crust (see page 266)

In a skillet, heat oil over medium heat.
Add onion and sauté for 3-5 minutes; set aside.
Steam spinach until just wilted; strain and set aside.
In a saucepan, melt ghee over medium heat.
Add flour and cook, while stirring, for 1 minute.
While stirring, slowly add milk and spices; stir until thickened.
Hint: If milk is pre-heated before it's added to sauce pan, sauce will thicken more quickly.
Add cheese and stir until melted.
Stir in onions and spinach.
Pour or scoop into prepared pie crust of choice.
Bake at 375°F, uncovered, for 20-25 minutes.

• Makes 4-6 servings.

Variation
❖ *Replace 2 cups spinach with any other greens: kale, Swiss chard, or dandelion.*

Vegetable Curry Pie

(A delicious deep dish mixed vegetable pie with curry spices that also has an option for herbs)

Crust:
   1½ time's recipe for Rice Flour Pie Crust on page 267

Filling:
   1½ Tbsp. olive oil or ghee
   2 cloves garlic, minced
   1 red or white onion, finely chopped
   1 tsp. chili powder & cumin
   ½ tsp. coriander, paprika & turmeric
   ½ tsp. sea salt
   pinch or 2 of cayenne
   1 carrot, chopped
   1 small sweet potato, chopped
   1 cup cauliflower, chopped
   1½ cups vegetable stock
   1 cup broccoli, chopped
   ½ cup green beans, chopped
   ½ cup frozen peas
   ½-14 oz. can chickpeas, rinsed & drained
   2 Tbsp. fresh parsley
   1 cup plain nut or seed milk
   ¼ cup tapioca flour

To prepare crust:
   Prepare crust accordingly and pat into a 9" square baking dish.
   Reserve some dough for optional top crust.
   Bake crust accordingly.

To prepare filling:

In a saucepan, heat oil over medium heat.

Add garlic, onions and spices, and sauté for 2-3 minutes.

Add carrots, sweet potato, cauliflower and stock, and bring to a boil. Reduce heat and simmer for 15 minutes.

Add broccoli, green beans, peas, chickpeas and parsley, and continue simmering until vegetables are tender, about 10-15 minutes.

Combine milk and tapioca flour and add to saucepan; stir until thickened.

Pour or scoop into prepared baking dish.

This step is optional: roll out remaining dough and place on top.

Prick dough with fork or make a $\frac{1}{4}$" hole in center of dough.

Bake at 400°F, uncovered, for 25-35 minutes, until bubbly and crust is golden.

• Makes 4 or more servings.

Variations
❖ *Replace top crust with mashed sweet or red potatoes.*
❖ *Replace green beans and/or peas with fresh spinach.*
❖ *For **Herb Vegetable Pie**: replace spices with 1 tsp. each dried basil, and oregano, and $\frac{1}{2}$ tsp. each rosemary, sage and thyme. Replace sweet potato with red potato or turnips and replace chickpeas with bean of choice.*

Spinach Dumplings

$\frac{1}{2}$ cup plain nut or seed milk
1 Tbsp. olive oil or ghee
1 cup finely chopped spinach
$\frac{1}{4}$ tsp. dried basil & oregano
1/8 tsp. garlic powder
sea salt & pepper
$\frac{1}{2}$ cup brown rice flour
1 Tbsp. rice Parmesan cheese
2 eggs
$2\frac{1}{2}$-3 cups stock of choice

In a saucepan, bring milk, olive oil or ghee, spinach and spices to medium heat. Season with sea salt and pepper.
In a bowl, combine flour and cheese.
When spinach is cooked, add flour mixture to saucepan and cook for 1-2 minutes, stirring constantly. (The batter will form into a ball)
Remove from heat and let cool a few minutes.
Beat in eggs, one at a time. Set aside.
In another saucepan, bring stock to a simmer.
Scoop out a spoonful of dough and add to simmering stock; continue with all the dough.
Let dumplings simmer for 7 minutes or until they rise to the surface.
Ladle dumplings and some stock into soup bowls.

- Makes 3-4 servings.
- Dough can be chilled for 1 day.
- Add dumplings to any favourite soup recipe.

Variation
❖ *Add any vegetable and/or cooked meat to simmering stock. Simmer vegetables until tender then add the prepared dough.*

Rosemary Dumplings

(Make these wonderful flavoured dumplings when there is extra stock or broth on hand)

1 egg
¼ cup plain nut or seed milk
2 Tbsp. olive oil or melted ghee
1 cup brown rice flour
2 tsp. baking powder
1-1½ tsp. dried rosemary
4 cups stock of choice

In a bowl, beat the egg.
Beat in milk and oil or ghee until combined.
Combine flour, baking powder and rosemary, and add to wet mixture; stir to form a stiff batter.
In a saucepan, bring stock to a simmer.
Roll dough into small balls or drop by spoonfuls into simmering stock.
Cover and simmer for 15 minutes.
Note: Do not lift the cover during simmering time.
Ladle dumplings and some stock into soup bowls.

• Makes 4 servings.
• Dough can be chilled for up to 2 days.
• Add dumplings to any favourite soup recipe.
• Add any vegetable or cooked meat to simmering stock.

Salad Dressings, Sauces & Accompaniments

Tips for Dressings & Sauces   136

Herb Dressing   137

Lemon Ginger Dressing   138

'Thousand Island' Dressing   139

Garlic 'French' Dressing   140

Creamy Salad Dressing   141

Garlic Caesar Dressing   142

Orange Ginger Dressing   143

Raspberry Dressing   144

'Teriyaki' Marinade   145

Curry Marinade   146

Grilling Marinade   147

Onion & Yogurt Cheese Dip   148

Roasted Red Pepper Dip   149

Hazelnut Butter Dip   150

Nut Butter & Coconut Sauce   151

Tahini Sauce   152

Tandoori Sauce   153

Basic Curry Sauce   154

Lemon Garlic Sauce   155

Roasted Vegetable Sauce   156

Sweet & Sour Sauce   157

Barbecue Sauce   158

Basic Tomato Sauce   159

Quick & Creamy Tomato Sauce   161

Creamy Pesto   162

Mushroom Gravy   163

Cucumber & Tomato Salsa   164

Papaya Salsa   165

Roasted Garlic Winter Salsa   166

Roasted Garlic, Fennel & Sweet Peppers   167

Cajun Spice   168

Garam Masala   168

Sugar Toasted Almonds   169

Crispy Rice Noodles   169

Flatbread Crisps   170

Crepe Crisps   171

Tips for Dressings & Sauces

❖ Always use fresh and high quality ingredients (lemons, limes, oils, spices, etc.).

❖ Dressings and sauces are relatively easy to make. Compared to commercial brands, they are tastier and healthier. Commercial brands use poor oils that are high in trans fatty acids, contain sugar and many chemical additives and preservatives.

❖ Most dressings and sauces can be prepared in advance and stored in the refrigerator. Stir ingredients or shake container before using.

❖ When adding condiments such as, ketchup, mustards, mayonnaise, relish, etc. to dressings and sauces, purchase ones that; a) are sugar-free and either fruit sweetened or unsweetened, b) contain apple cider vinegar as the vinegar source, c) use non-hydrogenated and quality oils, and d) use non-irradiated or organic herbs and spices. All condiments can be found with these qualities.

❖ Hint: For dressings etc. that don't need a blender or food processor for mixing, and to save time and work; put all ingredients into an opaque container and shake vigorously to combine; store in the refrigerator in the same container.

Herb Dressing

(A simple oil & vinegar dressing that is quite aromatic)

2 Tbsp. olive oil
2 Tbsp. flax seed oil
2½ Tbsp. fresh lemon juice
2 Tbsp. apple cider vinegar
2 Tbsp. water
1 clove garlic, minced
1 tsp. grain or Dijon mustard (optional)
¼ tsp. each dried basil, oregano, parsley, rosemary, thyme & sea salt
1/8 tsp. pepper

In a small bowl, whisk or stir together all ingredients until well combined.

- Store in an opaque container and refrigerate for up to 7 days.
- Makes about 2/3 cup.

Variations
- ❖ *For **Lemon Dill Dressing**: Replace 1 Tbsp. water and dried herbs with 1 Tbsp. fresh lemon juice and 1 tsp. dried dill; omit mustard.*
- ❖ *Replace flax seed oil with hemp or pumpkin seed oil.*
- ❖ *Replace dried basil with 2-3 fresh minced basil leaves.*

Lemon Ginger Dressing

(A tangy dressing good over greens or as a marinade for meats)

3 Tbsp. lemon juice
2 Tbsp. liquid aminos
2 Tbsp. apple cider vinegar
2 tsp. olive oil
2 tsp. sesame oil
1 tsp. honey or brown rice syrup
1 tsp. fresh ginger, minced
1 clove garlic, minced
pinch of cayenne pepper

In a small bowl, whisk or stir together all ingredients until well combined.

- Refrigerate for up to 5 days.
- Use as a dressing for spinach salads or other salad greens.
- Use as a marinade for chicken, turkey or fish.
- Makes about $\frac{1}{2}$ cup.

'Thousand Island' Dressing

(A healthier version of the standard supermarket variety)

$1\frac{1}{2}$ Tbsp. olive oil
$1\frac{1}{2}$ Tbsp. flax seed or pumpkin seed oil
$1\frac{1}{2}$ Tbsp. apple cider vinegar
1 Tbsp. sugar-free ketchup (fruit sweetened or unsweetened)
1 Tbsp. mayonnaise
1 Tbsp. almond or cashew milk
3 Tbsp. sugar-free relish
1 tsp. minced onion

Combine all ingredients, except relish and onion, in a blender or food processor until smooth.
Stir in the relish and onions.

• Store in an opaque container and refrigerate for up to 7 days.
• Makes about 2/3 cup.

Variation
❖ *Replace relish with minced dill pickle.*

Garlic 'French' Dressing

(An easy to prepare healthier version of this classic dressing)

2 Tbsp. olive oil
2 Tbsp. flax, hemp or pumpkin seed oil
2 Tbsp. water
1½ Tbsp. apple cider vinegar
1 Tbsp. ketchup
1 tsp. tomato paste
2 cloves garlic, chopped
½ tsp. paprika
¼ tsp. chili powder & sea salt
½-1 tsp. honey

Combine all ingredients in a blender or food processor until smooth.

• Store in an opaque container and refrigerate for up to 7 days.
• Makes ½ cup.

Creamy Salad Dressing

(A light refreshing summertime dressing)

$\frac{1}{2}$ cup plain soy or goat's milk yogurt
2 Tbsp. flax seed oil
2 Tbsp. fresh lemon juice
1 Tbsp. apple cider vinegar
2 Tbsp. fresh parsley, finely chopped
1 clove garlic, minced
sea salt & pepper

In a small bowl, stir together all ingredients until smooth.
Season to taste.

- Store in an opaque container and refrigerate for up to 3 days.
- Serve over salad greens, with potato salads, etc.
- Makes about 2/3 cup.

Variations
❖ *Add any of the following: 1 tsp. dried basil, 1 tsp. dried tarragon or*
   1 tsp. dried dill and Dijon or grain mustard.
❖ *For **Creamy Cucumber Dressing**: add $\frac{1}{2}$ cup finely chopped*
   cucumber and 1 tsp. dried dill or $\frac{1}{2}$ cup finely chopped dill pickles.

Garlic Caesar Dressing

(A dressing with kick and a variation that will make it hard to decide which one to make; it's easy...just make both)

½ cup yogurt cheese (see page 148)
3 Tbsp. olive or flax seed oil
1 Tbsp. fresh lemon juice
1 Tbsp. apple cider vinegar
1 tsp. liquid aminos
1 tsp. grain or Dijon mustard (optional)
3 cloves garlic, minced
sea salt & pepper

Combine all ingredients in a blender or food processor until smooth. Season to taste.

- Store in a opaque container and refrigerate for up to 3 days.
- Add a little rice Parmesan cheese.
- Serve over salad greens or steamed vegetables.
- Makes about ¾ cup.

Variation
- ❖ For **Roasted Garlic Caesar Dressing**: replace garlic cloves with 1 whole garlic bulb, roasted (see page 167).

Orange Ginger Dressing

(A tangy dressing that is great with coleslaws)

$\frac{1}{4}$ cup fresh orange juice
3 Tbsp. apple cider vinegar
1$\frac{1}{2}$ Tbsp. liquid aminos
1$\frac{1}{2}$ Tbsp. pumpkin or hemp seed oil
2 tsp. sesame oil
$\frac{1}{2}$-1 Tbsp. honey or sucanat
$\frac{1}{2}$ Tbsp. fresh ginger, minced
1 clove garlic, minced

Combine all ingredients in a blender or food processor until smooth.

- Store in an opaque container and refrigerate for up to 4 days.
- Use for Tangy Coleslaw on page 106.
- Serve over spinach or any other salad greens and add segments of mandarin oranges and toasted almonds.
- Makes about 2/3 cup.

Raspberry Dressing

(A refreshing summertime dressing)

$\frac{1}{2}$ cup fresh raspberries
3 Tbsp. pumpkin or flax seed oil
2$\frac{1}{2}$ Tbsp. almond or walnut oil
2 Tbsp. fresh lemon juice
2 Tbsp. apple cider vinegar
2 Tbsp. water
$\frac{1}{4}$ tsp. dried mint

Combine all ingredients in a blender or food processor until smooth.

- Store in an opaque container and refrigerate for up to 3 days.
- Serve over any salad greens.
- Add toasted almonds, sesame seeds or crumbled goat's milk feta cheese.
- Makes 7/8-1 cup.

'Teriyaki' Marinade

(A healthier version to this classic marinade)

3 Tbsp. apple cider vinegar
3 Tbsp. water
2 Tbsp. liquid aminos
1 Tbsp. olive oil
1 Tbsp. sesame oil
½-1 Tbsp. honey or sucanat
½ Tbsp. fresh ginger, minced
1-2 cloves garlic, minced

In a small bowl, stir together all ingredients until well combined.

- Use marinade for meat, poultry or fish. Marinate for a minimum of 30 minutes.
- Marinade can be stored for up to 3 days in the refrigerator.
- Makes about 2/3 cup.

Variations
- ❖ For **Orange Teriyaki Marinade**: replace water with 3-4 Tbsp. fresh orange juice.
- ❖ For **Lemon or Lime Ginger Marinade**: replace 2 Tbsp. apple cider vinegar and 1 Tbsp. liquid aminos for 3-4 Tbsp. fresh lemon or lime juice.

Curry Marinade

¼ cup fresh lemon or lime juice
2 Tbsp. olive oil
2 Tbsp. water
2 cloves garlic, minced or ¼ tsp. garlic powder
½ tsp. fresh ginger, minced (optional)
½ tsp. cumin seeds, crushed
¼ tsp. chili flakes & coriander seeds, crushed
1/8 tsp. paprika & turmeric
sea salt & pepper

In a small bowl, stir together all ingredients until well combined.
Season to taste.

- Use marinade for meat, poultry or fish. Marinate for a minimum of 2 hours.
- Marinade can be stored for up to 3 days in the refrigerator.
- Makes about ½ cup.

Variation
❖ *For **Tandoori Marinade**: replace water with 1/3-1/2 cup plain soy or goat's milk yogurt.*

Grilling Marinade

(This marinade is wonderful for vegetables or meats)

2 Tbsp. olive oil
2 Tbsp. fresh lemon or lime juice
2 Tbsp. apple cider vinegar
1 Tbsp. liquid aminos
1 Tbsp. water
2 cloves garlic, minced or $\frac{1}{4}$ tsp. garlic powder
$\frac{1}{2}$ tsp. chili powder
$\frac{1}{4}$ tsp. dried oregano & parsley
sea salt & pepper

In a small bowl, stir together all ingredients until well combined. Season to taste.

- Use marinade for vegetables, meat, poultry or fish before grilling.
- Marinate for 30 minutes to 2 hours.
- Marinade can be stored for up to 3 days in the refrigerator.
- Makes $\frac{1}{2}$ cup.

Onion & Yogurt Cheese Dip

1 cup yogurt cheese
1½-2 Tbsp. olive oil or ghee
2 Spanish onions, finely chopped
1-2 tsp. spice of choice (see below)
sea salt & pepper

To make yogurt cheese: Line a colander with cheesecloth or a cotton
   cloth. Add 2 cups (500 grams) plain goat's milk or soy milk yogurt.
   Cover top with another cloth. Place colander in a bowl and let
   yogurt strain at room temperature for 6-8 hours. (Can also be
   strained in the refrigerator for 12 or more hours.) When yogurt is
   no longer straining liquid and has thickened somewhat like cream
   cheese, remove yogurt cheese and place in a covered container, and
   refrigerate for 3-5 days. This makes 1 cup yogurt cheese.

Dip: In a skillet, heat oil or ghee over medium-low heat.
Add onions and sauté until caramelized, approximately 15-20 minutes.
In a blender or food processor, combine yogurt cheese, onions and
spice of choice until smooth. Season to taste.

• Use as a dip for raw vegetables, rice crackers/crisps, etc. Can also
   be used as a sandwich spread.
• Store in a covered container and refrigerator for up to 3 days.
• Makes 1 cup.

Variations
❖ *Spice combinations: a) herb mix; dried basil, oregano and parsley or
   dried rosemary and thyme, b) paprika, or c) curry mix; cumin, chili
   powder, coriander and turmeric.*
❖ *For **Roasted Garlic Dip**: replace Spanish onions with 2 whole garlic
   bulbs, roasted (see page 167).*

Roasted Red Pepper Dip

(Roasted red pepper adds awesome flavour to this yogurt cheese dip)

1 cup yogurt cheese (see page 148)
1 roasted red pepper, diced (see page 167)
2 Tbsp. mayonnaise
1-2 cloves garlic, minced
2-3 Tbsp. fresh basil or thyme, chopped
sea salt & pepper

Combine all ingredients in a blender or food processor until smooth. Season to taste.

- Use as a dip for raw vegetables, rice crackers/crisps, etc., or as a spread for flatbreads, rice paper, crepes, etc.
- Store in a covered container and refrigerator for up to 3 days.
- For a chunkier dip: process only $\frac{1}{2}$ of the pepper with other ingredients and stir in remaining pepper.
- Makes just over 1 cup.

Hazelnut Butter Dip

(A pleasing tasteful dip that goes well with many things)

1/3 cup hazelnut butter
$\frac{1}{2}$ cup plain nut or seed milk
2 Tbsp. fresh lemon juice
2 Tbsp. flax seed oil
2 Tbsp. liquid aminos
2 cloves garlic, minced
1 tsp. chili powder
1 tsp. fresh ginger, minced or $\frac{1}{2}$ tsp. ground ginger
$\frac{1}{2}$ tsp. guar gum
$\frac{1}{4}$ tsp. sea salt

Combine all ingredients in a blender or food processor until smooth.

- Use as a dip for raw vegetables, rice crackers/crisps, etc., or as a spread for flatbreads, rice paper, crepes, etc.
- Store in an opaque container and refrigerate for up to 7 days.
- Makes 1 cup.

Variation
❖ *Replace hazelnut butter with any other kind of nut or seed butter.*

Nut Butter & Coconut Sauce

(This sauce has Asian flare & goes well with an array of foods/dishes)

$\frac{1}{4}$ cup nut butter of choice
$\frac{1}{2}$ cup coconut milk
3 Tbsp. liquid aminos
2 Tbsp. apple cider vinegar
2-3 cloves garlic, minced
1 tsp. fresh ginger, minced
$\frac{1}{2}$-1 tsp. chili powder
$\frac{1}{2}$ tsp. coriander & cumin (optional)
sea salt & pepper

Combine all ingredients in a blender or food processor until smooth. Season to taste.

- Use as a poaching sauce for fish or poultry.
- Heat sauce in a saucepan and serve as a hot sauce over rice noodles, cooked grains, steamed vegetables, meat, poultry or fish.
- Use as a dipping sauce for Curried Lamb Wraps, etc.
- Store in a covered container and refrigerator for up to 3 days.
- Makes almost 1 cup.

Tahini Sauce

(A creamy seed butter sauce)

$\frac{1}{4}$ cup tahini
$\frac{1}{4}$ cup olive oil
$\frac{1}{4}$ cup water
2 Tbsp. fresh lemon juice
2-3 cloves garlic, minced
$\frac{1}{2}$ tsp. each cumin, paprika & sea salt
$\frac{1}{4}$ tsp. chili powder

Combine all ingredients in a blender or food processor until smooth.

- Heat sauce in a saucepan and serve as a hot sauce over rice noodles, grains, steamed vegetables, meat, poultry or fish.
- Use as a dressing for salad greens or coleslaw.
- Add $\frac{1}{2}$ tsp. guar gum to recipe and use as a dip for raw vegetables, rice crackers, etc.
- Store in a covered container and refrigerate for up to 5 days.
- Makes about 7/8 cup.

Variations
- ❖ *Replace all or part of the olive oil with flax or hemp seed oil and use as a dip or dressing. Do not heat the sauce.*
- ❖ *Replace cumin, paprika and chili powder with 1 tsp. fresh minced ginger or $\frac{1}{2}$ tsp. ground ginger and $\frac{1}{4}$ tsp. cinnamon; or add with cumin, etc.*

Tandoori Sauce

(A refreshing light curry sauce)

1 cup plain goat's milk or soy milk yogurt
1 Tbsp. fresh lemon or lime juice
2 cloves garlic, minced
1 tsp. chili powder & cumin
$\frac{1}{2}$ tsp. turmeric
$\frac{1}{4}$ tsp. sea salt
$\frac{1}{4}$ tsp. coriander (optional)

In a small bowl, stir together all ingredients until smooth.

- Use as a dipping sauce for Rice Paper Samosas, Curried Lamb Wraps, Chicken Crepes, etc.
- Use as a marinade for chicken or fish; add 2 more Tbsp. lemon or lime juice and 2 Tbsp. olive oil.
- Store in a covered container and refrigerate for up to 3 days.
- Make 1 cup.

Basic Curry Sauce

(Caramelized onion adds character to this tomato-based sauce)

1½ Tbsp. ghee or olive oil
1 large Spanish onion, chopped
3-4 cloves garlic, minced
½-1 Tbsp. fresh ginger, minced
1 tsp. cumin & coriander seeds, crushed
½-1 tsp. chili flakes, crushed
½ tsp. fennel seeds, crushed (optional)
½ tsp. paprika & turmeric
½ tsp. garam masala (optional)
2-3 cups pureed tomatoes (fresh or canned)
sea salt & pepper

In a skillet, heat ghee or oil over medium-low heat.
Add onion and sauté until caramelized, approximately 15-20 minutes.
Add garlic, ginger and spices, and cook for 2-3 minutes.
Add tomatoes and simmer, covered for 10-15 minutes.
Season to taste.

- Serve as a sauce over cooked grains, rice noodles, steamed vegetables, meat poultry or fish.
- Store in a covered container and refrigerate for up to 5 days or freeze.

Variations
❖ *For a chunkier sauce: replace ½ of pureed tomatoes with chopped tomatoes.*
❖ *For **Creamy Curry Sauce**: add ½-1 cup plain goat's milk or soy yogurt. Add yogurt to last 3-5 minutes of simmering time.*

Lemon Garlic Sauce

(This sauce will add zest to a number of dishes)

$\frac{1}{4}$ cup fresh lemon juice
$\frac{1}{4}$ cup vegetable stock
$\frac{1}{4}$ cup white wine or water
4-6 cloves garlic, minced
$\frac{1}{4}$ tsp. sea salt
$\frac{1}{2}$ Tbsp. tapioca flour

Combine all ingredients in a blender until smooth.
Transfer mixture to a saucepan and bring to medium heat, stirring constantly until thickened.

- Serve as a sauce over rice noodles, cooked grains, steamed vegetables, meat, poultry or fish.
- Store in a covered container and refrigerate for up to 3 days.

Variations

❖ *For **Creamy Lemon Garlic Sauce**: add $\frac{1}{4}$ cup cashew or other nut milk, or $\frac{1}{4}$ cup plain goat's milk yogurt and add $\frac{1}{2}$ tsp. more tapioca flour.*
❖ *Add $\frac{1}{2}$-1 tsp. of any spice: cumin, chili powder, basil, thyme, etc.*

Roasted Vegetable Sauce

(An awesome flavoured sauce that goes with many different foods)

2 red peppers, roasted (see page 167)
1 cup sliced fennel, roasted (see page 167)
6-10 garlic cloves, roasted (see page 167)
½ cup unsweetened apple juice
2 Tbsp. white wine or lemon juice
1 Tbsp. apple cider vinegar
½ tsp. dried thyme
¼ tsp. sea salt

Combine all ingredients in a blender or food processor until smooth.

- Makes about 1 cup thick sauce; can be thinned by adding vegetable stock or water.
- Heat in a saucepan and serve as a sauce over rice noodles, cooked grains, meat, poultry or fish.
- Thin sauce, one to one, with vegetable stock or water and use as a marinade and/or a cooking medium for meat, poultry or fish.
- Store in a covered container and refrigerate for up to 5 days or freeze.

Variation
❖ *Replace thyme with chili powder and add ½ Tbsp. liquid aminos.*

Sweet & Sour Sauce

(An fast & easy sauce to prepare)

$\frac{1}{2}$ cup unsweetened apple juice
$\frac{1}{2}$ cup apple cider vinegar
1/3-1/2 cup sugar-free apricot jam
$\frac{1}{4}$ cup liquid aminos
2-3 Tbsp. honey or brown rice syrup
2 cloves garlic, minced or $\frac{1}{4}$ tsp. garlic powder
$\frac{1}{2}$ Tbsp. tapioca flour mixed in 2 Tbsp. water

Combine all ingredients, except tapioca mixture, in a blender until smooth.
Transfer blender mixture to a saucepan and bring to a boil.
Lower heat and let simmer for 5 minutes; stir occasionally.
Add tapioca mixture and stir until thickened.

- Serve over meat, poultry, fish, cooked grains or use in stir fry's.
- Can also be used as a dipping sauce for Chicken Strips, etc.
- For a sweeter sauce: add all the jam and sweetener called for.
- Makes 1$\frac{1}{2}$-2 cups.
- Store in a covered container and refrigerate for up to 7 days.
- Sauce becomes quite thick when chilled. To thin: heat briefly and/or use less tapioca flour.

Barbecue Sauce

(A healthier version of barbecue sauce that is very easy to make)

½ cup ketchup (fruit-sweetened or unsweetened)
2 Tbsp. olive oil
½ Tbsp. liquid aminos (optional)
2 Tbsp. minced onion (optional)
2 cloves garlic, minced or ¼ tsp. garlic powder
1-2 tsp. chili powder
1 tsp. honey
½ tsp. cumin (optional)
sea salt & pepper

In a small bowl, stir together all ingredients until well combined. Season to taste.

- Brush over meat or poultry before grilling.
- Store in a covered container and refrigerate for up to 7 days.
- Makes 2/3-3/4 cup.

Basic Tomato Sauce

(With a number of variations to this sauce, more time might be spent on deciding which one to make than the actual preparation time)

2 Tbsp. olive oil
4-6 cloves garlic, minced
1 onion, finely chopped
1 leek (white part only), finely chopped
1 cup vegetable stock
5 lbs. fresh tomatoes, diced
9-12 oz. tomato paste
1 tsp. ground kelp (optional)
spice combination of choice
$\frac{1}{4}$ cup fresh parsley, finely chopped
sea salt & pepper

Spice Combinations:
   a) 2 tsp dried basil, 1 tsp. dried oregano, sage & thyme, $\frac{1}{2}$ tsp. dried rosemary and $\frac{1}{4}$ tsp cayenne pepper.
   b) 2 tsp. cumin, 1$\frac{1}{2}$ tsp. chili powder, 1 tsp coriander & turmeric, $\frac{1}{2}$ tsp. paprika & oregano and $\frac{1}{4}$ tsp. cayenne pepper.
   c) Spices of choice.

In a stockpot, heat oil over medium-low heat.
Add garlic, onion and leek and sauté for 5 minutes.
Add remaining ingredients, except parsley, and bring to a light boil.
Reduce heat and simmer, covered, for 45 minutes.
Add parsley and simmer for 15 more minutes.
Season to taste.

• Serve over rice noodles, cooked grains, vegetables, meat, poultry or fish.

- Store in cover containers and refrigerate for up to 2 weeks or freeze.
- Makes a minimum of 6 cups.

Variations

❖ *Replace any dried herb with fresh herbs.*

❖ *Canned tomatoes can be used in place of all or part of fresh tomatoes; use approximately 3-28 oz. cans of diced or chopped tomatoes to replace all 5 lbs. of fresh.*

❖ *Replace $\frac{1}{2}$ cup vegetable stock with $\frac{1}{2}$ cup red wine.*

❖ *For **Meat Tomato Sauce**: add 12-16 oz. of ground turkey, lamb, etc. Add meat with oil and cook until no longer pink then add garlic, etc.*

❖ *For **Tofu Tomato Sauce**: add 16 oz., or more, crumbled tofu. Add tofu with garlic, etc.*

❖ *For **Primavera Tomato Sauce**: add one or more cups of finely chopped, mixed vegetables to simmering sauce, such as: carrots, peppers, eggplant, spinach, Swiss chard, zucchini, etc.*

❖ *For **Roasted Garlic Tomato Sauce**: replace garlic with 3 or more whole roasted garlic bulbs (see page 167) and spice of choice. Add to simmering sauce.*

❖ *For **Roasted Red Pepper Tomato Sauce**: add 2 or more roasted red peppers (see page 167) and add spice of choice (rosemary and/or thyme go well).*

Quick & Creamy Tomato Sauce

1-1½ Tbsp. olive oil
2 cloves garlic, minced
1 small onion or 2 shallots, finely chopped
2-3 tomatoes, chopped
2 Tbsp. tomato paste
¼ cup plain nut or seed milk
2 Tbsp. fresh basil, chopped
1 Tbsp. fresh parsley, chopped
sea salt & pepper

In a skillet, heat oil over medium heat.
Add garlic and onion or shallots, and sauté for 2-3 minutes.
In a blender, combine tomatoes, tomato paste and milk until smooth.
Add tomato mixture and fresh herbs to skillet, and simmer, covered,
for 10-13 minutes.
Season to taste.

- Can be made ahead of time and refrigerated for up to 3 days.
- Makes 1-1¼ cups.

Variations
❖ *Replace all or part of fresh herbs with fresh oregano, rosemary*
  and/or thyme.
❖ *Add chopped olives with fresh herbs.*
❖ *Add 1-2 Tbsp. pine nuts or any other chopped nut; sauté with*
  garlic.
❖ *For **Quick & Creamy Tomato Curry Sauce**: replace basil and*
  parsley with ¼-½ tsp. each chili powder, cumin, paprika, turmeric
  and 1-2 Tbsp. fresh cilantro.
❖ *For **Fresh Tomato Sauce**: omit tomato paste and milk; add chopped*
  tomatoes to skillet and simmer for 5-10 minutes.

Creamy Pesto

(A rich tasting pesto made with hazelnuts)

1½ cups fresh basil, tightly-packed
1/3 cup hazelnuts
3 or more garlic cloves
½ tsp. sea salt
1/3 cup olive oil
1/3 cup hemp or flax seed oil
1/3 cup plain nut or seed milk
¼ cup rice Parmesan cheese (optional)

In a blender or food processor, combine basil, hazelnuts, garlic and salt until finely chopped.
With machine running, add oils in a slow, steady stream; blend until smooth.
Add milk and blend until smooth.
Add Parmesan (if using) and blend until combined.

- Serve with rice noodles or use as a topping for vegetables, poultry or fish.
- Do not heat Pesto. If using pesto in a recipe where it needs to be heated, replace flax or hempseed oil with olive oil.
- Store in covered container and refrigerate for up to 5 days or freeze by omitting the cheese.
- Makes about 1¼-1½ cups.

Variations
❖ For **Creamy Pesto with Rosemary**: replace ¼-½ cup basil with fresh rosemary.
❖ Pesto can be made without the milk.

Mushroom Gravy

(A quick rich tasting sauce)

1 Tbsp. ghee
1¼ cups cremeni or chanterelle mushrooms, sliced
1½ Tbsp. chickpea or millet flour
¾ cup sesame seed milk
1 Tbsp. liquid aminos
½ tsp. paprika
pinch of cayenne pepper

In a saucepan, heat ghee over medium heat.
Add mushrooms and sauté for 3-5 minutes, until tender.
Add chickpea or millet flour and cook for 1 minute, stirring constantly.
Stir in milk, liquid aminos and spices.
Reduce heat and simmer until thickened; stirring occasionally.

- Add extra milk to make thinner.
- Serve over cooked grains, noodles, vegetables, meat or poultry.
- Can be prepared a day in advance; refrigerate.
- Makes about 1¼ cups.

Variation
❖ *For a richer sauce: replace sesame milk with almond, cashew or soy milk.*

Cucumber & Tomato Salsa

1 onion, finely chopped
1 field cucumber, finely chopped
2 tomatoes, diced
1 chili pepper of choice, finely chopped
2 cloves garlic, minced
2 Tbsp. fresh cilantro or mint, finely chopped
2 Tbsp. fresh lime or lemon juice
2 Tbsp. apple cider vinegar
1 Tbsp. olive oil
$\frac{1}{2}$ tsp. cumin
$\frac{1}{4}$ tsp. sea salt

In a bowl, stir together all ingredients; mix well.
Remove 1 cup of mixture and puree in a blender or food processor.
Return pureed mixture to bowl and stir to combine.

- Serve with Rice Paper Chili Tacos, Black Bean Tostadas, Turkey Burrito Crepes, cooked poultry, or as dip for rice crackers/crisps, etc.
- Add 1 diced avocado.
- Store in a covered container and refrigerate for up to 5 days.
- Makes about $2\frac{1}{2}$ cups.

Papaya Salsa

(The mild sweetness of papaya & roasted red pepper makes this salsa 'to die for')

2 cups peeled and diced tomatoes (about 2 large)
1 papaya, diced
1 roasted red pepper, finely chopped (see page 167)
3-4 green onions, finely chopped
1 Tbsp. fresh parsley, finely chopped
1 small chili pepper of choice, finely chopped
              or
1 tsp. chili/pepper sauce of choice
3 Tbsp. fresh lime or lemon juice
1 Tbsp. olive oil
1 Tbsp. apple cider vinegar
1 Tsp. honey
$\frac{1}{4}$ tsp. sea salt

In a bowl, stir together tomatoes, papaya, roasted pepper, onions, parsley and chili pepper (if using).
In a small bowl, stir or whisk together remaining ingredients until well combined.
Pour over tomato mixture and stir to mix.

- Serve with Rice Paper Chili Tacos, Black Bean Tostadas, Turkey Burrito Crepes, cooked poultry, or as dip for rice crackers/crisps, etc.
- Add 1 diced avocado.
- Store in a covered container and refrigerate for up to 7 days.
- Makes about 3 cups.

Roasted Garlic Winter Salsa

(This is good in recipes that require cooking)

1-14 oz. can diced tomatoes
6-8 garlic cloves, roasted (see page 167)
½ green or roasted red pepper, finely chopped
2 green or 2 Tbsp. red onions, finely chopped
1-2 Tbsp. fresh cilantro or parsley, finely chopped
½ Tbsp. olive oil
½ Tbsp. apple cider vinegar
½ tsp. chili powder & cumin
¼ tsp. sea salt

In a bowl, stir together all ingredients; mix well.

- Serve with Rice Paper Chili Tacos, Black Bean Tostadas, Turkey Burrito Crepes, on top of Mexican Lasagna, cooked poultry, or as dip for rice crackers/crisps, etc.
- This salsa is good in the winter time or when fresh tomatoes are not available.
- Store in a covered container and refrigerate for up to 5 days.
- Makes about 1½ cups.

Roasted Garlic, Fennel & Sweet Peppers

How to roast garlic, choose 1 of 3 ways:
1) Cut off top (about $\frac{1}{4}$") of whole garlic bulb to expose garlic. Drizzle exposed garlic with a little olive oil and wrap bulb in tinfoil. Roast in 425°F oven for 35-45 minutes. Let cool, and squeeze out each clove.
2) Remove all cloves from bulb and peel. Wrap garlic cloves in tinfoil with a little olive oil. Roast in 425°F oven for 30-35 minutes.
3) Place peeled cloves in a bowl and drizzle on a little olive oil. Stir to coat and transfer to a baking sheet. Roast at 425°F for 15-20 minutes; watching closely to not burn.
   Note: If there is a concern with the aluminum from the tinfoil, wrap the garlic bulb in parchment paper first and then cover with tinfoil.

How to roast fennel:
1) Cut fennel bulb into slices and place into a bowl. Drizzle with a little of olive oil and stir to coat. Transfer to a baking sheet and roast at 425°F for 20-25 minutes; watch closely to not burn.

How to roast red sweet peppers:
1) Cut peppers into quarters and seed. Place peppers, skin side up, on a baking sheet. Broil until charred and blistered, about 20 minutes. Turn off heat and let cool; peel off skin.
   Note: Some methods recommend putting the peppers in a paper bag after roasting. This makes the peppers steam and sweat, further loosening their skin as they cool. This step is not necessary. Also, roasting peppers whole will take longer than quartered peppers.

- All of these roasted vegetables can be refrigerated for up to 7 days in an airtight container.

Cajun Spice

(A spice that has kick & adds heat)

1 Tbsp. paprika
1½ tsp. sea salt
1 tsp. onion powder
1 tsp. garlic powder
1 tsp. cayenne pepper
1 tsp. black or white pepper
½ tsp. each dried basil, oregano & thyme

In a blender, food processor or coffee bean/nut/seed grinder, process all ingredients until well blended.

- Store in a spice jar.
- Double or triple recipe.

Garam Masala

(A spicy East Indian seasoning)

1 Tbsp. cumin seeds
1 Tbsp. cardamom seeds
1 Tbsp. black or white peppercorns
½ Tbsp. allspice berries
12 whole cloves
1-4" long piece of cinnamon stick, mashed into pieces

Bring a skillet to medium-low heat.
Add all ingredients, except cinnamon, and toast for 3-5 minutes, until fragrant.
Using a seed or spice grinder, grind together all spices into a powder.

- Store in a spice jar.

Sugar Toasted Almonds

2-3 tsp. ghee
$\frac{1}{2}$ cup slivered or sliced almonds
1-2 tsp. sucanat

In a skillet, heat ghee over medium heat.
Add almonds and stir to coat with melted ghee.
Sprinkle on sucanat.
Sauté almonds, stirring occasionally, until lightly brown; about 5 minutes.

• Store in a covered container and refrigerate.

Crispy Rice Noodles

8 oz. brown rice spaghetti noodles

Cook noodles accordingly; rinse and drain.
Spread noodles evenly onto a lightly oiled baking sheet (or parchment paper); don't let noodles bunch up.
Bake at 375°F for 30 minutes; turning noodles once after 15 minutes. (The noodles will have stuck together, so just pick up the whole mass with your hands and turn over.)
Watch noodles carefully so they don't burn.
Once noodles are nicely brown, turn off oven and let noodles continue to bake and dry out. Noodles become crispy when cooled.
Note: Some brands of rice noodles are thicker and therefore will take up to 20 minutes longer to bake.
Once noodles are cooled, break them into pieces and store them at room temperature in an airtight container, indefinitely.

• Use as a topping for salads, stir fry's, etc.

Flatbread Crisps

(A Melba toast-like cracker that is a little time consuming, but worth it)

$1\frac{1}{4}$ cups water
$\frac{3}{4}$ cup brown rice flour
$\frac{1}{4}$ cup amaranth or hemp seed flour
1 Tbsp. olive oil
$\frac{1}{4}$ tsp. sea salt
1 egg white
2 Tbsp. water
seasoning of choice

In a bowl, mix together water, flours, oil and salt until well combined; batter will be thin.
Heat a skillet over medium-high heat. No oil is required if using a non-stick skillet.
Pour a little batter, enough to make a 3" round flatbread, onto hot skillet and cook until flatbread looks almost dry, about 30 seconds.
Turn and cook the other side; about 20 seconds.
Finish with remaining batter.
Place breads, in a single layer, onto an oiled baking sheet or, line the baking sheet with parchment paper.
Note: It's a possibility crisps may stick to pan; using parchment paper will guarantee crisps will not stick to pan.
In a small bowl, mix together egg white and water.
Brush egg wash over topside of flatbreads.
Sprinkle on seasoning of choice.
Bake at 375°F for 20-25 minutes, until golden brown.

- Flatbreads will become crispy as they cool. They can be left in the oven after baking to dry out and make crispy. Watch that they don't burn.
- Use as a cracker with dips, salsa, soups, etc.

- Store in an airtight metal tin at room temperature, indefinitely.
- Makes 2-2½ dozen
- For seasoning, choose any of the following in any combination: sea salt, pepper, cumin, chili powder, dried herbs, garlic or onion powder, sesame seeds, rice Parmesan cheese, sucanat and cinnamon.
- Seasoning can also be added to batter.

Crepe Crisps

(A paper-thin cracker)

2 egg whites
3 Tbsp. water
12 crepes, cut into 6 wedges or quarters
seasoning of choice

Place crepes, in a single layer, onto a baking sheet lined with parchment paper.
In a small bowl, mix together egg whites and water.
Brush egg wash over topside of crepes.
Sprinkle on seasoning of choice.
Bake at 375°F for 7-10 minutes, until lightly brown. Watch closely, so they don't burn.

- Crepes will become crispy as they cool.
- Use as a cracker with dips, salsa, soups, etc.
- Store in an airtight metal tin at room temperature, indefinitely.
- Use same seasoning as Flatbread Crisps.

Meat, Poultry & Fish

Tips for Meat, Poultry & Fish   174
Turkey Strips   176
Chicken & Vegetables in Rosemary Yogurt Sauce   177
Chicken with Creamed Spinach   178
Turkey with Nut Butter & Coconut Sauce   179
Chicken Pot Pie   180
Roasted Cajun Chicken & Vegetables   182
Turkey & Spaghetti Squash Parmigiana   183
Turkey Biryani   184
Tarragon Turkey with Roasted Fennel & Tomatoes   185
'Sloppy Joes'   186
Herb Meatballs   187
Curry Meatballs   188
Honey & Garlic Grilled Lamb Chops   189
Lamb & Sweet Potato Curry   190
Grilled Rosemary Venison with Roasted Vegetable Sauce   191
Sweet Potato Meatloaf   192
Chicken Ragu   193
Rabbit Ragu   194
Curried Cornish Hens   195
Roasted Garlic Duck Breasts   196
Orange Ginger Roast Duck   197
Fish Fillets with Tomatoes, Fennel & Saffron   198
Fish Fillets with Roasted Vegetable Sauce   199
Cajun Fish with Orange Salsa   200
Roast Salmon with Asian Sauce   201
Citrus Fish Fillets with Star Anise   202
Fish Steaks With Teriyaki   203
Grilled Curried Fish Steaks   204

Tips for Meat, Poultry & Fish

❖ Purchase organic and free-range meats and poultry. These animals have been raised more humanely. If unavailable, purchase meats and poultry that are chemical-free. Chemical-free usually means they have not been given any antibiotics or hormones, but is not guaranteed. These quality meats and poultry can be purchased from farmers markets, some butcher chops, any health food store that carries meat and some major grocery chains.

❖ Favour fresh over frozen meats, poultry and fish. This is not always possible because organic or chemical-free meats, etc. especially bacon, wieners, luncheon meat, etc., can spoil quite quickly if left refrigerated. When these are purchased fresh, freeze into serving size portions within a day or 2.

❖ Purchase meats with tender, slightly moist flesh and a fresh smell. Purchase poultry with moist skin, not slimy, tender flesh and a fresh smell. Purchase fish that have a bright colour, a firm texture (skin or flesh will spring back when pressed lightly), and a fresh ocean-like smell.

❖ Fresh meat, poultry and fish, when tightly wrapped, can be kept refrigerated for up to three days in the coldest part of the refrigerator. Sometimes it is good to wash, with fresh water, and pat dry before wrapping and storing.

❖ To avoid the development of harmful bacteria, always defrost meats, etc. in the refrigerator.

❖ Never refreeze raw meats, etc. after thawing, unless they are cooked first.

❖ Always cook poultry and meat until no longer pink and juices run clear. Do not over cook, or meat and poultry becomes dry. Never serve rare, especially poultry, because all harmful bacteria may not have been killed during the cooking process.

❖ Always cook fish until moist, tender and flakes easily when tested with a fork. Over cooked fish will be dry. Do not consume raw fish.

❖ A general rule of thumb for cooking fresh fish: Cook 10 minutes for every inch of thickness. If fish is wrapped or stuffed, add 5-10 minutes total cooking time. (This may vary depending on the cooking method used.)

❖ Be cautious with any of the following fish, they usually contain mercury: halibut, shark, swordfish and shellfish. The following fish contain PCB's (polychlorinated biphenyls), chemical pollutants found to cause cancer: striped bass, bluefish, carp, catfish, king mackerel, tilefish and shellfish. All fish, to some degree, may contain PCB's. Recently, farmed raised fish have been found to contain PCB's and other chemical pollutants.
Note: Shellfish is not used in any recipe nor is it recommended, because they contain high amounts of mercury, PCB's and other chemicals. Shellfish are 'bottom feeders'; therefore they consume all the garbage on the water floors. Shellfish are also highly allergenic.

❖ Meat and poultry are interchangeable in any given recipe.

❖ Although beef is not used in any recipe, because of author's preference, it may be substituted in any recipe containing red meat.

Turkey Strips

(Kids of all ages will love these)

1 lb. boneless & skinless turkey, cut into strips
$\frac{1}{4}$ cup mayonnaise
2 Tbsp. water
1 Tbsp. olive oil
$\frac{3}{4}$ cup ground almonds or sesame seeds
2 Tbsp. brown rice flour
$\frac{1}{2}$ tsp. each dried basil, oregano & parsley
$\frac{1}{4}$-$\frac{1}{2}$ tsp. chili powder (optional)
2 Tbsp. rice or soy Parmesan cheese (optional)
sea salt & pepper

In a small bowl, mix together mayonnaise, water and oil until smooth.
In another bowl, mix together ground almonds or sesame seeds, flour, spices and cheese (if using).
Season to taste.
Dip turkey strips into mayonnaise mixture to coat; or brush strips.
Dip into dry mixture and turn to coat.
Arrange strips on to an oiled baking sheet.
Bake at 375°F for 20-25 minutes; turning once after 10 minutes.

- Makes 3-4 servings.
- Double, triple, etc. recipe and freeze. Strips do not need to be pre-cooked before freezing.

Variations
❖ *Replace all or part of the ground almonds or sesame seeds with crushed rice crisp cereal.*
❖ *Chicken can be used in place of turkey.*

Chicken & Vegetables in Rosemary Yogurt Sauce

1½ Tbsp. ghee or olive oil
12-16 oz. boneless & skinless chicken, cut into strips
3-4 cloves garlic, minced
1 large onion or 2-3 shallots, finely chopped
2 green or red sweet peppers, finely chopped
1½-2 cups shitake mushrooms, sliced
2 cups chopped spinach
1 cup chicken or vegetable stock
1 cup white wine or water
1 cup plain goat's milk yogurt
1½ Tbsp. tapioca flour
2½ tsp. dried or 3-4 Tbsp. fresh rosemary
sea salt & pepper

In a small Dutch oven, heat ½ Tbsp. ghee or oil over medium heat.
Add chicken and brown all sides. Remove and set aside.
Add remaining ghee or oil, garlic, onion or shallots, peppers and mushrooms, and sauté for 5 minutes.
Add chicken, spinach, stock and wine or water, and bring to a light boil.
Reduce heat and simmer, covered, for 7-10 minutes, until chicken is cooked through.
Combine yogurt, tapioca flour and rosemary, and add to Dutch oven; stir until thickened.
Season to taste.
• Makes 4 servings.

Variation
❖ For **Chicken & Vegetables in Rosemary Tomato Sauce**: *replace white wine, yogurt and tapioca flour with red wine, 2-3 diced tomatoes and 5-6 Tbsp. tomato paste. Add ingredients with stock.*

Chicken with Creamed Spinach

(A pleasing combination of chicken, spinach & herbs)

2 Tbsp. olive oil or ghee
12-16 oz. boneless & skinless chicken, cut into strips
2 onions or 2 leeks (white part only), chopped
2-3 cloves garlic, minced
5-6 cups chopped spinach
$\frac{1}{2}$ tsp. each dried basil, oregano, parsley, tarragon & thyme
2 cups plain nut or seed milk
$1\frac{1}{2}$ Tbsp. tapioca flour
sea salt & pepper

In a small Dutch oven, heat 1 Tbsp. oil or ghee over medium heat.
Add chicken and sauté until cooked through. Remove and set aside.
Add remaining oil or ghee and onions or leeks, and sauté for 5-7
minutes, until softened.
Add garlic and sauté 1 minute.
Add spinach and cook until just wilted.
Add chicken and spices.
In a bowl combine milk and tapioca flour, and add to Dutch oven; stir
until thickened.
Season to taste.
• Makes 4 servings.

Variations
❖ *Add extra vegetables such as strips of sweet pepper and zucchini.
    Add and sauté with onions or leeks.*
❖ *Any dried herb can be replaced with 1 Tbsp. fresh.*
❖ *For **Chicken & Spinach Crepes**: divide mixture among 8-12 crepes;
    heat if desired.*
❖ *Turkey can be used in place of chicken.*

Turkey with Nut Butter & Coconut Sauce

(A wonderful tasty combination)

2 tsp. olive oil or ghee
12-16 oz. boneless & skinless turkey, cut into strips
sea salt & pepper

Sauce:
$\frac{1}{4}$ cup nut butter of choice
$\frac{1}{2}$ cup coconut milk
3 Tbsp. liquid aminos
2 Tbsp. apple cider vinegar
2-3 cloves garlic, minced
1 tsp. fresh ginger, minced
$\frac{1}{2}$-1 tsp. chili powder
$\frac{1}{2}$ tsp. coriander & cumin (optional)

Combine all ingredients for sauce in a blender or food processor until smooth.
In a skillet, heat oil or ghee over medium heat.
Add turkey and brown all sides.
Add sauce and simmer, covered, for 10-12 minutes.
Season to taste.

• Makes 4 servings.
• Serve over cooked brown rice or noodles.
• Chicken or lamb can be used in place of turkey.

Chicken Pot Pie

(A delicious deep dish chicken & vegetable pie with an optional top crust)

Top crust:
   1 cup brown rice flour
   $\frac{1}{4}$ tsp. sea salt
   3-4 Tbsp. ghee or unsalted butter
   2-3 Tbsp. water

Filling:
   $1\frac{1}{2}$ Tbsp. ghee or olive oil
   1 leek (white part only), finely chopped
   2 carrots, chopped
   1 sweet potato, cut into cubes
   $1\frac{1}{4}$ cups chopped mixed vegetables of choice (cauliflower, peas, celery, broccoli, spinach, etc.)
   $1\frac{1}{2}$ cups chicken or vegetable stock
   $\frac{1}{4}$ cup fresh parsley, chopped
   $1\frac{1}{2}$ tsp. dried or 2-3 Tbsp. fresh tarragon
   $\frac{1}{2}$ tsp. sea salt
   pinch or 2 of cayenne pepper
   10 oz. (about 2 cups) cooked chicken, cubed
   1 cup plain nut or seed milk
   $\frac{1}{4}$ cup tapioca flour

To prepare crust:
   In a bowl, combine flour and salt.
   With fingers, rub in 3 Tbsp. ghee or butter until crumbly; add 1 more Tbsp. if needed.
   Add 2 Tbsp. water and stir with fork to mix; add 1 more Tbsp., if necessary, to make dough hold together.
   Form into a ball and chill.

180

To prepare filling:

In a saucepan, heat ghee or oil over medium heat.

Add leek and sauté for 3-5 minutes.

Add carrots, sweet potato, mixed vegetables, stock, and spices, and bring to a light boil.

Reduce heat and simmer, covered, for 10 minutes.

Add chicken and simmer for 10-15 more minutes or until vegetables are tender.

In a small bowl, combine milk and tapioca flour, and add to saucepan; stir until thickened.

Pour mixture into a deep 9" square baking dish.

On a floured surface, roll out dough and place on top of mixture; use hands to form crust. (there may dough leftover)

Prick dough with fork or make a $\frac{1}{4}$" hole in center.

Bake at 400°F, uncovered, for 25-35 minutes, until bubbly and golden.

- Makes 4-6 servings.

Variations
- ❖ *Replace $\frac{1}{4}$ cup rice flour with $\frac{1}{4}$ cup buckwheat, tapioca or chickpea flour.*
- ❖ *Replace chicken with turkey or rabbit.*
- ❖ *Frozen vegetables can be used in place of mixed vegetables. Add to last 5 minutes of simmering time.*
- ❖ *Replace crust with 2-3 cups of garlic mashed sweet or red potatoes. To make: boil 4-6 cloves garlic with 2-4 potatoes (about 2 lbs.). Strain and add 2-3 tsp. ghee or olive oil and $\frac{1}{4}$ cup plain nut or seed milk; mix until smooth. Replace sweet potatoes (optional) in filling with turnips or rutabagas.*
- ❖ *For **Vegetable Pot Pie**: replace chicken with 10 oz. cooked beans of choice.*

Roasted Cajun Chicken & Vegetables

(A one-pot meal with kick)

1 whole chicken, 3-4 lbs.
2 cloves garlic, chopped
3 carrots, chopped
2 sweet potatoes, chopped
1-2 celery stalks, chopped
6-10 pearl onions
1 turnip, chopped (optional)
1 cup vegetable or chicken stock
$\frac{1}{4}$ cup white wine (optional)
olive oil or melted ghee
Cajun spice (see page 168)

Place chicken into a small roasting pan.
Add vegetables, stock and wine. Add more stock or water, if needed, to cover vegetables.
Brush chicken with oil or ghee to coat.
Sprinkle or rub chicken with Cajun spice; coat well.
Roast at 350°F, covered, for $1\frac{1}{4}$-$1\frac{1}{2}$ hours or until juices run clear when chicken is pierced with fork.

- Makes 6-8 servings.
- Add millet stuffing.
- Uncover for last 20 minutes of cooking time, for a crispy coating.

Variation
❖ *Replace chicken with Cornish hens or 1 rabbit.*

Turkey & Spaghetti Squash Parmigiana

1 spaghetti squash
2 cups or more tomato sauce of choice
2-3 cloves garlic, sliced
½ cup ground nuts or seeds
¼ rice or soy Parmesan cheese
½ tsp. dried basil & oregano
sea salt & pepper
1 egg white
2 Tbsp. water
1 tbsp. olive oil or ghee
4 turkey cutlets, 3-4 oz. each
2-3 oz. shredded cheese of choice

Cook squash accordingly. (see page 115)
Remove spaghetti-like strands of flesh with a fork and place into an oiled baking dish.
Add 1 cup of tomato sauce and place sliced garlic on top.
In a bowl, stir together ground nuts or seeds, Parmesan and spices. Season to taste.
In another bowl, stir together egg white and water.
Dip each turkey cutlet into egg wash and then into dry mixture to coat.
In a skillet, heat oil or ghee over medium heat.
Add cutlets and brown both sides, about 2-3 minutes per side.
Place cutlets over squash in prepared baking dish.
Pour on remaining tomato sauce.
Sprinkle on cheese.
Bake at 375°F, uncovered, for 15-20 minutes or until bubbly and cheese is melted.

• Makes 4 servings.

Turkey Biryani

(An East Indian cream-like dish)

1$\frac{1}{2}$ Tbsp. ghee
12-16 oz. boneless & skinless turkey, cut into serving size pieces
2 cloves garlic, minced
1 shallot, minced
$\frac{1}{2}$ cup vegetable stock
$\frac{1}{2}$ cup red wine
1 tsp. cumin & garam masala
$\frac{1}{2}$ tsp. saffron threads
$\frac{1}{2}$ tsp. chili powder & paprika
1/3 cup yogurt cheese (see page 148)
sea salt & pepper

In a large skillet, heat ghee over medium-high heat.
Add turkey and brown both sides.
Add garlic and shallot, and cook for 1-2 minutes.
Add remaining ingredients, except yogurt cheese, and reduce heat to medium-low.
Cover and simmer for 7-10 minutes or until turkey is cooked through.
Remove cover and increase heat to high; boil until liquid is reduced in half.
Stir in yogurt cheese.
Season to taste.

• Serve with brown rice or noodles cooked with saffron; add saffron to cooking liquid.
• Makes 4 servings.

Variations
❖ *Replace yogurt cheese with rice, soy or goat's milk sour cream.*
❖ *Replace turkey with chicken or red meat of choice.*

Tarragon Turkey with Roasted Fennel & Tomatoes

(A wonderful combination of ingredients gives this dish an exotic taste experience)

1 Tbsp. ghee
12-16 oz. boneless & skinless turkey, cut into serving size pieces
2 cloves garlic, minced
1 shallot, minced
$\frac{1}{2}$ cup vegetable stock
$\frac{1}{2}$ cup red wine
3 tomatoes, diced
1 roasted fennel bulb (see page 167)
$\frac{1}{2}$ Tbsp. dried or 3 Tbsp. fresh tarragon
sea salt & pepper

In a large skillet, heat ghee over medium-high heat.
Add turkey and brown both sides.
Add garlic and shallot, and cook for 1-2 minutes.
Add remaining ingredients and reduce heat to medium-low.
Cover and simmer for 7-10 minutes or until turkey is cooked through.
Season to taste.

- Serve with brown rice noodles.
- Makes 4 servings.

Variations
- ❖ *Replace 3-4 Tbsp. red wine with sambuca, for an added licorice flavour.*
- ❖ *Replace turkey with chicken or red meat of choice.*

'Sloppy Joes'

(An easy and quick dish/meal to prepare)

1½ Tbsp. olive oil
1 lb. ground turkey
3 cloves garlic, minced
1 onion, finely chopped
1 green sweet pepper, finely chopped
2 Tbsp. liquid aminos
2½ cups tomato sauce of choice
4 tsp. chili powder
½ tsp. sea salt

In a skillet, heat oil over medium heat.
Add ground turkey, garlic, onion and pepper, and sauté until turkey is cooked through, occasionally stirring to break up meat.
Stir in remaining ingredients and simmer, covered, for 7-10 minutes.
Season to taste.

- Serve over toasted rice bread, rice pasta or brown rice.
- Makes 4-6 servings.

Variations
❖ *Replace ground turkey with ground chicken, lamb, emu or venison.*
❖ *For **Tofu Sloppy Joes**: replace ground turkey with 1¼ lbs. crumbled tofu. Sauté vegetables for 3 minutes and add tofu; sauté until brown.*

Herb Meatballs

(A fun dish for the young at heart)

1 lb. ground turkey, chicken, lamb, emu or venison
1 egg or 1 Tbsp. ground flax seeds mixed in 3 Tbsp. water
1 clove garlic, minced
1-2 green onions, finely chopped
$\frac{1}{4}$ cup ground almonds
$\frac{1}{2}$ tsp. each dried basil, oregano, parsley, rosemary & thyme
$\frac{1}{4}$ tsp. sea salt
1/8 tsp. black or white pepper
2 Tbsp. Parmesan cheese of choice (optional)

In a bowl, add all ingredients and stir or work with hands until well combined.
With wet hands, form mixture into 1" balls.
Place meatballs onto an oiled baking sheet.
Bake at 375°F for 25-30 minutes.

- Serve as is or with brown rice noodles and/or tomato sauce, or any other sauce. Can also be added to soups or stews.
- Cover and refrigerate for up to 2 days; or freeze.
- Makes 24 meatballs.
- Mixture can also be made into 4-6 hamburger patties.

Variation
❖ *For **Lemon Dill Meatballs**: replace herbs with $1\frac{1}{2}$-2 tsp. dried dill and add 2 tsp. lemon juice + $\frac{1}{2}$-1 tsp. (optional) grated lemon peel.*

Curry Meatballs

(Meatballs dressed with East Indian flare)

1 lb. ground turkey, chicken, lamb, emu or venison
1 egg or 1 Tbsp. ground flax seeds mixed in 3 Tbsp. water
2 Tbsp. plain goat's milk or soy yogurt
1 tsp. fresh lemon or lime juice (optional)
1 clove garlic, minced
2 green onions, finely chopped (optional)
¼ cup ground sesame seeds
1 tsp. fresh ginger, minced or ¼ tsp. ground ginger
½ tsp. or more chili powder & cumin
¼ tsp. each coriander, turmeric, garam masala & sea salt
1/8 tsp. cayenne or white pepper

In a bowl, add all ingredients and stir or work with hands until well combined.
With wet hands, form mixture into 1" balls.
Place meatballs onto an oiled baking sheet.
Bake at 375°F for 25-30 minutes.

- Serve as is or with brown rice noodles or cooked grains and/or curry sauce, curry tomato sauce, or Tandoori sauce. Can also be added to soups or stews.
- Cover and refrigerate for up to 2 days or freeze.
- Makes 24 meatballs.
- Mixture can also be made into 4-6 hamburger patties.

Honey & Garlic Grilled Lamb Chops

(The marinade in this dish softens the strong flavour of lamb)

4 shoulder or 8 loin lamb chops
  Marinade:
    2-3 Tbsp. olive oil
    $\frac{1}{4}$ cup liquid aminos
    $\frac{1}{4}$ cup vegetable stock or water
    $1\frac{1}{2}$ Tbsp. honey
    4 cloves garlic, minced or $\frac{1}{2}$ tsp. garlic powder
    1 tsp. dried mint
    1 tsp. dried chervil or rosemary
    sea salt & pepper

In a bowl, stir together all ingredients for marinade until well combined.
In a shallow dish, add lamb chops and pour marinade over top.
Cover and refrigerate for a minimum of 1 hour, and up to 24 hours.
Arrange lamb in a single layer on a broiling pan.
Broil lamb chops about 4" from heat for 7-10 minutes per side.

• Makes 4 servings.
• Lamb chops can also be grilled on the barbecue.

Lamb & Sweet Potato Curry

(A lightly spiced meat, or meatless, & vegetable dish with a couple of variations for the lamb)

1-2 Tbsp olive oil
1 lb. ground lamb
2-3 cloves garlic, minced
1 red or white onion, finely chopped
½ Tbsp. fresh ginger, minced
1 tsp. each chili powder, cumin & turmeric
½ tsp. coriander & sea salt
pinch or 2 of cayenne or white pepper
2 sweet potatoes, cut into cubes
2 cups vegetable stock
2 Tbsp. tomato paste
2 cups chopped spinach
1 cup frozen peas
¼ cup fresh parsley, chopped

In a Dutch oven, heat oil over medium heat.
Add lamb and cook until no longer pink, about 7 minutes; occasionally stirring to break up meat.
Add garlic, onion, ginger and spices, and sauté for 3-5 minutes.
Add sweet potatoes, stock and tomato paste, and bring to a light boil.
Reduce heat and simmer, covered, for 15 minutes.
Stir in spinach, peas and parsley, and simmer for 10 more minutes, until potatoes are tender.

• Makes 4-6 servings.

Variations
❖ *Replace lamb with ground chicken, turkey, emu or venison.*
❖ *For* **Tofu & Sweet Potato Curry***: replace ground lamb with 1-1¼ lbs. crumbled tofu. Sauté with garlic, etc. until brown and continue.*

Grilled Rosemary Venison with Roasted Vegetable Sauce

(Adding a combination of rosemary & roasted vegetable sauce to venison;
makes a delicious dish that all will be asking for the recipe)

4 venison steaks of choice (enough for 4 servings)
  Marinade:
    2 Tbsp. olive oil
    2 Tbsp. liquid aminos
    $\frac{1}{2}$ cup vegetable stock or water
    $\frac{1}{2}$ cup red wine
    2 cloves garlic, minced or $\frac{1}{4}$ tsp. garlic powder
    2 tsp. dried or 3-4 Tbsp. fresh rosemary
    sea salt & pepper
1 recipe roasted vegetable sauce on page 156

In a bowl, stir together all ingredients for marinade until well
combined.
In a shallow dish, add venison steaks and pour marinade over top.
Cover and refrigerate for a minimum of 1 hour, and up to 24 hours.
Arrange venison in a single layer on a broiling pan.
Broil venison steaks about 4" from heat for 7-10 minutes per side.
Warm vegetable sauce and serve over steaks.

• Makes 4 servings.
• Steaks can also be grilled on the barbecue.

Variations
❖ *Replace venison with lamb chops or red meat of choice. Boneless
   and skinless chicken or turkey works well too; use 1 lb.*
❖ *Can also be made with meat roasts; roast meat with marinade.*

Sweet Potato Meatloaf

(Adding the variation to this meatloaf will make it a complete meal)

1 lb. ground meat of choice
1 lb. sweet potatoes, cooked and mashed
1 egg, beaten
½ cup tomato sauce of choice
½ cup ground almonds
2 cloves garlic, minced
1 shallot, minced
2 Tbsp. ketchup
1 tsp. chili powder
½ tsp. each dried basil, oregano, parsley & rosemary
sea salt & pepper

In a bowl, add all ingredients and stir or work with hands until well combined.
Season to taste.
Lightly press mixture into an oiled loaf pan or baking dish.
Bake at 375°F, uncovered, for 45-55 minutes.

- Serve tomato sauce, mushroom gravy or roasted vegetable sauce over top.
- Makes 4-6 servings.

Variation
❖ *Add 1½-2 cups mixed sautéed vegetables to top of loaf (lightly pressed), for the last 15 minutes of baking time.*

Chicken Ragu

(An easy one-pot meal)

2 Tbsp. olive oil
4-6 chicken thighs, bone in (about 1½ lbs.)
2 cloves garlic, minced
1 leek, chopped
2 large carrots, chopped
2 celery stalks, chopped
4 oz. shitake or brown mushrooms, sliced
1 green sweet pepper, chopped
4 cups chopped Swiss chard or kale
2 cups chicken or vegetable stock
1 cup red wine
2-2½ cups chopped tomatoes
1-6 oz. can tomato paste
1 tsp. dried or 2 Tbsp. fresh sage & savory
¼ tsp. cayenne pepper
sea salt & pepper

In a Dutch oven, heat 1 Tbsp. olive oil over medium heat.
Add chicken and brown all sides. Remove and set aside.
Add remaining oil, garlic, leek, carrots, celery, mushrooms and green pepper, and sauté for 7-10 minutes, until softened.
Add remaining ingredients, including chicken, and bring to a light boil.
Reduce heat and simmer, covered, for 25 minutes and chicken is cooked through.
Season to taste.

• Serve with or over cooked brown or wild rice.
• Makes 4-6 servings.

Variation
❖ *Replace chicken with ½ rabbit or young turkey wings or drums.*

Rabbit Ragu

(A Cajun style ragu)

2 Tbsp. ghee & olive oil
8 oz. okra, tips removed & cut into ½" rounds
½ rabbit (about 2 lbs.), cut into pieces
2 cloves garlic, minced
2 shallots, finely chopped
2 carrots, cut into chunks
2 celery stalks, cut into chunks
1 fennel bulb, cut into chunks
1 lb. chopped tomatoes
1-6 oz. can tomato paste
2 cups vegetable stock
1 cup white wine or water
1 Tbsp. Cajun spice (see page 168)
3 Swiss chard leaves, chopped
¼ cup fresh parsley, chopped
sea salt & pepper

In a Dutch oven, heat ghee over medium-low heat.
Add okra and sauté for 10-15 minutes, until browned. Remove and set aside.
Add olive oil and rabbit, and brown all sides over medium heat.
Add garlic, shallots, carrots, celery and fennel, and sauté for 2-3 minutes.
Add tomatoes, tomato paste, stock, wine or water and Cajun spice, and bring to a light boil.
Reduce heat and simmer, covered, for 40 minutes.
Add Swiss chard and parsley, and simmer for 20 more minutes.
Stir in okra and season to taste.

• Makes 4-6 servings.

Curried Cornish Hens

2 large Rock Cornish hens
$\frac{1}{4}$ cup ghee or unsalted butter, melted
$\frac{1}{4}$ fresh lemon juice
3 cloves garlic, minced
1 tsp. chili powder & cumin
$\frac{1}{2}$ tsp. coriander & paprika
$\frac{1}{4}$ tsp. each dried oregano sea salt & turmeric
1/8 tsp. cayenne or white pepper

Place hens in a small roasting pan or baking dish.
In a bowl, stir together remaining ingredients until well combined.
Brush hens with sauce to coat well.
Roast at 400°F, uncovered, for 30 minutes; baste occasionally.
Reduce heat to 350 and continue roasting and basting for 30 more minutes or until skin is deep brown and juices run clear when hens are pierced with fork.

• Makes 4 servings.
• Hens can be stuffed with millet or wild rice stuffing (page 238).
• Serve with yogurt or Tandoori sauce (page 153).

Roasted Garlic Duck Breasts

(All the different flavours combine for an exotic tasting duck)

2 boneless & skinless duck breasts (or enough for 4 servings)
1 whole garlic bulb, roasted (see page 167)
¼ cup vegetable stock
¼ cup white wine
2 Tbsp. melted ghee or olive oil
1 tsp. chili powder
½ tsp. saffron threads
½ tsp. cumin (optional)
¼ tsp. sea salt

Place duck breasts into an oiled baking dish.
In a bowl, stir together remaining ingredients until well combined.
Pour sauce over duck breasts.
Bake at 375°F, covered, for 30-40 minutes or until juices run clear when duck is pierced with fork.

• Makes 4 servings.
• Muscovy is a lean, meaty and tasty breed of duck.

Variation
❖ Replace duck with 2 boneless and skinless chicken breasts or 1 turkey breast cut in half.

Orange Ginger Roasted Duck

(An perfect dish to help celebrate any holiday)

1 duck (about 4lbs.)
1½ cups fresh orange juice
1 cup vegetable stock
½ cup white wine
2 Tbsp. olive oil
¼ cup chopped fresh ginger
4 cloves garlic, finely chopped
2 tsp. dried sage
sea salt & pepper
2-3 tsp. tapioca flour mixed in 2 Tbsp. water

Truss duck and place into a roasting pan.
In a bowl, stir together orange juice, stock, wine, oil, ginger, garlic and sage until well combined.
Pour sauce over duck and season.
Roast duck at 350°F, uncovered, for 1¼-1½ hours or until juices run clear when duck is pierced with fork, basting often with sauce.
Note: Tent duck with parchment paper or tinfoil if browning to fast.
Cut up duck and place on a serving platter; keep warm.
Put roasting pan on stove and bring to medium-high heat, or transfer juices to a saucepan. (Juices can be strained before thickening.)
Add tapioca mixture and stir until thickened.
Serve sauce over duck.

- Makes 6 or more servings.
- Duck can be stuffed with millet or wild rice stuffing (page 238).
- Muscovy is a lean, meaty and tasty breed of duck.

Variations
❖ *Replace duck with chicken or Cornish hens.*
❖ *Replace ¼ cup wine with ¼ cup liquid aminos.*

Fish Fillets with Tomatoes, Fennel & Saffron

(An exotic tasting fish dish that is easy to prepare)

1 lb. fish fillets of choice
2 Tbsp. olive oil or ghee
2 shallots, finely chopped
2 cups finely chopped fennel
2 large tomatoes, chopped
1 tsp. saffron threads
1 cup vegetable stock
$\frac{1}{4}$ cup white wine or fresh lemon juice
sea salt & pepper

In a large skillet, heat oil or ghee over medium heat.
Add shallots and fennel, and sauté for 5 minutes.
Add tomatoes and saffron, and cook for 2 minutes.
Add stock, wine or lemon juice and arrange fish fillets in a single layer over top; bring to a boil.
Reduce heat and simmer, covered, for 4-6 minutes or until fish is opaque and flakes easily when tested with a fork.
Season to taste.

• Makes 4 servings.

Variations

❖ *After fish is cooked: with a slotted spoon, remove fish and some vegetables to a serving platter, reserving poaching liquid in skillet. Combine 1$\frac{1}{2}$ tsp. tapioca flour with 2-3 Tbsp. water, and add to skillet. Stir until thickened and spoon sauce over fish.*

❖ *For **Tofu with Tomatoes, Fennel & Saffron**: replace fish with 1 lb. sliced tofu. Sauté tofu for 2 minutes per side, remove and set aside. Continue as above, add tofu in place of fish and simmer for 10 minutes.*

Fish Fillets with Roasted Vegetable Sauce

(The roasted vegetable sauce softens the flavour of most fish)

1 lb. fish fillets of choice
   Sauce:
      1 red pepper, roasted (see page 167)
      $\frac{1}{2}$ cup sliced fennel, roasted (see page 167)
      6 garlic cloves, roasted (see page 167)
      $\frac{1}{4}$ cup unsweetened apple juice
      $\frac{1}{2}$ cup vegetable stock
      $\frac{1}{2}$ cup water
      2 Tbsp. white wine or lemon juice
      1 Tbsp. apple cider vinegar
      $\frac{1}{2}$ tsp. dried thyme
      $\frac{1}{4}$ tsp. sea salt

Combine all ingredients for sauce in a blender or food processor until smooth.
Divide fish into serving sized pieces and arrange in a single layer, in an oiled baking dish.
Pour sauce over fish.
Bake at 425°F, uncovered, for 10-13 minutes or until fish is opaque and flakes easily when tested with a fork.

- Makes 4 servings.
- Use fish with a red colour flesh (artic char, salmon, trout, etc.).

Variation
❖ For **Tofu with Roasted Vegetable Sauce**: *replace fish with 1 lb. sliced tofu. Sauté tofu in a little oil for 2 minutes per side. Continue as above, add tofu in place of fish and bake for 10-15 minutes.*

Cajun Fish with Orange Salsa

(Spicy flavoured fish balanced with orange salsa)

1 lb. Orange Roughy fillets
1 Tbsp. olive oil
Cajun spice (see page 168)
2 Tbsp. ghee
  Salsa:
    2 oranges, finely chopped
    2 Tbsp. fresh lime or lemon juice
    $\frac{1}{2}$ Tbsp. apple cider vinegar
    $1\frac{1}{2}$-2 Tbsp. finely chopped red or green onions
    1 Tbsp. finely chopped fresh cilantro or mint
    sea salt & pepper

In a bowl, stir together all ingredients for salsa.
Season to taste, set aside and chill.
Brush fish with olive oil and then rub with as much Cajun spice as
wanted.
In a skillet, heat ghee over medium-high heat.
Add fillets and sauté both sides until brown and crisp or fish is opaque
and flakes easily when tested with a fork; about 4 minutes per side.

• Serve with salsa.
• Makes 4 servings.

Variations
❖ *Replace Orange Roughy with any white coloured flesh fish, sole,*
  pike, whitefish, etc.
❖ *Replace oranges in salsa with mandarins, Ugli (Unique) fruit or*
  papaya.

Roast Salmon with Asian Sauce

(Salmon covered in a rich tasting sauce & sesame seeds)

1 lb. salmon fillet(s)
1 Tbsp. ground sesame seeds
  Sauce:
    $\frac{1}{4}$ cup liquid aminos
    juice of 2 limes
    2 Tbsp. water
    2 Tbsp. maple syrup
    2 tsp. olive oil
    1 tsp. sesame oil
    $\frac{1}{2}$ Tbsp. grain or Dijon mustard
    1 Tbsp. finely chopped fresh cilantro or mint

In a bowl, stir together ingredients for sauce until well combined.
Divide fish into serving sized pieces and arrange in a single layer, in an oiled baking dish.
Pour sauce over fish and sprinkle with ground sesame seeds.
Bake at 425°F, uncovered, for 10-13 minutes or until fish is opaque and flakes easily when tested with a fork.

• Makes 4 servings.

Variations
❖ *Replace salmon with any red coloured flesh fish, trout, artic char, etc.*
❖ *For **Roasted Tofu with Asian Sauce**: replace fish with 1 lb. sliced tofu. Sauté tofu in a little oil for 2 minutes per side. Continue as above, add tofu in place of fish and bake for 10-15 minutes.*

Citrus Fish Fillets with Star Anise

(Oven-steamed fish with a combination of tangy citrus and licorice-like flavour)

1 lb. white coloured flesh fish fillets (sole, cod, haddock, etc.)
2 Tbsp. olive oil or melted ghee
1 lemon
sea salt & pepper
1 small tangerine, sliced
1 lime, sliced
10-12 fresh sage or basil leaves
4-6 whole star anise

Lay fish, in a single layer, on a piece of parchment paper, with a larger piece of tinfoil lying underneath the parchment paper.
Note: Parchment paper is optional, but is used to prevent aluminum from leaching into fish.
Brush fish with olive oil or melted ghee.
Squeeze the juice from lemon over fish.
Season to taste.
Line fish with tangerine and lime slices.
Line with sage or basil and star anise.
Fold paper over fish and seal in tinfoil.
Place on a baking sheet.
Bake at 425°F for 15 minutes.

• Makes 4 servings.

Fish Steaks with Teriyaki

(A classic Asian style dish combination)

1 lb. fish steaks of choice (salmon, tuna, etc.)
1 Tbsp. ground sesame seeds
  Marinade:
    3 Tbsp. red wine or 3 Tbsp. apple cider vinegar
    2 Tbsp. water
    2 Tbsp. liquid aminos
    4 tsp. olive oil
    2 tsp. sesame oil
    1 Tbsp. honey or sucanat
    $\frac{1}{2}$ Tbsp. fresh ginger, minced
    1-2 cloves garlic, minced

In a bowl, stir together ingredients for marinade until well combined.
Divide fish into serving sized pieces and arrange in a single layer, in an oiled baking dish.
Pour marinade over fish; cover and refrigerate for 30 minutes.
Sprinkle fish with ground sesame seeds.
Bake at 425°F, uncovered, for 12-15 minutes or until fish is opaque and flakes easily when tested with a fork.

• Makes 4 servings.

Variations
❖ *Replace steaks with fillets and poach in a skillet for 4-6 minutes.*
❖ *For* **Teriyaki Tofu**: *replace fish with 1 lb. sliced tofu. Sauté tofu in a little oil for 2 minutes per side. Continue as above, add tofu in place of fish and bake for 15 minutes (no need to marinade).*

Grilled Curried Fish Steaks

(This marinade is sure to spice up any fish)

1 lb. fish steaks of choice
  Marinade:
    $\frac{1}{4}$ cup fresh lemon or lime juice
    2 Tbsp. olive oil
    2 Tbsp. water
    2 cloves garlic, minced or $\frac{1}{4}$ tsp. garlic powder
    $\frac{1}{2}$ tsp. fresh ginger, minced (optional)
    $\frac{1}{2}$ tsp. cumin seeds, crushed
    $\frac{1}{4}$ tsp. chili flakes & coriander seeds, crushed
    1/8 tsp. paprika & turmeric
    sea salt & pepper

In a bowl, stir together ingredients for marinade until well combined.
Season to taste.
Divide fish into serving sized pieces and arrange in a single layer, in a
shallow dish.
Pour marinade over fish; cover and refrigerate for 30 minutes to 2
hours.
Grill fish on a grill or in a grilling pan for 3-5 minutes per side or until
fish is opaque and flakes easily when tested with a fork.

- Makes 4 servings.
- Fish can also be done under the broiler, about 4" from heat.

Pasta, Grains & Legumes

Tips for Pasta, Grains & Legumes   206
Macaroni & Cheese Bake   210
Baked Rice Noodles with Pesto   211
Sweet Potato Casserole   212
Roasted Vegetables & Rice Noodles   213
Brown Rice Pasta Primavera   214
Mexican Lasagna   215
Sweet & Red Potato Lasagna   216
Spaghetti Pie   217
Lemon Garlic Chicken with Basil & Rice Noodles   218
Chicken Vegetable & Rice Noodle Casserole   219
Rice Noodles with Bean Sauce   220
Chili   211
Toasted Cumin & Navy Bean Chili   223
Chili Pasta   224
Turkey & Roasted Vegetable Casserole   226
Brown Rice Balls   227
Rice Meatloaf   228
Millet & Tomato Risotto   229
Millet & Saffron Risotto   230
Millet Vegetable Risotto   231
Island Millet   232
Barbecue Baked Beans   233
Black Bean Tostadas   234
Curried Lentils   235
Sweet & Sour Lentils   236
Veggie Patties   237
Millet Stuffing   238
Spaghetti Salad 'Italian Style'   239
Spaghetti Salad 'Asian Style'   240
Wild Rice & Vegetable Salad   241
Quinoa Salad   242
Mixed Bean & Vegetable Salad   243

Tips for Pasta, Grains & Legumes

❖ **Pasta**

1. For its nutritional superiority, choose brown rice pastas over white varieties.

2. How to cook rice pasta:
   a. Bring a pot of water to a boil and add noodles.
   b. Cook pasta at a light boil until firm to the bite, 'al Dente', or tender. Times will vary from one type of pasta to the next, because noodles come in different size and thickness. Some noodles will only require soaking in hot water and others need to be cooked for up to 13 minutes.
   c. If noodles are overcooked, they become mushy and fall apart.
   d. Most noodles, when cooked, will have expanded about 3 times their original size.

3. *Note:* Other types of pastas are also available in selective areas. Grain pastas (quinoa, millet, etc.) usually contain corn as the first ingredient, and as the recipes in this book are also corn-free, these are not recommended. Legume (lentil, pea, etc.) pastas, although fairly new, are showing great promise because they are quite low on the Glycemic Index. These pastas are a wonderful alternative for those with blood sugar handling problems.

❖ **Grains & Legumes**

1. Sort through grains and legumes and remove any foreign looking objects, gravel or small stones, dirt balls and any broken or misshapen grains or legumes.

2. Brown and wild rice, quinoa and legumes need to be pre-washed and rinsed. Although, it is recommended to wash and rinse all grains for health and sanitary reasons.

3. In general, grains and legumes, except for wild rice and dried beans, do not need pre-soaking. But because grains and legumes contain phytates, which hinders absorption of minerals, pre-soaking is recommended. Pre-soaking breaks down the phytates and makes grains and legumes easier to digest.
4. Grains and legumes need to be cooked at a low heat. If heat is too high, they will burn on the outside and be undercooked in the center.
5. Do not stir grains or legumes during the cooking process or they will stick and possibly burn.
6. Cook grains and legumes until they are tender and easy to chew. Do not overcook them or they become too soft, mushy and fall apart.
7. To reheat cooked grains or legumes add a little liquid and cook, covered, on low heat until heated through.
8. 1 cup of dry grains or legumes yields about 2-3 cups cooked.

❖ Preparation for Individual Grains & Legumes
Short & Long Grain Brown Rice.
Wash and rinse rice to remove dirt and excess starch. Use 2 cups of liquid to 1 cup of rice. Bring rice and liquid to a boil; reduce heat and simmer, covered, for 40-50 minutes until tender and easy to chew. For less starchy and chewier texture: use $1\frac{3}{4}$ cups liquid to 1 cup rice. This is good for fried rice or when rice needs a second cooking. For creamier rice: use $2\frac{1}{4}$-$2\frac{1}{2}$ cups liquid to 1 cup rice. This is good for rice puddings, rice balls and when a creamier consistency is wanted.

Wild Rice.
Wash and rinse rice thoroughly. Soak 1 cup of wild rice in $2\frac{1}{2}$-3 cups of liquid for 2-3 hours. Bring rice and liquid to a boil, reduce heat and simmer, covered, for 60-75 minutes until tender, fluffy and each grain of rice is split.

Millet.
For a soft texture: use 3-3$\frac{1}{2}$ cups of liquid to 1 cup millet. This has a porridge-like texture.
For a crumbly texture: use 2-2$\frac{1}{2}$ cups of liquid to 1 cup millet. This has a fluffier texture.
Bring millet and liquid to a boil, reduce heat and simmer, covered, for 20-30 minutes; until most of the liquid is absorbed.

Quinoa.
Wash and rinse thoroughly before cooking. Use 2-3 cups liquid to 1 cup quinoa. Bring quinoa and liquid to a boil, reduce heat and simmer, covered, for 20-30 minutes, until tender, the grains have turned transparent, and the spiral-like germ has split.

Lentils & Split Peas.
Wash and rinse lentils and split peas thoroughly.
For un-soaked lentils or split peas: use 3 cups liquid to 1 cup lentils or split peas. Bring lentils or split peas and liquid to a boil, reduce heat and simmer, covered, for 35-45 minutes until most of the liquid is absorbed.
For soaked lentils or split peas: soak 1 cup of lentils or split peas in water for 8 hours or overnight. Rinse and drain. Bring lentils or split peas and 2 cups of water to a boil, reduce heat and simmer, covered, for 25-35 minutes; until most of the liquid is absorbed.

Dried Beans.
Canned beans are used in all recipes that contain beans. This is done for convenience sake and because many people hesitate at recipes that require dried beans. Many are afraid of cooking beans improperly and the time required in preparing them. For those that prefer to make their own beans, replace canned beans with home made in any given recipe. One 14 oz. can of beans yields 1$\frac{1}{2}$ cups.

How to prepare and cook beans properly and for easy digestion:

a. Sort through the beans and discard any shriveled, misshapen or discoloured beans. Remove any stones or dirt balls.

b. Fill a container with water and swish beans with hands. Discard any beans that float.

c. Rinse and drain several times, until water runs clear.

d. Cover beans with fresh water, enough water to cover beans by 2 inches. Soak beans for a minimum of 8 hours.

e. Discard the soaking water, rinse, and drain again with fresh water.

f. Put beans in a pot and cover with water. Boil beans for 10 minutes. Pour off boiling water, rinse, and drain one more time. Some flavours and nutrients may be lost during this step, but the beans become more digestible. This procedure also eliminates the element that causes intestinal gas.

   Note: The boiling water does not necessarily need to be discarded. If this is the case, just remove all the froth that forms on top during boiling time and continue on with next step.

g. Put beans back into a pot and add enough water to cover beans by $1-1\frac{1}{2}$".

h. Simmer beans over low heat and cook for $1\frac{1}{4}$ hours, or more, until beans are tender or quite soft. Simmer pinto, kidney and mung beans for $1\frac{1}{2}$ hours and chickpeas for $2\frac{1}{2}$ hours

i. Do not add salt at any point in the process until after beans are cooked, otherwise they will not become tender.

j. Adding 1 tsp. dried savory or ground fennel seeds to cooking water improves the digestibility of beans.

k. Overall, navy (white) beans, split peas and lentils are the easiest legumes do digest.

l. All cooked beans freeze well.

Macaroni & Cheese Bake

(A favourite enjoyed by many)

2 2/3 cups plain nut or seed milk
3 Tbsp. ghee or unsalted butter
3 Tbsp. chickpea or millet flour
1 tsp. dried parsley & sea salt
pinch or 2 of nutmeg & cayenne pepper
8 oz. dry brown rice elbows or penne, cooked
2¼ cups shredded cheese (rice, soy or goat's milk)
4-6 oz. cooked turkey sausage, crumbled or ground turkey (optional)
     Or
2 cups mixed sautéed vegetables (optional)
¼ cup ground almonds
¼ cup Parmesan cheese (rice, soy or goat's milk)

In a saucepan, heat milk over medium heat and keep warm.
In another saucepan, heat ghee or butter over medium heat.
Add flour and cook for 1-2 minutes, stirring constantly.
Slowly stir in milk, a little at a time, until thickened.
Stir in spices and rice noodles.
Stir in turkey or vegetables (if using).
Add cheese and stir until melted.
Transfer to an oiled baking or casserole dish.
Sprinkle ground almonds and Parmesan over top.
Bake at 375°F, uncovered, for 30 minutes or until bubbly and top is golden brown.

• Makes 4 or more servings.

Variations
❖ *Use 2 or 3 kinds of different or flavoured cheeses.*
❖ *Add ½ tsp. each dried basil and oregano or 1 tsp. of favourite spice or herb.*

Baked Rice Noodles with Pesto

(A good summertime dish)

1½ cups plain nut or seed milk
¼ cup tapioca flour
½ cup pesto (see page 162)
1 tsp. dried parsley
¼ cup Parmesan cheese, rice or soy
8 oz. dry rice elbows or penne, cooked
sea salt & pepper
¼ shredded cheese, rice or soy
¼ cup ground nuts or seeds

In a saucepan, whisk together milk and tapioca until well combined.
While stirring, heat milk mixture over medium heat until thickened.
Stir in pesto, parsley and Parmesan, until well combined.
Stir in noodles.
Season to taste.
Transfer to an oiled baking or casserole dish.
Sprinkle shredded cheese and ground nuts or seeds over top.
Bake at 375°F, uncovered, for 25-30 minutes or until bubbly, cheese
is melted and top is golden brown.

• Makes 4 or more servings.
• Use pesto made with only olive oil and with or without milk.

Sweet Potato Casserole

(A pleasant taste experience)

4 oz. brown rice noodles, penne or elbows
3 medium sweet potatoes, peeled & cut into chunks
1½ Tbsp. melted ghee or unsalted butter
1/3 cup plain sesame seed milk
½ tsp. each chili powder, cumin & dried parsley
3 green onions, finely chopped (optional)
2 cloves garlic, minced
3 slices cooked turkey bacon, crumbled (optional)
     Or
½ cup cooked ground turkey (optional)
2 Tbsp. ground almonds
2 Tbsp. rice Parmesan cheese

Cook noodles accordingly; rinse and set aside.
Steam or boil sweet potatoes until tender, about 15 minutes. Drain water.
In a large bowl, mash potatoes.
Mix in milk and spices until well combined.
Stir in onions (if using), garlic, cooked turkey (if using) and noodles.
Transfer to an oiled baking or casserole dish.
Sprinkle ground almonds and Parmesan over top.
Bake at 375°f, uncovered, for 20-30 minutes or until bubbly and top is golden brown.

• Makes 4 or more servings.

Roasted Vegetables & Rice Noodles

8 oz. brown rice noodles, elbows or penne
4 small red potatoes, chopped into bite-sized pieces
10-12 cloves garlic
1 fennel bulb, sliced
3 Tbsp. olive oil
6 Tbsp. ghee or unsalted butter
2 shallots, chopped
1 zucchini chopped
¼ cup chopped nuts of choice
1 tsp. dried or 2 Tbsp. fresh chopped parsley, rosemary & thyme
1 roasted red pepper, chopped (see page 167)
2 Tbsp. Parmesan cheese (rice, soy or goat's milk)
sea salt & pepper

Cook noodles accordingly; rinse and set aside.
Place potatoes, garlic and fennel in a baking dish. Add olive oil and stir to coat.
Bake at 425°F for 25 minutes or until potatoes are tender. Set aside.
In a large saucepan or Dutch oven, heat ghee or butter over medium heat.
Add shallots and zucchini, and sauté for 3 minutes.
Add nuts and sauté for 1 minute.
Add herbs, roasted vegetables and rice noodles, and stir to coat with ghee or butter; heat through.
Sprinkle on Parmesan and season to taste.

• Serve warm or cold
• Makes 4 or more servings.

Variation
❖ *Add 8 oz. roast turkey, cubed or cooked turkey sausage, chopped.*

Brown Rice Pasta Primavera

(Noodles & vegetables in a cream-like sauce)

6 oz. brown rice fettuccini noodles
1 Tbsp. olive oil or ghee
2 cloves garlic, minced
2 carrots, julienne
1 celery stalk, sliced
1 cup chopped asparagus
$\frac{1}{2}$ cup sliced mushrooms or julienne zucchini
$1\frac{1}{2}$ Tbsp. chickpea or millet flour
$1\frac{1}{4}$-$1\frac{1}{2}$ cups plain nut or seed milk at room temperature
2-3 Tbsp. Parmesan or $\frac{1}{4}$ cup shredded cheese of choice
1 Tbsp. fresh lemon juice or white wine
1 tsp. dried or 2 Tbsp. fresh rosemary or thyme
sea salt & pepper

Cook noodles accordingly; rinse and set aside.
In a saucepan, heat oil or ghee over medium heat.
Add garlic, carrots, celery, asparagus and mushrooms or zucchini, and sauté for 5 minutes.
Add flour and cook for 1 minute, stirring constantly.
While stirring, slowly add milk and cook until thickened, about 5-7 minutes.
Stir in noodles, cheese, lemon juice or wine and herb of choice; cook until noodles are heated through.
Season to taste.

• Makes 2-4 servings.

Variation
❖ *Replace any vegetable with any fresh vegetable on hand.*

Mexican Lasagna

(Noodles, refried beans & optional tofu cooked in roasted red pepper tomato sauce & salsa; make extra, because dinner companions will be asking for seconds & thirds)

12 brown rice lasagna noodles
8-12 oz. tofu, crumbled (optional)
2½ cups roasted red pepper tomato sauce (see page 160)
1-16 oz. can refried beans
1 tsp. chili powder & cumin
1 roasted garlic winter salsa recipe (see page?) or salsa of choice
6 oz. shredded goat's milk cheese, mozzarella or Monterey

Cook noodles accordingly; rinse and set aside.
If using tofu: sauté in a skillet with 2 tsp. olive oil until brown.
In a bowl, stir together 2 cups tomato sauce, refried beans, chili powder and cumin until smooth.
In a 9"x13" or lasagna baking dish, spread remaining tomato sauce over bottom and top with 4 noodles.
Cover noodles with ½ bean mixture and tofu (if using); top with 4 noodles.
Add remaining bean mixture and noodles.
Cover top with salsa.
Sprinkle cheese over top.
Bake at 375°F, uncovered, for 30-40 minutes, until hot and bubbly.

• Makes 6-8 servings.

Sweet & Red Potato Lasagna

(A unique blend of ingredients creates this unusual but delicious lasagna)

12 brown rice lasagna noodles, cooked & rinsed
3 Tbsp. ghee or olive oil
2 large red onions, sliced
20 oz. peeled & chopped sweet potatoes
20 oz. peeled & chopped red potatoes
4 cloves garlic, chopped
½ cup plain nut or seed milk
½ tsp. dried parsley & sea salt
1 cup yogurt cheese (see page 148)
        Or
10 oz. soft goat's milk, rice cream or soy cream cheese
4 oz. shredded mozzarella cheese of choice

In a skillet, heat 2 Tbsp. ghee or oil over medium heat.
Add onions and sauté for 5-7 minutes, until lightly browned. Set aside.
In a pot of water, add sweet potatoes, red potatoes and garlic, and cook over medium-high heat until tender, about 20 minutes.
Drain water, and mash potatoes and garlic.
Add remaining ghee or oil, milk, parsley and sea salt; stir until smooth.
Stir in soft cheese of choice, until smooth.
In a well-oiled lasagna baking dish, cover bottom with 4 noodles.
Top with ½ potato mixture and top with 4 noodles.
Add remaining potato mixture and noodles.
Sprinkle on shredded cheese and top with onions.
Bake at 375°F, covered, for 30-40 minutes, until hot and bubbly.

• Makes 6-8 servings.

Spaghetti Pie

(An easy to prepare noodle dish that is baked in the oven)

10 oz. brown rice spaghetti noodles
½ cup plain almond milk
1 tsp. tapioca flour
3 eggs
1 cup tomato sauce of choice (optional)
¼ cup rice or goat's milk Parmesan cheese
6 oz. shredded cheese of choice
6 oz. cooked turkey sausage, chopped (optional)
½ Tbsp. dried parsley
sea salt & pepper

Cook noodles accordingly; rinse and set aside.
In a small bowl, combine almond milk and tapioca flour.
In a large bowl, beat eggs.
Mix in almond milk mixture and tomato sauce (if using).
Stir in cheeses, turkey (if using) and parsley, until well combined.
Season to taste.
Stir in pasta.
Transfer mixture to a well-oiled baking dish or large pie plate.
Bake at 375°F, uncovered, for 30 minutes, until hot and cheese is melted.
Cut spaghetti pie into wedges and serve as is or, with sauce of choice.

• Makes 4 or more servings.

Variations
❖ *Sprinkle ground almonds over top before baking.*
❖ *Add 1 tsp. of favourite spice or herb.*
❖ *Replace turkey sausage with any kind of cooked meat or sautéed tofu.*

Lemon Garlic Chicken with Basil & Rice Noodles

(An Asian-style chicken dish with zesty lemon, garlic & fresh basil)

12 oz. brown rice noodles, spaghetti or fettuccini
1-2 Tbsp. olive oil
12-16 oz. boneless & skinless chicken, cut into strips
6-8 cloves garlic, minced
2 shallots, minced
2 cups chopped spinach
2-3 tbsp. fresh lemon juice
1 cup chicken or vegetable stock
1 cup fresh basil, chopped
2 tsp. tapioca flour mixed in 2 Tbsp. water
sea salt & pepper

Cook noodles accordingly; rinse and set aside.
In a saucepan, heat oil over medium heat.
Add chicken and sauté until cooked through.
Add garlic and shallots, and cook 1 minute.
Add spinach and cook until just wilted.
Add lemon juice, stock and basil, and simmer, covered for 5 minutes.
Add tapioca mixture and stir until thickened.
Season to taste.
Stir in noodles or serve mixture over top of noodles.

• Makes 4 servings.

Variation
❖ *Replace spinach with baby bok choy or broccoli.*

Chicken Vegetable & Rice Noodle Casserole

8 oz. brown rice elbows
2 Tbsp. olive oil or ghee
2-3 cloves garlic, minced
4 cups mixed chopped vegetables of choice
2 cups vegetable or chicken stock
2 tsp. dried tarragon
1 tsp. dried parsley & sage
12 oz. cooked chicken, cubed
1 cup plain nut or seed milk
2 Tbsp. tapioca flour
$\frac{1}{2}$ cup shredded cheese of choice
$\frac{1}{4}$ cup ground nuts or seeds
sea salt & pepper

Cook noodles accordingly; rinse and set aside.
In a saucepan, heat oil over medium heat.
Add garlic and vegetables, and sauté for 5-7 minutes.
Add stock and dried herbs, and bring to a light boil.
Reduce heat and simmer, covered, for 10 minutes, until vegetables are tender.
Stir in chicken.
Combine milk and tapioca flour, and add to pan; stir until thickened.
Stir in noodles.
Season to taste.
Transfer mixture to an oiled baking or casserole dish.
Sprinkle on cheese and ground nuts or seeds over top.
Bake at 375°F, uncovered, for 25-30 minutes, until bubbly and hot.

• Makes 4 or servings.
• For vegetables choose: carrots, celery, onions, mushrooms, Swiss chard, kale, green beans, rutabaga, etc.

Rice Noodles with Bean Sauce

(A delicate flavoured noodle dish)

12 oz. brown rice spaghetti
2 cups cooked navy beans (about 1-19 oz. can)
1 cup vegetable stock
$\frac{1}{4}$ cup liquid aminos
$1\frac{1}{2}$ Tbsp. ghee
2-3 cloves garlic, minced
1 shallot, finely chopped
12 oz. regular tofu, cubed (optional)
2-3 tomatoes, diced
1 tsp. dried or 2 Tbsp. finely chopped fresh parsley & oregano
pinch or 2 of cayenne pepper
sea salt & pepper

Cook noodles accordingly; rinse and set aside.
In a blender, combine 1 cup beans, stock and liquid aminos until smooth.
In a large skillet or saucepan, heat ghee over medium heat.
Add garlic, shallot and tofu (if using), and sauté for 3 minutes.
Add tomatoes, herbs and cayenne, and cook 1-2 minutes.
Add sauce and remaining beans; heat through.
Add noodles and cook until heated through.
Season to taste.

• Makes 4 servings.

Variations
❖ *Replace spaghetti with any other type of brown rice noodles.*
❖ *Replace $\frac{1}{4}$-$\frac{1}{2}$ cup vegetable stock with same amount of white wine.*
❖ *Replace tofu with 12 oz. boneless and skinless chicken, cut into strips. Sauté chicken until cooked through, then add garlic, etc.*

Chili

(A wonderful wintertime dish with many variations)

2 Tbsp. olive oil
1 lb. ground turkey
4-6 cloves garlic, minced
2 onions, finely chopped
1 leek, finely chopped
1 cup finely chopped carrots
1 cup finely chopped celery
1 cup finely chopped cauliflower
1-2 sweet peppers of choice, finely chopped
1½ cups vegetable stock
2 lbs. fresh tomatoes, finely chopped
1-6 oz. can tomato paste
2 Tbsp. liquid aminos
1 Tbsp. chili powder
1½ tsp. cumin seeds, crushed
1 tsp. dried oregano & ground kelp
¼ tsp. cayenne or white pepper
1-14 oz. can navy beans, rinsed & drained
1-14 oz. can pinto beans, rinsed & drained
¼ cup fresh parsley, finely chopped
sea salt & pepper

In a Dutch oven, heat oil over medium heat.
Add ground turkey and sauté until browned, occasionally stirring to break up meat.
Add garlic, onions and leek, and sauté for 3-5 minutes, until softened.
Add carrots, celery, cauliflower and sweet peppers, and cook for 5 more minutes.
Add remaining ingredients, except parsley, and bring to a light boil.
Reduce heat and simmer, covered, for 30 minutes.

Add parsley and simmer for 15-25 minutes more.
Season to taste.

• Makes 8 or more servings.

Variations
❖ *Replace ground turkey with ground chicken, lamb, venison or meat of choice.*
❖ *For **Vegetarian Chili**: replace ground turkey with 1¼-1½ lbs. crumbled tofu. Sauté tofu with garlic, etc.*
> *Or*
> *Replace ground turkey with 1½-2 cups cooked brown rice. Add rice with parsley.*
❖ *For **Three Bean Chili**: replace ground turkey with 1-14 oz. can of black beans or, beans of choice.*
❖ *Canned tomatoes can be used in place of fresh tomatoes.*
❖ *Replace ½ cup vegetable stock with ½ cup red wine.*
❖ *Add 2 leaves finely chopped Swiss chard or 1 cup finely chopped spinach. Add with parsley.*

Toasted Cumin & Navy Bean Chili

(Chili with an earthy nut-like flavour)

1 Tbsp. olive oil
2 cloves garlic, minced
1 onion, finely chopped
1 small chili pepper, finely chopped (optional)
1½ lbs. fresh tomatoes, diced (or 28 oz. can)
1-6 oz. can tomato paste
1¼ cups vegetable stock
1 Tbsp. toasted cumin seeds, ground
½-1 tsp. chili flakes (if not using chili pepper)
½ Tbsp. dried parsley
2-14 oz. cans navy beans, rinsed & drained
2-3 sweet potatoes, cut into bite-sized pieces
1 Tbsp. fresh lime juice
sea salt & pepper

How to toast cumin seeds (and other spice seeds):
   Heat a skillet over medium-low heat.
   Add whole seeds and cook for 3-5 minutes, until fragrant. Do not
   over cook seeds or they become bitter.
   Crush, or grind seeds.

In a saucepan or small Dutch oven, heat oil over medium heat.
Add garlic, onion and chili pepper (if using), and sauté 3-5 minutes;
until softened.
Add remaining ingredients, except lime juice, and bring to a light boil.
Reduce heat and simmer, covered, for 35-45 minutes.
Stir in lime juice.
Season to taste.

• Makes 6 or more servings.

Chili Pasta

(A beautiful mix of ingredients, with a number of variations, is sure to please all)

6 oz. brown rice elbows or penne noodles
1½ Tbsp. olive oil
8-10 oz. ground turkey
2 cloves garlic, minced
1 leek (white part only), finely chopped
1 small green sweet pepper, finely chopped
1 cup chopped spinach or kale
2 tsp. chili powder
1 tsp. cumin seeds, ground
½ tsp. dried oregano
pinch or 2 of cayenne pepper
¼ cup vegetable stock or water
½ cup plain nut or seed milk
1 Tbsp. liquid aminos (optional)
1 lb. fresh tomatoes, diced (or 14 oz. can)
2 Tbsp. tomato paste
¼ cup rice Parmesan or ½ cup shredded rice cheese
sea salt & pepper

Cook noodles accordingly; rinse and set aside.
In a saucepan, heat oil over medium heat.
Add ground turkey and sauté until browned, occasionally stirring to break up meat.
Add garlic, leek and green pepper, and cook for 3-5 minutes, until softened.
Add spinach or kale and spices, and cook until just wilted.
Add stock or water and milk, and bring to a light boil.
Reduce to medium heat and simmer, uncovered, until most of the liquid is absorbed.

Stir in liquid aminos (if using), tomatoes and tomato paste, and simmer, uncovered, on medium heat for 5-7 minutes, until slightly thickened.
Stir in noodles and cook until heated through.
Stir in cheese of choice.
Season to taste.

• Makes 4 servings.

Variations
❖ *Replace ground turkey with ground chicken, lamb, venison or meat of choice.*
❖ *For **Vegetarian Chili Pasta**: replace ground turkey with 12-16 oz. crumbled tofu. Sauté tofu with garlic, etc.*
    Or
Replace ground turkey with 1-1½ cups cooked brown rice. Add rice with tomatoes, etc.
❖ *For **Baked Chili Pasta**: transfer mixture to an oiled casserole dish and bake at 375°F for 20-25 minutes, until hot and bubbly.*
❖ *Add ½-1 can of favourite beans. Add beans with tomatoes.*
❖ *Replace rice cheese with goat's milk cheese.*

Turkey & Roasted Vegetable Casserole

6 oz. brown rice elbows or penne noodles
1½ Tbsp. olive oil
12 oz. ground turkey
1 large onion, finely chopped
2 red peppers, roasted & chopped (see page 167)
1 fennel bulb, roasted & chopped (see page 167)
1 whole garlic bulb, roasted & chopped (see page 167)
1½ cups vegetable or turkey stock
5 Tbsp. tomato paste
1 tsp. paprika & ground safflower (or 1½ tsp. paprika)
½ tsp. sea salt
pinch or 2 of cayenne pepper
4-5 oz. shredded cheese of choice
1/3 cup ground almonds
3 Tbsp. Parmesan cheese of choice (optional)

Cook noodles accordingly; rinse and set aside.
In a Dutch oven, heat oil over medium heat.
Add ground turkey and onion, and sauté until turkey is browned,
occasionally stirring to break up meat.
Add roasted vegetables, stock, tomato paste and spices, and simmer,
covered, for 15-20 minutes.
Remove from heat; stir in pasta and shredded cheese.
Transfer mixture to an oiled casserole dish.
Sprinkle ground almonds and Parmesan (if using) over top.
Bake at 375°f for 25-30 minutes, until hot and bubbly.
• Makes 4 servings.

Variation
❖ *For **Tofu & Roasted Vegetable Casserole**: replace ground turkey
   with 1 lb. crumbled tofu. Sauté tofu with onion until browned.*

Brown Rice Balls

(Croquettes)

1 Tbsp. ghee or unsalted butter
¼ cup finely chopped leeks or shallots
½ cup brown basmati rice
1¼ cups vegetable or chicken stock
1 large egg, beaten
¼ tsp. each dried basil, parsley, rosemary & thyme
pinch of cayenne pepper
1/3 cup ground almonds
3 Tbsp. rice Parmesan
sea salt & pepper

In a saucepan, heat ghee or butter over medium-low heat.
Add leeks or shallots, and sauté for 3-5 minutes.
Add rice and sauté for 2 minutes.
Add stock and bring to a boil.
Lower heat and simmer, covered, for 35-45 minutes, until liquid is absorbed and rice is tender.
Let rice cool.
Stir in egg, spices, ground almonds and Parmesan, until well combined.
Season to taste.
With wet hands form mixture into 1" balls.
Place rice balls onto an oiled baking sheet.
Brush or spray rice balls with olive oil.
Bake at 375°F for 15-20 minute, until crisp and browned.

• Serve as a side dish, as is, or with sauce of choice.
• Makes 12-16 rice balls.

Variation
❖ *Add spices to simmering rice.*

Rice Meatloaf

(An interesting dish that can be served with any favourite sauce)

4 cups cooked brown rice
1 lb. ground chicken or turkey
$\frac{1}{2}$ cup brown rice flour
2 eggs, beaten
1 cup ground almonds
1 onion, finely chopped
2 cloves garlic, minced
8 oz. shredded rice cheese (about 2 cups)
$\frac{1}{2}$ tsp. each dried basil, oregano, parsley & rosemary
sea salt & pepper

In a bowl, mix together all ingredients until well combined.
Season to taste.
Press mixture into an oiled loaf pan or baking dish.
Bake at 350°F, uncovered, for 60 minutes.

- Serve as is, or with sauce of choice, such as: tomato sauce,
  mushroom gravy, roasted vegetable sauce, lemon garlic sauce, etc.
- Makes 4 or more servings.

Variations
❖ *Replace ground chicken or turkey with meat of choice.*
❖ *Replace rice cheese with goat's milk cheese.*

Millet & Tomato Risotto

(Millet cooked in a tomato wine sauce to a creamy-like consistency)

$\frac{1}{2}$ cup millet
1 cup vegetable stock
1 Tbsp. ghee or unsalted butter
2 cloves garlic, minced
1 cup tomato sauce of choice
$\frac{1}{2}$ cup red wine or water
$\frac{1}{4}$ cup fresh basil, chopped
2 oz. shredded rice or goat's milk cheddar cheese
sea salt & pepper

Wash and rinse millet, then soak millet with stock for 3 hours, or longer.
In a saucepan, heat ghee or butter over medium heat.
Add garlic and sauté for 1 minute.
Add millet, stock, tomato sauce and wine or water, and bring to a boil.
Reduce heat and simmer, covered, for 25-30 minutes, until liquid is absorbed.
Stir in basil and cheese.
Season to taste.

- Makes 4 servings.
- If millet is not pre-soaked: sauté millet with garlic for 2 minutes before adding stock, etc.

Millet & Saffron Risotto

(A creamy textured millet dish cooked in white wine & saffron)

½ cup millet
1¾ cups vegetable stock
2 Tbsp. ghee or unsalted butter
2 shallots, minced
½-1 tsp. saffron threads
½ cup white wine
¼ cup rice, soy or goat's milk Parmesan cheese
sea salt & pepper

Wash and rinse millet, then soak millet with stock for 3 hours, or longer.
In a saucepan, heat 1 Tbsp. ghee or butter over medium heat.
Add shallots and sauté for 2-3 minutes.
Add saffron and cook 1 minute.
Add millet, stock and wine, and bring to a boil.
Reduce heat and simmer, covered, for 25-30 minutes, until liquid is absorbed.
Stir in remaining ghee or butter and Parmesan of choice.
Season to taste.

- Makes 4 servings.
- If millet is not pre-soaked: sauté millet with saffron for 1-2 minutes before adding stock, etc.

Millet Vegetable Risotto

(Millet cooked to a creamy-like consistency with mixed vegetables)

$\frac{1}{2}$ cup millet
$1\frac{1}{2}$ cups vegetable stock
2 Tbsp. ghee or unsalted butter
2 cloves garlic, minced
1 small onion or 1 shallot, minced
$\frac{1}{2}$ cup diced carrots
$\frac{1}{2}$ cup diced celery
$\frac{1}{2}$ cup diced red or orange sweet peppers
$\frac{1}{2}$ cup sliced mushrooms (shitake, oyster or portabella)
$1\frac{1}{2}$ cups plain nut or seed milk
1 tsp. dried tarragon
$\frac{1}{4}$ cup rice, soy or goat's milk Parmesan cheese
sea salt & pepper

Wash and rinse millet, then soak millet with stock for 3 hours, or longer.
In a saucepan, heat 1 Tbsp. ghee or butter over medium heat.
Add garlic, onion or shallot, carrots, celery, pepper and mushrooms, and sauté for 5-7 minutes.
Add millet, stock, milk and tarragon, and bring to a boil.
Reduce heat and simmer, covered, for 25-30 minutes, until liquid is absorbed.
Stir in remaining ghee or butter and Parmesan of choice.
Season to taste.

• Makes 4 servings.
• If millet is not pre-soaked: sauté millet with vegetables for last 2 minutes of sautéing time, then add stock, etc.

Island Millet

(A tropical tasting millet dish)

Cooking sauce:
$\frac{3}{4}$ cup vegetable stock
$\frac{1}{2}$ cup coconut milk
$1\frac{1}{2}$ Tbsp. fresh lime juice
$1\frac{1}{2}$ Tbsp. liquid aminos
$\frac{1}{2}$ Tbsp. brown rice syrup or honey
1 clove garlic, chopped
$\frac{1}{2}$-1 tsp. fresh ginger, minced
2 green onions, chopped
1 tsp. dried or 2 Tbsp. fresh finely chopped basil & parsley
$\frac{1}{2}$ Tbsp. ghee
$\frac{1}{2}$ Tbsp. sesame oil
1 clove garlic, minced
1 green onion, finely chopped
$\frac{1}{2}$ cup millet, washed & rinsed
$\frac{1}{4}$ cup chopped almonds, pecans or hazelnuts
sea salt & pepper

In a blender, combine all ingredients for cooking sauce until smooth.
In a saucepan, heat ghee and sesame oil over medium heat.
Add garlic and onion, and sauté for 1 minute.
Add millet and cook for 1-2 minutes.
Add nuts of choice and cooking sauce, and bring to a boil.
Reduce heat and simmer, covered, for 20-25 minutes, until most of the liquid is absorbed.
Season to taste.

• Makes 2-4 servings.

Variation
❖ *Replace millet with brown rice and simmer for 40-45 minutes.*

Barbecue Baked Beans

(Slow baked beans with a robust earth-like flavour)

1 Tbsp. olive oil
1 onion, finely chopped
1 small green pepper or 1 chili pepper, finely chopped (optional)
2 cloves garlic, minced
1¼ cups vegetable stock
¼ cup ketchup
2 Tbsp. tomato paste
1½ Tbsp. apple cider vinegar
1 Tbsp. liquid aminos
3 Tbsp. brown rice syrup or 2 Tbsp. molasses
½ Tbsp. chili powder
½ Tbsp. toasted cumin seeds, crushed (see page 223)
½ tsp. sea salt
2-14 oz. cans navy beans, rinsed & drained
2-3 slices cooked turkey bacon, crumbled (optional)
        Or
½ cup crumbled tofu (optional)

In a saucepan, heat oil over medium heat.
Add onion and pepper (if using), and sauté for 3-5 minutes, until softened.
Add garlic and cook for 1 minute.
Add remaining ingredients, except beans and turkey bacon or tofu, and simmer for 7-10 minutes.
Stir in beans and turkey bacon or tofu (if using).
Transfer mixture to an oiled baking dish.
Bake at 350°F, uncovered, for 1 hour.

• Makes 4-8 servings.

Black Bean Tostadas

(A flatbread sandwich great for lunch or as a snack)

1 Tbsp. olive oil
2 cloves garlic, minced
1 small onion, diced
1 small green sweet pepper, diced
1 small chili pepper, diced or 2 tsp. chili powder
1-14 oz. can black beans, rinsed & drained
1 lb. fresh tomatoes, diced (or 14 oz. can)
2 Tbsp. tomato paste
sea salt & pepper
8-12 flatbreads of choice, toasted until crisp
4-6 green onions, finely chopped
4 oz. shredded goat's milk Monterey or rice cheddar cheese
2-4 romaine lettuce leaves, shredded
1 cup plain goat's milk yogurt

In a saucepan, heat oil over medium-low heat.
Add garlic onion, green pepper and chili pepper or chili powder, and sauté for 3-5 minutes.
Add beans, tomatoes, and tomato paste, and simmer for 10-15 minutes. Season to taste.
Spoon bean mixture over each flatbread, and sprinkle with cheese.
At this point, tostadas can be heated under the broiler until cheese is melted, or continue on with next step.
Sprinkle top with onions and lettuce, and top with a little yogurt.

• Makes 4-6 servings.
• Cover and refrigerate any leftover bean mixture for up to 3 days.

Variations
❖ *Replace romaine lettuce with any other salad greens.*
❖ *Add sliced avocado to top of tostadas.*

Curried Lentils

(A dish with a couple of interesting variations served hot)

1 cup lentils
2 Tbsp. ghee or unsalted butter
1 large red or white onion, chopped
2 cloves garlic, minced
1 tsp. cumin seeds, crushed
$\frac{1}{2}$ tsp. chili flakes & coriander seeds, crushed
$\frac{1}{4}$ tsp. paprika & turmeric
1 tsp. garam masala
2 cups vegetable stock or water
3 tomatoes, diced
1 tsp. dried mint or parsley
1 Tbsp. fresh lemon juice
sea salt & pepper

Soak lentils for 6 hours or overnight; rinse and drain.
In a saucepan, heat ghee or butter over medium-low heat.
Add onion and sauté until caramelized, approximately 15-20 minutes.
Add garlic and spices, and sauté for 2 minutes.
Add lentils, stock, tomatoes and mint or parsley, and bring to a boil.
Reduce heat and simmer, covered, for 25-35 minutes, until most of the liquid is absorbed.
Stir in lemon juice.
Season to taste.

- Makes 4 servings.
- If lentils are not pre-soaked: add 1 more cup of liquid and simmer for 10-15 minutes longer.

Variations
❖ *Replace $\frac{1}{2}$ cup lentils with $\frac{1}{2}$ cup millet*
❖ *Replace $\frac{1}{2}$ cup stock with $\frac{1}{2}$ cup coconut milk.*

Sweet & Sour Lentils

(A tangy lentil dish that is good served hot or cold)

1 cup lentils
1½ Tbsp. ghee or unsalted butter
1 Tbsp. sesame oil
1 large red or Spanish onion, chopped
1½ cups vegetable stock
2 Tbsp. apple cider vinegar
2 Tbsp. liquid aminos
1 tsp. dried parsley
3 Tbsp. brown rice syrup or honey

Soak lentils for 6 hours or overnight; rinse and drain.
In a saucepan, heat ghee or butter and sesame oil over medium heat.
Add onion and sauté for 3-5 minutes, until softened.
Add lentils, stock, apple cider vinegar, liquid aminos and parsley, and bring to a boil.
Reduce heat and simmer, covered, for 25-35 minutes, until most of the liquid is absorbed.
Stir in brown rice syrup or honey.

- Serve hot or cold.
- Cover and refrigerate for up to 3 days.
- Makes 4 servings.
- If lentils are not pre-soaked: add 1 more cup of liquid and simmer for 10-15 minutes longer.

Veggie Patties

½ cup millet, washed & rinsed
1¼ cups vegetable stock or water
1 cup cooked adzuki beans
¾ cup rolled rice or soy
½ cup tomato sauce of choice
1 egg or egg substitute (see page 13)
2 tbsp. fresh basil, finely chopped
sea salt & pepper

In a saucepan, bring millet and stock or water to a boil.
Reduce heat and simmer, covered, for 20-25 minutes, until most of the liquid is absorbed.
In a bowl, stir together all ingredients until well combined.
Season to taste.
With wet hands, form mixture into 3-4" patties.
Place patties onto an oiled baking sheet.
Bake at 350°F for 20-25 minutes.

- Serve as is, or top with tomato sauce, or sauce of choice.
- Patties can also be served on flatbreads with melted cheese, sliced onions, etc.
- Makes 8-10 patties.
- Patties can be frozen.

Variations
- ❖ *Replace rolled rice or soy with quinoa or rice flakes.*
- ❖ *Replace ¼ cup rolled rice or soy with ¼ ground nuts or seeds.*
- ❖ *Replace fresh basil with any fresh herb. (Use same herb as in tomato sauce)*
- ❖ *Replace adzuki beans with any other bean. Beans can also be mashed.*

Millet Stuffing

(An awesome stuffing without the bread)

1 Tbsp. ghee or olive oil
1 onion, finely chopped
1 carrot, finely chopped
1 celery stalk, finely chopped
1/3 cup dried cranberries
½ tsp. cinnamon
1½ cups cooked millet
sea salt & pepper

In a skillet, heat ghee or oil over medium heat.
Add onion, carrot and celery, and sauté for 5-7 minutes, until softened.
Add cranberries and cinnamon, and cook for 1-2 minutes, stirring constantly.
Remove from heat and stir in millet.
Season to taste.

• Use to stuff chicken, turkey, duck or Cornish hens.
• Millet stuffing can also be used as a side dish.
• Makes about 2¼ cups.

Variations
❖ *Replace all or part of the millet with cooked wild rice. Brown basmati rice or quinoa.*
❖ *Replace cranberries with raisins, currants or dried blueberries.*
❖ *Add any other finely chopped vegetable, such as: shallots, leeks, garlic, cauliflower, mushrooms, sweet peppers, fennel, etc.*
❖ *Add 1 tsp. mix of curry spices (cumin, chili powder, coriander, turmeric) or dried herbs (basil, oregano, rosemary, sage).*

Spaghetti Salad 'Italian Style'

(A delicious summer's day salad)

12 oz. brown rice spaghetti noodles, broken into quarters
1 small English cucumber, sliced
1 small green sweet pepper, sliced into thin strips
1 small orange sweet pepper, sliced into thin strips
1 red onion, sliced
2 tomatoes, diced
2 cups broccoli, florets
6-8 radishes, sliced
$\frac{1}{4}$ cup fresh basil & parsley, finely chopped
   Dressing:
      $\frac{1}{4}$ cup flax or pumpkin seed oil
      2 Tbsp. olive oil
      3 Tbsp. apple cider vinegar
      3 Tbsp. fresh lemon juice
      1 tsp. dried oregano & thyme
      2 cloves garlic, minced or $\frac{1}{4}$ tsp. garlic powder
      sea salt & pepper
rice Parmesan or crumbled goat's milk feta cheese

Cook noodles accordingly; rinse and drain. Let cool.
In a salad bowl, toss together noodles, cucumbers, peppers, onion, tomatoes, broccoli, radishes, basil and parsley.
In another bowl, whisk or stir together ingredients for dressing until well combined. Season to taste.
Pour dressing over salad mix and toss to coat.
Sprinkle with a little cheese of choice; chill.

• Makes 4-8 servings.
• Cover and refrigerate for up to 3 days.
Variation
❖ *Replace any vegetable with sliced carrots, celery or cauliflower.*

Spaghetti Salad 'Asian Style'

(A refreshing & delicious summer's day salad with Asian flare)

12 oz. brown rice spaghetti noodles, broken into quarters
3 cups daikon (white radish), sliced
2 carrots, sliced
2 celery stalks, sliced
2 cups snow peas
6-8 green onions, finely chopped
$\frac{1}{4}$ cup parsley, finely chopped
  Dressing:
    $\frac{1}{4}$ cup plain goat's milk or soy yogurt
    3-4 Tbsp. mayonnaise
    4 tsp. sesame oil
    2 Tbsp. apple cider vinegar
    2 Tbsp. fresh lime juice
    2 Tbsp. liquid aminos
    $\frac{1}{2}$ tsp. ground ginger
    pinch or 2 of cayenne pepper
    2 cloves garlic, minced or $\frac{1}{4}$ tsp. garlic powder
sesame seeds

Cook noodles accordingly; rinse and drain. Let cool.
In a salad bowl, toss together noodles, daikon, carrots, celery, snow peas, onions and parsley.
In another bowl, whisk or stir together ingredients for dressing until well combined.
Pour dressing over salad mix and toss to coat.
Sprinkle with sesame seeds; chill.

- Makes 4-8 servings.
- Cover and refrigerate for up to 3 days.
- Add water chestnuts and/or $\frac{1}{4}$ cup fresh basil, finely chopped.
- Sesame seeds can be toasted and/or ground.

Wild Rice & Vegetable Salad

(An excellent salad with robust flavour; a crowd favourite)

1 cup wild rice
2½ cups vegetable stock or water
1 cup chopped broccoli
1 carrot, chopped
1 celery stalk, chopped
1 red sweet pepper, diced (raw or roasted; see page 167)
2 tomatoes, diced
  Dressing:
    2 Tbsp. flax or pumpkin seed oil
    1 Tbsp. olive oil
    1½ Tbsp. fresh lemon juice
    1-2 cloves garlic, minced
    ½ tsp. each dried basil, oregano, parsley, rosemary & thyme
¼ cup crumbled goat's milk feta cheese
sea salt & pepper

Wash and rinse rice, then soak rice with stock for 2-3 hours.
In a saucepan, bring rice and stock to a boil.
Reduce heat and simmer, covered, for 60-70 minutes or until tender, fluffy and each grain of rice is split. Let cool.
In a large bowl, stir together rice and vegetables.
In a small bowl, whisk or stir together ingredients for dressing until well combined.
Pour dressing over salad mix and stir to coat.
Stir in cheese and season to taste; chill.

• Makes 4-8 servings.
• Cover and refrigerate for up to 4 days.

Variation
❖ *Replace broccoli with sliced fennel (raw or roasted; see page 167).*

Quinoa Salad

(A refreshing salad with mango & cucumber)

1 cup quinoa
2½ cups vegetable stock or water
½ English cucumber, sliced
1 mango, diced
3 green onions, diced
¼ cup sugar toasted almonds (see page 169)
2 Tbsp. fresh parsley, finely chopped
1 Tbsp. fresh mint, finely chopped
  Dressing:
    2 Tbsp. flax or pumpkin seed oil
    3 Tbsp. fresh lemon or lime juice
    ½ tsp. cumin
    ¼ tsp. coriander
    1/8 tsp. chili powder (optional)
    sea salt & pepper

Wash and rinse quinoa thoroughly; drain excess water. (Pre-soak in stock or water if desired)
In a saucepan, bring quinoa and liquid to a boil.
Reduce heat and simmer, covered, for 20-30 minutes, until tender, the grains have turned transparent, and the spiral-like germ has split. Let quinoa cool.
In a salad bowl, stir together quinoa, cucumber, mango, onions, almonds, parsley and mint.
In a small bowl, whisk or stir together ingredients for dressing until well combined. Season to taste.
Pour dressing over salad mix and stir gently to coat; chill.

• Makes 4-8 servings.
• Cover and refrigerate for up to 4 days.
• Use papaya in place of mango.

Mixed Bean & Vegetable Salad

(A tasty combination of mixed beans & veggies with a zesty earth-like dressing)

1-14 oz. can black or pinto beans, rinsed & drained
1-14 oz. can navy beans, rinsed & drained
1-14 oz. can adzuki beans, rinsed & drained
1-14 oz. can chickpeas, rinsed & drained
2 small shallots, finely chopped
1 carrot, finely chopped
1 celery stalk, finely chopped
1 cup finely chopped cauliflower
1 small red or orange sweet pepper, diced
$\frac{1}{4}$ cup fresh basil or oregano, finely chopped
2-3 Tbsp. fresh cilantro or parsley, finely chopped
  Dressing:
    2 Tbsp. flax seed oil
    2 Tbsp. olive oil
    3 Tbsp. fresh lemon juice
    $1\frac{1}{2}$ Tbsp. apple cider vinegar
    $\frac{1}{2}$ Tbsp. toasted cumin seeds, ground (see page 223)
    1 tsp. toasted mustard seeds, ground (optional) (see page 223)
    1 clove garlic, minced (optional)
    sea salt & pepper

In a salad bowl, stir together beans, shallots, carrot, celery, cauliflower, pepper and fresh herbs.
In a small bowl, whisk or stir together ingredients for dressing until well combined. Season to taste.
Pour dressing over salad mix, and stir gently to coat; chill.

- Makes 6 or more servings.
- Cover and refrigerate for up to 4 days.
- Add rice Parmesan or shredded cheese of choice.

Wraps & Pie Crusts

Rice Wraps 246

Rice Paper Samosas 248

Rice Paper Spring Rolls 249

Rice Paper Chili Tacos 250

Vegetable Manicotti Wraps 251

Rolled Squash Surprise 253

Rice Paper Enchiladas 254

Chili & Rice Wraps 255

Basic Crepes 256

Chicken Crepes 258

Chicken Tandoori Wraps 260

Curried Lamb Wraps 261

Turkey Burrito Crepes 262

Grilled Veggie Wraps 263

Vegetable Korma Wraps 264

Turkey Club Crepes 265

Potato Pie Crust 266

Sweet Potato Pie Crust 266

Rice Flour Pie Crust 267

Rice Crisp Pie Crust 268

Rice & Almond Pie Crust 269

Rice Wraps

Rice wraps or 'rice paper' is ground rice and water made into a round thin piece of 'noodle paper', which resembles pasta. Rice paper is quite common in Asian cuisine. Rice paper comes in different diameter sizes, ranging from 6" to 12". The most common size, and the recommended one for most of the following recipes, is 8-10" diameter. Rice paper can be purchased in any Asian super market. Some health food, specialty (gluten-free) shops or grocery stores also carry them. If grocery stores carry rice paper, they can be found in the international or specialty sections. Rice wraps or paper will always be labeled as 'Rice Paper'. Rice paper is wonderful for wrapping almost any type of food for a snack or a main course; e.g. cooked grains, grilled vegetables, fresh vegetables and nut butter sauce, chicken salads, egg salad, lentils, beans, etc. Once filled and rolled, they can then be dipped into sauces or dips, eaten as is, chilled, heated or reheated another day in the oven. When heated in the oven, rice paper becomes crispy. Combinations are endless. Filled and rolled rice paper travels well, making them great for packed lunches, day trips, etc. Depending on the type of filling used, rice wraps freeze well. The following recipes are a few examples as to what can be done with rice paper.

To prepare rice paper for filling:

1. Dip rice paper, one at a time, in fairly warm water and let it sit for about half a minute or until softened. (The warmer the water the faster rice paper will soften. If water is too hot rice paper tends to tear easily.)
2. Once softened, remove rice paper from the water and place it on a flat surface. (If placed on top of a towel, the towel will absorb some of the water.)
3. Place the appropriate amount of filling or ingredients on the lower (bottom) end of the rice paper (a).
4. Starting from the bottom, start to roll the rice paper (b), rolling as tight as possible. When rolled halfway, fold in the sides (c) and continue to roll (d).

Note: a) In order to make a better seal after rolling, it is better to add the filling right after the paper has been softened.
b) Some types of rice paper are fairly thin. Two sheets can be used together.

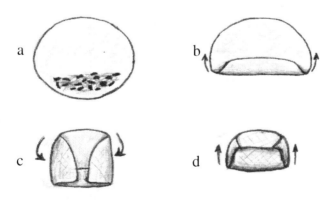

Rice Paper Samosas

(Mixed vegetables in a chickpea & tahini sauce rolled in rice paper)

1 onion, finely chopped
2 carrots, chopped
1 large sweet potato, peeled & cubed
1 cup fresh or frozen peas
fresh water
1-14 oz. can chickpeas
2 Tbsp. tahini
$\frac{1}{2}$ tsp. chili powder & cumin
$\frac{1}{4}$ tsp. sea salt
rice paper

In a saucepan, add onion, carrots, sweet potato and peas (if fresh).
Add enough fresh water to just cover vegetables and bring to a boil.
Reduce heat and simmer until vegetables are tender, about 15 minutes.
Add frozen peas to last 3 minutes of cooking time.
Strain water and reserve $\frac{1}{2}$ cup.
In a bowl, mash chickpeas. Add reserved water and tahini, and stir
until fairly smooth. (This can be done in a blender or food processor.)
Stir in vegetables and spices to coat.
Scoop 1 large spoonful of mixture onto a piece of rice paper and roll
accordingly. Continue with remaining mixture.
Transfer wraps to an oiled baking pan and brush or spray lightly with
olive oil or melted ghee.
Bake at 350°F for 15-20 minutes.

• Serve with plain yogurt or Tandoori sauce.
• Makes about 12-18 wraps.
• Wraps can be frozen before heating in the oven.

Variation
❖ *Replace 1 carrot with 1-1$\frac{1}{2}$ cup chopped cauliflower.*

Rice Paper Spring Rolls

2 tsp. olive oil
1 lb. ground turkey or chicken
3-5 green onions, finely chopped
2 carrots, finely shredded
1 celery stalk, finely chopped
1 small zucchini, coarsely shredded (optional)
1 head baby bok choy, finely chopped
1 tsp. sesame oil
2-3 Tbsp. liquid aminos
1 tsp. fresh minced ginger or $\frac{1}{4}$ tsp. ground ginger
1 tsp. dried parsley
1 Tbsp. tapioca flour mixed in $\frac{1}{4}$ cup water
sea salt & pepper
rice paper

In a skillet, heat oil over medium heat.
Add ground turkey or chicken and sauté until browned, occasionally stirring to break up meat.
Add onions, carrots, celery, zucchini (if using) and bok choy, and cook for 3 minutes.
Stir in sesame oil, liquid aminos, ginger and parsley.
Add tapioca mixture and stir until thickened. Season to taste.
Scoop 1 large spoonful of mixture onto a piece of rice paper and roll accordingly. Continue with remaining mixture.
Serve as is, or brush or spray lightly with olive oil or melted ghee and bake at 350°F for 15-20 minutes.
• Makes about 12-18 wraps.
• Wraps can be frozen before heating in the oven.
Variations
❖ *Replace bok choy with* $1\frac{1}{2}$ *cups finely chopped spinach or cabbage.*
❖ *For **Vegetarian Spring Roll**: replace ground meat with* $1\frac{1}{4}$ *lbs. tofu.*

249

Rice Paper Chili Tacos

1 Tbsp. olive oil
1 lb. ground meat of choice
3 cloves garlic, minced
1 onion, finely chopped
3 tomatoes, peeled & diced
½ cup tomato sauce or salsa of choice
2 tsp. chili powder
1 tsp. cumin (optional)
1-14 oz. can refried beans
4 oz. shredded goat's milk Monterey or mozzarella cheese
sea salt & pepper
rice paper

In a large skillet, heat oil over medium heat.
Add ground meat of choice, garlic and onions, and sauté until meat is browned; occasionally stirring to break up meat.
Add tomatoes, tomato sauce or salsa of choice, spices and beans, and cook for 3 minutes; occasionally stirring.
Remove from heat and stir in cheese. Season to taste.
Scoop 1 large spoonful of mixture onto a piece of rice paper and roll accordingly. Continue with remaining mixture.
Transfer wraps to an oiled baking pan and brush or spray lightly with olive oil or melted ghee.
Bake at 350°F for 15-20 minutes.

• Serve with plain yogurt.
• Makes about 12-18 wraps.
• Wraps can be frozen before heating in the oven.
Variations
❖ For **Vegetarian Chili Tacos**: replace ground meat with 1¼ lbs. tofu.
❖ Replace goat's milk cheese with rice or soy cheese.

Vegetable Manicotti Wraps

(Vegetables rolled in rice paper and cooked in a cream-like cheese sauce)

1 Tbsp. olive oil
2 cloves garlic, minced
2 shallots or 1 onion, finely chopped
$2\frac{1}{2}$ cups mixed vegetables, finely chopped
3 cups chopped spinach
   Sauce:
    2 Tbsp. ghee
    2 Tbsp. chickpea or millet flour
    2 cups plain nut or seed milk
    1 tsp. dried oregano
    $\frac{1}{2}$ tsp. dried parsley
    6 oz. soft goat's milk cheese
    sea salt & pepper
rice paper

In a saucepan, heat oil over medium heat.
Add garlic, shallots or onion and mixed vegetables, and sauté for 5-7 minutes, until softened.
Add spinach and cook until just wilted. Set aside vegetables.
In another saucepan, melt ghee over medium heat.
Add flour and cook for 1 minute, stirring constantly.
Slowly stir in milk and spices, and cook until thickened; about 10-15 minutes and stirring constantly.
Add cheese and stir until melted.
Season to taste.
Remove $\frac{1}{2}$ cup of sauce and stir into vegetables.
Spread $\frac{3}{4}$ cup of sauce into bottom of a lasagna dish.
Scoop 1 large spoonful of vegetable mixture onto a piece of rice paper and roll accordingly. Continue with remaining mixture.
Transfer wraps to prepared lasagna dish.

251

Pour remaining sauce over top.
Bake at 375°F, uncovered, for 25-30 minutes, until hot and bubbly.

- Makes about 12-16 wraps.
- Prepared dish can be frozen before heating in the oven.
- For mixed vegetables, choose: carrots, celery, mushrooms, sweet peppers, green beans, asparagus, cauliflower, etc.
- Frozen vegetables can be used; cook accordingly and add after spinach is cooked.

Variations

❖ *Sprinkle shredded mozzarella, cheddar or Parmesan cheese of choice over top before baking.*
❖ *Replace 1 cup of mixed vegetables with 1-1½ cups crumbled tofu. Cook tofu with mixed vegetables.*
❖ *Replace soft goat's milk cheese with rice or soy cream cheese.*
❖ *Replace sauce, except soft cheese, with 2-2½ cups of tomato sauce of choice. Mix ½ cup tomato sauce with vegetables and the soft cheese and use remaining tomato sauce as above.*
Or
❖ *Replace 1 cup of sauce with 1 cup of tomato sauce of choice. Use only 1 Tbsp. of ghee and flour, and 1 cup of milk; cook as above, then add 1 cup of tomato sauce and the soft cheese.*

Rolled Squash Surprise

(A good Thanksgiving Day, or anytime, snack or meal accompaniment)

2 cups cooked squash, delicata or buttercup
1 Tbsp. ghee or unsalted butter, melted
$\frac{1}{4}$ cup plain nut or seed milk
$\frac{1}{2}$ tsp. chili powder
$\frac{1}{2}$ tsp. ground safflower
$\frac{1}{4}$ tsp. sea salt
1/8 tsp. garlic powder
$\frac{1}{4}$ cup ground almonds or hazelnuts
$\frac{1}{4}$ cup crushed rice crisp cereal
2 oz. shredded rice cheese
rice paper

In a bowl, mix together squash, ghee or butter, milk and spices until well combined.
Stir in ground nuts, rice cereal and cheese.
Scoop 1 large spoonful of mixture onto a piece of rice paper and roll accordingly. Continue with remaining mixture.
Transfer wraps to an oiled baking pan and brush or spray lightly with olive oil or melted ghee.
Bake at 350°F for 15-20 minutes.

- Serve with plain yogurt or favourite sauce.
- Makes about 12-18 wraps.
- Wraps can be frozen before heating in the oven.
- If safflower is unavailable, $\frac{1}{2}$ tsp. paprika can be used.

Variation
❖ *Replace chili powder, safflower and garlic powder with 1$\frac{1}{4}$ Tsp. dried sage and add 1 finely chopped caramelized onion (sauté onion with 1 Tbsp. ghee or olive oil on medium-low for 15-20 minutes).*

Rice Paper Enchiladas

2 tsp. olive oil
1 lb. ground meat of choice
1 onion, chopped
3-4 cloves garlic, minced
2 Tbsp. chickpea or millet flour
1 Tbsp. chili powder
½ tsp. cumin & sea salt
¼ tsp. dried oregano
1-14 oz. can diced tomatoes (or 1 lb. fresh)
6 oz. shredded cheese of choice
2½ cups tomato sauce
rice paper

In a saucepan, heat oil over medium heat.
Add ground meat of choice and onion, and sauté until meat is browned, occasionally stirring to break up meat.
Add garlic and cook for 1 minute.
Stir in flour and spices, and cook for 1 minute.
Add tomatoes and bring to a boil.
Reduce heat and simmer, covered, for 15-20 minutes.
Spread 1 cup of tomato sauce into bottom of a baking (lasagna) dish.
Scoop 1 large spoonful of mixture onto a piece of rice paper.
Sprinkle with a little cheese and roll accordingly. Continue with remaining mixture.
Transfer wraps to prepared baking dish.
Pour remaining tomato sauce over top and sprinkle on any remaining cheese.
Bake at 375°F, uncovered, for 25-30 minutes, until hot and bubbly.
• Makes about 12-16 wraps.
• Prepared dish can be frozen before heating in the oven.
• For **Vegetarian Enchiladas**: replace meat with 1¼-1½ lbs. tofu.

Chili & Rice Wraps

(A great quick meal for using leftover chili and cooked rice)

3 cups chili
1½ cups cooked brown rice
3 oz. shredded rice cheese
rice paper

In a bowl, stir together chili, rice and cheese.
Scoop 1 large spoonful of mixture onto a piece of rice paper and roll accordingly. Continue with remaining mixture.
Transfer wraps to an oiled baking pan and brush or spray lightly with olive oil or melted ghee.
Bake at 350°F for 20-25 minutes.

- Serve with plain yogurt and sliced avocado.
- Makes about 12-16 wraps.
- Wraps can be frozen before heating in the oven.

Variations
- ❖ *Leave cheese out of filling and sprinkle over top of wraps. Top with sliced onions and cook as above.*
- ❖ *Replace rice with cooked millet.*

Basic Crepes

(A thin pancake-like tortilla)

3 eggs
1½ cups plain nut or seed milk
3 Tbsp. olive oil or melted ghee
1 cup brown rice flour
pinch of sea salt

In a bowl, beat eggs until light and foamy.
Beat in milk and oil or ghee until combined.
Mix in flour and sea salt until smooth.
Lightly oil or butter a 10" skillet or crepe pan and bring to medium-high heat.
Add ¼ cup of batter to hot pan and swirl to cover bottom of pan.
Cook until crepe no longer sticks to pan and edges begin to curl up, less than 1 minute.
Turn crepe over and cook the other side for about 20-30 seconds, until golden.
Repeat with remaining batter, not necessary to re-oil pan.

- Makes 12-16 crepes.
- Use basic crepes as a 'wrap'. Wonderful for wrapping almost any type of food for a snack, sandwich or a main course; e.g. chicken salads, egg salad, grilled vegetables, fresh vegetables and nut butter sauce, cooked grains, lentils, beans, etc.
- Crepes can be eaten warm or cold. When filled, they can be heated in the oven for 10-15 minutes; this makes crepes crispy.
- Once filled and rolled, crepes can be covered with sauces.
- To avoid sticking together, stack crepes between wax paper.
  Note: If there is a corn allergy, some brands of wax paper contain cornstarch.
- Refrigerate crepes for up to three days or freeze.

Variations

❖ *Add ¼-1 tsp. of favourite spice to batter.*
❖ *Replace ¼ cup of rice flour with ¼ cup tapioca flour.*
  Note: This is recommended for crepes that will be frozen. The tapioca flour makes crepes hold together better after freezing. Sometimes crepes made with straight rice flour tend to tear after they have been frozen (this can also happen with tapioca flour). To avoid this, it is best to warm crepes in the oven before using.

Variations for dessert crepes:

❖ *Use sweetened nut or seed milk.*
❖ *Replace olive oil with almond or walnut oil.*
❖ *Add ½ tsp. vanilla extract or extract of choice.*
❖ *Add ½ tsp. grated orange or lemon peel.*
❖ *Add ½-1 tsp. of any or combination of following spices to batter; cinnamon, nutmeg, cardamom, cloves, ginger, etc.*

The following recipes are a few examples of what can be done with crepes.

Chicken Crepes

(Chicken and vegetables rolled in crepes with a number of tasty variations)

1½ Tbsp. olive oil
8-12 oz. boneless & skinless chicken, cut into strips
2 cloves garlic, minced
3 green onions or 1 shallot, finely chopped
2½ cups mixed vegetables, julienne
½ tsp. chili powder & cumin
¼ tsp. coriander & turmeric
1 Tbsp. fresh parsley, finely chopped
1 cup plain nut or seed milk
2 Tbsp. tapioca flour
sea salt & pepper
8 crepes

In a saucepan, heat ½ Tbsp. oil over medium heat.
Add chicken and cook until no longer pink, about 5-7 minutes.
Remove chicken and set aside.
Heat remaining oil.
Add garlic, onions or shallot and mixed vegetables, and sauté until tender, about 5 minutes.
Stir in spices and cook for 1 minute.
Add chicken and parsley.
In a small bowl, combine milk and tapioca flour until smooth.
Add to saucepan and stir until thickened.
Season to taste.
Divide among 8 crepes and roll like a wrap.

- Makes 4 servings.
- Serve with Tandoori Sauce, Basic Curry Sauce or Lemon Garlic Sauce.

- For mixed vegetables, choose; carrots, celery, sweet peppers, zucchini, turnips, mushrooms, sweet potato, etc.
- Heat filled crepes in 375 degree oven for 10-15 minutes.

Variations
❖ *Replace ½ cup of nut or seed milk with ½ cup coconut milk.*
❖ *Replace ¼ cup of nut or seed milk with ¼ cup plain goat's milk or soy yogurt.*
❖ *For **Vegetable Crepes**: replace chicken with 1 cup of cooked (canned) chickpeas or beans of choice.*
❖ *For **Herb Chicken Crepes**: replace chili powder, cumin, coriander and turmeric with ½ tsp. each dried basil, oregano and rosemary or thyme (or 1 Tbsp. each finely chopped fresh herbs). Replace ½ cup nut or seed milk with ½ cup chicken stock. Serve with Lemon Garlic Sauce or Mushroom Gravy.*
❖ *For **Herb Vegetable Crepes**: do same as Herb Chicken Crepes, but use vegetable stock, and replace chicken with 1 cup cooked beans of choice.*

Chicken Tandoori Wraps

(A curried chicken dish rolled in crepes or rice paper)

Marinade:
  2 Tbsp. olive oil
  juice of 1 lemon
  2 Tbsp. water
  2 cloves garlic, minced or $\frac{1}{4}$ tsp. garlic powder
  1 tsp. dried mint
  $\frac{1}{2}$ tsp. each crushed chili flakes , coriander & cumin seeds
  $\frac{1}{4}$ tsp. sea salt
1 lb. boneless & skinless chicken, cut into strips
2 tomatoes, diced
1 small red onion, sliced
$\frac{1}{2}$ English cucumber, finely chopped
$\frac{1}{4}$-$\frac{1}{2}$ cup plain goat's milk or soy yogurt
2 tsp. fresh lime or lemon juice
8-12 crepes

In a shallow dish, stir together ingredients for marinade until well combined.
Add chicken and let marinate for $\frac{1}{2}$ hour or longer in the refrigerator.
In a skillet, sauté chicken over medium heat until cooked through.
In a bowl, stir together tomatoes, onion, cucumber, yogurt and juice.
Stir in chicken to coat.
Divide among crepes and roll like a wrap.

• Makes 4 servings.

Variations
❖ *Replace chicken with meat of choice.*
❖ *Replace crepes with rice paper.*

Curried Lamb Wraps

2 tsp. olive oil
1 lb. ground lamb
2 cloves garlic, minced
1 onion, finely chopped
$\frac{1}{4}$ cup tomato sauce (curried)
$\frac{1}{2}$ tsp. chili powder & cumin
$\frac{1}{4}$ tsp. each coriander, paprika & turmeric
pinch or 2 of cayenne or white pepper
$\frac{1}{2}$ tsp. dried mint or parsley
1 Tbsp. tapioca flour mixed in $\frac{1}{4}$ cup water
$\frac{1}{2}$ cup ground almonds or sesame seeds
sea salt & pepper
4-8 crepes

In a skillet, heat oil over medium heat.
Add ground lamb, garlic and onion, and sauté until meat is browned, occasionally stirring to break up meat.
Stir in tomato sauce and spices; heat through.
Add tapioca mixture and stir until thickened.
Remove from heat and stir in ground almonds or sesame seeds.
Divide among 4-8 crepes; roll them up like a wrap and serve as is, or heated in 375°F degree oven for 10-15 minutes.
• Makes 4 servings.
• Serve with plain yogurt, Tandoori Sauce or Basic Curry Sauce.
• Add slices of onion, tomato and cheese before rolling.
Variations
❖ *Replace ground lamb with ground meat of choice.*
❖ *For **Curried Vegetarian Wraps**: replace ground meat with 1$\frac{1}{4}$ lbs. crumbled tofu, or $\frac{1}{2}$ lb. crumbled tofu and $\frac{1}{2}$-1 cup beans of choice. Add beans with tomato sauce.*
❖ *Replace crepes with rice paper.*

Turkey Burrito Crepes

(An awesome Mexican flavoured dish good as a snack or lunch)

2 tsp. olive oil
8 oz. boneless & skinless turkey, cut into strips
2 cloves garlic, minced
1 shallot or small onion, finely chopped
1-14 oz. can black or pinto beans, rinsed & drained
1 cup cooked brown or wild rice
1 cup Roasted Garlic Winter Salsa or salsa of choice
1 cup shredded rice or soy cheese of choice
8-12 crepes

In a large skillet, heat oil over medium heat.
Add turkey and sauté until cooked through.
Add garlic and shallot or onion, and cook 1-2 minutes.
Stir in beans, rice and salsa of choice, and heat through.
Divide among crepes and roll like a wrap.
Transfer crepes to a baking pan and sprinkle with cheese.
Broil for 2-3 minutes, until cheese is melted.

• Makes 4 servings.

Variations
❖ *Replace turkey with meat of choice. Ground meat can also be used.*
❖ *For **Vegetarian Burritos**: replace turkey with ¾ lb. crumbled tofu.*
❖ *For **Bean Burritos**: replace turkey with another ½-14 oz. can beans of choice (use 2 types of beans) + ½ cup more rice.*
❖ *Replace rice with cooked millet.*
❖ *Replace rice or soy cheese with any kind of goat's milk cheese.*
❖ *Replace crepes with rice paper.*

Grilled Veggie Wraps

(An excellent summertime or barbecue accompaniment)

4 cups mixed vegetables, cut into slices or strips
1 recipe Grilling Marinade (see page 147)
4-8 crepes
3-4 oz. shredded cheese of choice (optional)

In a large bowl, add mixed vegetables and marinade, and toss to coat.
Cover vegetables and let marinate for 30 minutes to 2 hours in the
refrigerator.
Heat a grilling pan over medium-high heat.
Add vegetables and grill both sides until tender. Reserve marinade.
Add ½-1 cup grilled vegetables to each crepe.
Sprinkle with a little cheese (if using) and roll like a wrap.
Serve as is, or continue with next step.
Transfer wraps to a baking pan and bake at 350°F for 10-12 minutes,
until golden.
With reserve marinade: add ¼ cup vegetable stock or water and ½
Tbsp. tapioca flour; stir to combine.
In a saucepan, heat sauce until thickened, constantly stirring.
Serve sauce over veggie wraps.

• Makes 4 servings.
• Vegetables can also be grilled on the barbecue or under the broiler.
• Rice paper can also be used.

Vegetable Korma Crepes

(A curried vegetable dish wrapped in crepes)

2 Tbsp. ghee or olive oil
2 cloves garlic, minced
1 small red onion, finely chopped
½ tsp. cumin seeds, ground
¼ tsp. chili flakes & coriander seeds, ground
¼ tsp. garam masala & sea salt
1/8 tsp. turmeric
2 sweet potatoes (about 20 oz.), cubed
2¼ cups vegetable stock
2 cups finely chopped cauliflower
1/3 cup chopped hazelnuts or almonds
½ cup frozen peas
¼ cup dried cranberries, raisins or currants (optional)
1 Tbsp. tapioca flour mixed in ¼ cup plain goat's milk or soy yogurt
8-12 crepes

In a saucepan, heat ghee or oil over medium heat.
Add garlic, onion and spices, and sauté for 2-3 minutes.
Add sweet potatoes and stock, and bring to a boil.
Reduce heat to medium and cook for 8-10 minutes.
Add cauliflower and nuts, and cook for 7 more minutes.
Add peas and dried fruit (if using), and cook for 3-5 minutes, until vegetables are tender.
Turn off heat and stir in tapioca mixture until thickened.
Divide among crepes and roll like a wrap.
Serve as is, or heat crepes at 375°F for 10-15 minutes, until golden.

• Makes 4 or more servings.

Turkey Club Crepes

(A delicious sandwich for kids of all ages)

1 avocado
2 tsp. fresh lime or lemon juice
2 Tbsp. mayonnaise
2 Tbsp. plain goat's milk or soy yogurt, or sour cream
1/8 tsp. chili powder
pinch of sea salt
1 tomato, finely chopped
2-3 green onions, finely chopped
$1\frac{1}{4}$-$1\frac{1}{2}$ cups chopped romaine lettuce or spinach
4 slices roast turkey breast
4 slices cooked turkey bacon
4 slices rice or soy cheese
4 crepes

In a small bowl, mix together pulp from avocado, lime or lemon juice, mayonnaise, yogurt or sour cream, chili powder and sea salt until smooth.
In another bowl, stir together tomatoes, onions and lettuce or spinach.
Spread avocado mixture over each crepe.
Layer each crepe with a slice of turkey breast, turkey bacon and cheese.
Spoon on tomato mixture.
Roll like a wrap and serve.

• Makes 2-4 servings.

Potato Pie Crust

(These potato pie crust recipes are an excellent companion for veggie pies)

12-14 oz. peeled & chopped red potatoes
2 tsp. olive oil
1¼ cups cooked brown rice
2 Tbsp. ground nuts

In a pot of water, boil potatoes until tender, about 20 minutes.
Drain water and mash potatoes.
Stir in oil, cooked rice and ground nuts until well combined.
Press mixture into a lightly oiled pie plate.
Bake at 400°F, covered with tinfoil or parchment paper, for 20 minutes.
Remove cover and bake another 15-20 minutes.
Turn off heat and let pie crust continue to cook and 'dry out'.
Remove when oven has cooled.

- Use for vegetable pies, pot pies, quiche etc.
- Non-stick pans work the best. Don't use glass ovenware for this recipe.

Variation
❖ *Replace cooked rice with cooked millet.*

Sweet Potato Pie Crust

10-12 oz. peeled & chopped sweet potatoes
2 tsp. olive oil
1¼ cups cooked brown rice
1/3 cup brown rice flour

Prepare the same as Potato Pie Crust, but bake 5 minutes more before turning off heat.

Rice Flour Pie Crust

1¼ cups brown rice flour
¼ tsp. sea salt
3-4 Tbsp. unsalted butter
2-3 Tbsp. water

In a bowl, combine flour and salt.
With fingers, rub in 3 Tbsp. butter until crumbly; add 1 or more Tbsp. if needed.
Add 2 Tbsp. water and stir with fork to mix; add 1 or more Tbsp., if necessary, to make dough hold together.
Press dough into a lightly oiled pie plate.
For baked pies: bake at 350°F for 5 minutes.
For no-bake pies: bake at 350°F for 10-12 minutes or until golden.

• Use this pie crust for quiche, pot pies, vegetable pies, etc.
• For recipes with a top crust, use 1½ times this recipe.

Variations
❖ *Replace ½ cup rice flour with ½ cup millet flour or chickpea flour.*
❖ *Replace ¼ cup rice flour with ¼ cup tapioca flour.*
❖ *Replace ½ cup rice flour with ¼ cup tapioca flour and ¼ cup hemp flour.*

Rice Crisp Pie Crust

(A very easy to make pie crust made from rice cereal)

1½ cups crushed rice crisp cereal
3-4 Tbsp. almond oil or walnut oil
2-3 Tbsp. water

In a bowl, stir together cereal, 3 Tbsp. oil and 2 Tbsp. water until well combined.
Add 1 more Tbsp. oil or water, if necessary, to make dough hold together.
Press mixture into a lightly oiled pie plate.
For baked pies: do not bake; refrigerate to cool.
For no-bake pies: bake at 325°F for 7-10 minutes.

• Use this pie crust for dessert pies, cheese cakes, etc.
• For large pies, use 1½ times this recipe.

Variations
❖ *Replace oil with melted ghee or unsalted butter.*
❖ *Add ¼-½ tsp. cinnamon and/or a dash of nutmeg.*

Rice & Almond Pie Crust

¾ cup brown rice flour
½ cup ground almonds
1 Tbsp. sucanat (optional)
pinch of sea salt
2-3 Tbsp. unsalted butter
½ tsp. vanilla or almond extract
2-3 Tbsp. water

In a bowl, combine flour, ground almonds, sucanat (if using) and salt.
With fingers, rub in 2 Tbsp. butter until crumbly; add 1 or more Tbsp.
if needed.
Add 2 Tbsp. water and extract, and stir with fork to mix; add 1 or
more Tbsp., if necessary, to make dough hold together.
Press dough into a lightly oiled pie plate.
For baked pies: bake at 325°F for 5 minutes.
For no-bake pies: bake at 325°F for 9-12 minutes or until golden.

- Use this pie crust for dessert pies, cheese cakes, etc.
- For large pies, use 1½ times this recipe.

Variations
❖ *Replace ¼ cup rice flour with ¼ cup tapioca flour.*
❖ *Add ¼-½ tsp. cinnamon and/or a dash of nutmeg.*
❖ *For **Rice & Hazelnut Pie Crust**: replace almonds with hazelnuts.*

Desserts & Sweets

Tips for Desserts & Sweets   272
Carob Chip Cookies #1   273
Carob Chip Cookies #2   274
Double Carob Cookies   275
Almond Carob Cookies   276
Cherry Cookies   277
Lemon Cookies   278
Lemon Pecan Cookies   279
Applesauce Cookies   280
Rice Crisp Cookies   281
Rice Bran Cookies   282
Rolled Rice Cookies   283
Banana Rice Flake Muffins   284
Carob Banana Muffins   285
Banana Cherry Muffins   286
Raspberry Muffins   287
Pumpkin Muffins   288
Pumpkin Orange Muffins   289
Banana Cake   290
Lemon Cake   291
Carob Marble Cake   292
Carob Carrot Cake   293
Pumpkin Cheese Cake   294
Carob Cheese Cake   295
Rice Crisp Squares   296
Jam Squares   297
Peanut Butter & Papaya Bars   298
Fruit Berry Crisp   299
Fudge   300
Mixed Fruit Crepes   301

Tips for Desserts & Sweets

❖ If available, use fresh organic flours. Keep flour stored in the refrigerator or in cool dark place.

❖ Non-stick or 'air' bakeware work well with all recipes.

❖ Unsalted butter is used in most recipes. Butter can be replaced with ghee or coconut butter of same amount.

❖ For baking powder use the gluten-free baking powder on page 28.

❖ Use free range and/or organic eggs. Free range does not necessarily mean organic.

❖ All cookie recipes that call for eggs: each egg can be substituted with 1 Tbsp. ground flax seeds mixed in 3 Tbsp. water.

❖ All recipes that call for almond milk can be substituted with any nut, seed, rice or soy milk. If homemade milks are sweetened, do not make too sweet or sweeteners in recipes may need adjusting. Store bought milks are fine to use; if sweetened, adjust recipes accordingly.

❖ Use sugar-free or sucanat (cane juice) sweetened carob chips. Check ingredients in carob chips, as they may contain hydrogenated oils. For chocolate lovers: use dairy-free and cane juice sweetened semi-sweet chocolate chips. Both kinds of chips can be found in any health food store.

❖ Always use pure extracts, not artificial.

❖ All muffin recipes can be made into cakes; pour batter into a small oiled cake pan and bake at 350 for 30-40 minutes or until a toothpick inserted in center of cake comes out clean.

Carob Chip Cookies #1

(A delicious cookie that can also be made with dairy-free chocolate chips)

$\frac{1}{2}$ cup unsalted butter, softened
1/3 cup sucanat
1 egg
1 tsp. vanilla extract
1 cup brown rice flour
$\frac{1}{4}$ cup tapioca flour
$\frac{1}{2}$ tsp. baking soda
$\frac{1}{2}$ tsp. cinnamon (optional)
dash of nutmeg (optional)
1/3 cup carob chips

In a bowl, cream together butter and sucanat.
Beat in egg and vanilla until smooth.
In another bowl, combine flours, baking soda and spices (if using), and add to wet mixture; mix well.
Stir in carob chips.
Drop by spoonful, or roll into 1" balls and press onto an oiled cookie sheet.
Bake at 350°F for 11-14 minutes until golden.

Variations
❖ For **Chocolate Chip Cookies**: *replace carob chips with dairy-free semi-sweet chocolate chips.*
❖ *Replace $\frac{1}{4}$ cup rice flour with $\frac{1}{4}$ cup amaranth flour.*
❖ *Replace $\frac{1}{2}$ tsp. vanilla extract with $\frac{1}{2}$ tsp. peppermint extract.*

Carob Chip Cookies #2

(A rich tasting cookie that is sugar-free)

$\frac{1}{4}$ cup unsalted butter, softened
$\frac{1}{4}$ cup macadamia nut butter
1/3 cup sugar-free raspberry jam
1 egg
$\frac{1}{2}$ tsp. vanilla extract (optional)
1$\frac{1}{2}$ cups brown rice flour
1 tsp. baking powder
$\frac{1}{2}$ tsp. baking soda
$\frac{1}{2}$ tsp. cardamom (optional)
1/3 cup carob chips

In a bowl, cream together butter, macadamia nut butter and jam.
Beat in egg and vanilla (if using) until smooth.
 In another bowl, combine flour, baking powder, baking soda and
cardamom (if using), and add to wet mixture; mix well.
Stir in carob chips.
Drop by spoonful, or roll into 1" balls and press onto an oiled cookie
sheet.
Bake at 350°F for 11-14 minutes until golden.

Variations
❖ *Replace carob chips with dairy-free semi-sweet chocolate chips.*
❖ *Replace $\frac{1}{4}$ cup rice flour with $\frac{1}{4}$ cup tapioca flour.*
❖ *Add $\frac{1}{4}$ cup chopped macadamia nuts or nuts of choice.*
❖ *Replace macadamia nut butter with almond or hazelnut butter.*
❖ *Replace raspberry jam with jam of choice or apple butter.*
❖ *Replace 1/3 cup rice flour with $\frac{1}{2}$ cup ground almonds.*

Double Carob Cookies

(A sugar-free cookie that is sure to please kids of all ages)

$\frac{1}{2}$ cup unsalted butter, softened
$\frac{1}{2}$ cup apple butter
2 eggs
1 tsp. vanilla extract
$1\frac{1}{2}$ cups brown rice flour
$\frac{1}{2}$ cup tapioca flour
$\frac{1}{4}$ cup carob powder
1 tsp. baking powder
1 tsp. baking soda
$\frac{1}{2}$ cup carob chips

In a bowl, cream together butter and apple butter.
Beat in eggs and vanilla until smooth.
In another bowl, combine flours, carob powder, baking powder and baking soda, and add to wet mixture; mix well.
Stir in carob chips.
Roll into 1" balls and press onto an oiled cookie sheet.
Bake at 350°F for 12 15 minutes until golden.

Variations
- ❖ *Replace $\frac{1}{4}$-$\frac{1}{2}$ cup apple butter with same amount of sugar-free apricot jam.*
- ❖ *For **Double Chocolate Cookies**: replace carob chips with dairy-free semi-sweet chocolate chips and carob powder with organic caffeine-free cocoa powder.*

Almond Carob Cookies

(A sugar-free frosted cookie)

1/3 cup unsalted butter, softened
1/3 cup apple butter
$\frac{1}{4}$ cup almond butter
1 Tbsp. ground flax seeds mixed with 3 Tbsp. water
$\frac{1}{2}$ tsp. almond extract
$\frac{1}{2}$ tsp. vanilla extract (optional)
1 cup ground almonds
1 cup quinoa flour
$\frac{1}{4}$ tapioca flour
2 tsp. baking powder

Frosting:
$\frac{1}{2}$ cup carob chips
$1\frac{1}{2}$ Tbsp. unsalted butter
3 Tbsp. almond milk
$\frac{1}{2}$ tsp. vanilla extract (optional)
1 Tbsp. rice syrup or honey (optional)
2 Tbsp. grated coconut (optional)

In a bowl, cream together butter, apple butter and almond butter.
Mix in flax seed mixture and extracts until smooth.
Stir in ground almonds.
In another bowl, combine flours and baking powder, and add to wet mixture; mix well.
Roll into 1" balls and press onto an oiled cookie sheet.
Bake at 350°F for 11-14 minutes until golden.
Frosting:
In a saucepan, heat all ingredients for frosting over medium-low until melted, constantly stirring. Spoon on top of baked cookies.

Variations
❖ *Replace quinoa flour with brown rice flour.*
❖ *Replace carob chips with dairy-free semi-sweet chocolate chips.*
❖ *Omit the frosting and add carob chips to batter.*
❖ *For **Hazelnut Almond Cookies**: replace almond butter with hazelnut butter.*

Cherry Cookies

(A sugar-free cookie with tahini and quinoa flour)

$\frac{1}{4}$ cup unsalted butter, softened
$\frac{1}{4}$ cup tahini
1/3 cup sugar-free cherry jam
1 Tbsp. ground flax seed mixed in 3 Tbsp. water
$\frac{1}{2}$ tsp. cherry extract
$\frac{1}{2}$ tsp. vanilla extract (optional)
1 cup quinoa flour
$\frac{1}{4}$ cup tapioca flour
1 tsp. baking soda
$\frac{1}{4}$ cup dried chopped figs or cherries

In a bowl, cream together butter, tahini and jam.
Mix in flax seed mixture and extracts until smooth.
In another bowl, combine flours and baking soda, and add to wet mixture; mix well.
Stir in dried figs or cherries.
Drop by spoonful, or roll into 1" balls and press onto an oiled cookie sheet.
Bake at 350°F for 11-14 minutes until golden.

Variation
❖ *Replace quinoa flour with brown rice flour.*

Lemon Cookies

(A lightly spiced zesty cookie)

$\frac{1}{4}$ cup unsalted butter, softened
$\frac{1}{4}$ cup sucanat
$\frac{1}{4}$ cup apple butter
1 Tbsp. ground flax seeds mixed in 3 Tbsp. water
3 Tbsp. fresh lemon juice
1 tsp. lemon extract
1$\frac{1}{4}$ cups brown rice flour
1/3 cup tapioca flour
2 tsp. grated lemon peel
1 tsp. baking powder
$\frac{1}{4}$-$\frac{1}{2}$ tsp. cardamom or cinnamon

In a bowl, cream together butter and sucanat.
Mix in apple butter, flax seed mixture, lemon juice and extract until smooth.
In another bowl, combine remaining ingredients and add to wet mixture; mix well.
Drop by spoonful, or roll into 1" balls and press onto an oiled cookie sheet.
Bake at 350°F for 11-14 minutes until golden.

Variations
❖ *Replace $\frac{1}{2}$ cup brown rice flour with $\frac{1}{2}$ cup quinoa or amaranth flour.*
❖ *For **Orange Cookies**: replace lemon juice, extract and peel with orange juice, extract and peel.*

Lemon Pecan Cookies

1/3 cup unsalted butter, softened
$\frac{1}{4}$ cup brown rice syrup
1 Tbsp. ground flax seeds mixed in 3 Tbsp. water
1 tsp. lemon extract
$1\frac{1}{2}$ cups brown rice flour
1 tsp. baking powder
$\frac{1}{2}$ tsp. grated lemon peel
$\frac{1}{4}$ tsp. each cardamom, cinnamon & ginger
$\frac{1}{4}$ cup chopped pecans

In a bowl, cream together butter, rice syrup, flax seed mixture and lemon extract until smooth.
In another bowl, combine flour, baking powder, lemon peel and spices, and add to wet mixture; mix well.
Stir in pecans.
Roll into 1" balls and press onto an oiled cookie sheet.
Bake at 350°F for 11-14 minutes until golden.

Variations
❖ *Replace $\frac{1}{2}$ cup brown rice flour with $\frac{1}{2}$ cup tapioca flour.*
❖ *Replace rice flour with 1 cup quinoa flour and $\frac{1}{2}$ cup tapioca flour.*
❖ *Add $\frac{1}{4}$ cup chopped dried cranberries or blueberries.*

Applesauce Cookies

(A soft moist cookie that is mildly sweet)

1/3 cup unsalted butter, softened
$\frac{1}{4}$ cup sucanat
$1\frac{1}{2}$ cups unsweetened applesauce
1 Tbsp. ground flax seeds mixed in 3 Tbsp. water
1 tsp. vanilla extract
$1\frac{1}{4}$ cups brown rice flour
1 cup quinoa flour
1 tsp. baking powder
$\frac{1}{2}$ tsp. baking soda
1 tsp. cinnamon
$\frac{1}{4}$ tsp. nutmeg
1/3 cup chopped pecans or walnuts
$\frac{1}{4}$ cup raisins (optional)

In a bowl, cream together butter and sucanat.
Mix in applesauce, flax seed mixture and vanilla until smooth.
In another bowl, combine flours, baking powder, baking soda and spices, and add to wet mixture; mix well.
Stir in chopped nuts and raisins (if using).
Drop by spoonful onto an oiled cookie sheet.
Bake at 350°F for 12-15 minutes until golden.

Variations
❖ *Replace quinoa flour with $\frac{1}{2}$ cup tapioca and amaranth flour.*
❖ *Use Apple Berry Sauce on page 309.*

Rice Crisp Cookies

(A sugar-free cookie made with rice cereal)

$\frac{1}{2}$ cup unsalted butter, softened
$\frac{1}{2}$ cup apple butter
1 Tbsp. ground flax seeds mixed in 3 Tbsp. water
1 tsp. vanilla extract
$1\frac{1}{4}$ cups brown rice flour
1 tsp. baking soda
$\frac{1}{2}$ tsp. cinnamon (optional)
$1\frac{1}{2}$ cups rice crisp cereal, (fruit sweetened)

In a bowl, cream together butter and apple butter.
Mix in flax seed mixture and vanilla until smooth.
In another bowl, combine flour, baking soda and cinnamon (if using),
and add to wet mixture; mix well.
Stir in rice cereal.
Drop by spoonful onto an oiled cookie sheet.
Bake at 350°F for 10-13 minutes until golden.

Variations
❖ *Replace $\frac{1}{4}$ cup rice flour with $\frac{1}{4}$ cup tapioca flour.*
❖ *Add $\frac{1}{4}$ cup carob chips; stir in with cereal.*

Rice Bran Cookies

(A light crunchy cookie with added fibre)

$\frac{3}{4}$ cup unsalted butter, softened
$\frac{1}{2}$ cup sucanat
2 eggs
1 tsp. almond & vanilla extract
$1\frac{3}{4}$ cups rice bran
$1\frac{1}{4}$ cups brown rice flour
1 tsp. baking powder
$1\frac{1}{4}$ cups rolled rice
$\frac{1}{2}$ cup carob chips

In a bowl, cream together butter and sucanat.
Beat in eggs and extracts until smooth.
Mix in rice bran.
In another bowl, combine flour and baking powder, and add to wet mixture; mix well.
Stir in rolled rice and carob chips.
Roll into 1" balls and press onto an oiled cookie sheet.
Bake at 350°F for 12-15 minutes until golden.

Variations
❖ *Replace carob chips with dairy-free semi-sweet chocolate chips.*
❖ *Replace $\frac{1}{2}$ cup rice flour with $\frac{1}{2}$ cup tapioca flour.*

Rolled Rice Cookies

(A crunchy delicious cookie)

$\frac{1}{2}$ cup unsalted butter, softened
1/3 cup sucanat
1 egg
2 Tbsp. almond or rice milk
1 tsp. almond or vanilla extract
$1\frac{1}{4}$ cups brown rice flour
$1\frac{1}{4}$ cups rolled rice
1 tsp. baking soda
$\frac{1}{2}$ tsp. cinnamon
$\frac{1}{4}$ tsp. nutmeg (optional)
$\frac{1}{4}$ cup chopped pecans or raisins
$\frac{1}{4}$ cup carob chips (optional)

In a bowl, cream together butter and sucanat.
Beat in egg, milk and extract until smooth.
In another bowl, combine flour, rolled rice, baking soda and spices, and add to wet mixture; mix well.
Stir in pecans or raisins and carob chips (if using).
Drop by spoonful, or roll into 1" balls and press onto an oiled cookie sheet.
Bake at 350°F for 12-15 minutes until golden.

Variations
❖ *Replace $\frac{1}{4}$ cup rice flour with $\frac{1}{4}$ cup tapioca flour.*
❖ *Replace carob chips with dairy-free semi-sweet chocolate chips.*
❖ *Replace rolled rice with quinoa flakes.*

Banana Rice Flake Muffins

¼ cup almond, macadamia or walnut oil
¼ cup sucanat
1 egg
3 bananas, mashed
½ cup almond or soy milk
1 tsp. vanilla extract
½ cup rice flakes
1 cup brown rice flour
2 tsp. baking powder
1 tsp. baking soda
½ tsp. cinnamon
½ tsp. grated orange peel (optional)
¼ cup carob chips (optional)

In a bowl, beat together oil, sucanat and egg.
Mix in bananas, milk and extract until smooth.
Stir in rice flakes.
In another bowl, combine flour, baking powder, baking soda, cinnamon
and orange peel (if using), and add to wet mixture; mix until
moistened.
Stir in chips (if using).
Pour or scoop batter into an oiled muffin pan.
Bake at 375°F for 18-20 minutes or until tops are firm to the touch.

Variations
❖ *Replace rice or soy milk with coconut milk.*
❖ *Replace ¼ cup rice flour with ¼ cup tapioca flour.*
❖ *Replace carob chips with dairy-free semi-sweet chocolate chips.*
❖ *For **Quinoa Banana Muffins**: replace rice flakes with quinoa flakes,
    and rice flour with ¾ cup quinoa flour + ¼ cup tapioca flour.*
❖ *Muffins can be frosted with Carob Frosting on page 306.*

Carob Banana Muffins

(A sugar-free muffin with optional crunchy topping)

1/3 cup unsalted butter, softened
¼ cup apple butter
1 egg
3 bananas, mashed
1 cup almond milk
1 tsp. vanilla or almond extract (optional)
1½ cups quinoa flour
¼ cup tapioca flour
¼ cup carob powder
1 Tbsp. baking powder
½ tsp. cardamom or cinnamon

Topping: (optional)
2 Tbsp. unsalted butter, melted
1½ Tbsp. honey or brown rice syrup
2-3 Tbsp. grated coconut or chopped nuts

In a bowl, cream together butter and apple butter.
Beat in egg.
Mix in bananas, milk and extract (if using) until smooth.
In another bowl, combine flours, carob powder, baking powder, and
spice (if using), and add to wet mixture; mix until moistened.
Pour or scoop batter into an oiled muffin pan.
Bake at 375°F for 10 minutes.
For optional topping: while muffins are baking, combine butter, honey
or brown rice syrup and coconut or nuts, spoon over muffins.
Bake for 10 more minutes; or until tops are firm to the touch.

Variations
❖ *Replace almond milk with coconut milk.*
❖ *Replace quinoa flour with brown rice flour.*
❖ *Replace carob powder with organic (caffeine-free) cocoa powder.*
❖ *If topping is not used: muffins can be frosted with Carob Frosting*
  on page 306 or frosting from Almond Carob Cookies (use double
  the recipe) on page 276.

Banana Cherry Muffins

(A sugar-free muffin with tahini)

½ cup unsalted butter, softened
½ cup sugar-free cherry jam
¼ cup tahini
2 eggs
3 bananas, mashed
½ cup almond milk
1 tsp. vanilla extract (optional)
2 cups brown rice flour
2 tsp. baking powder
1 tsp. baking soda
½ cup carob chips (optional)

In a bowl, cream together butter, jam and tahini.
Beat in eggs.
Mix in bananas, milk and vanilla until smooth.
In another bowl, combine flour, baking powder and baking soda, and add to wet mixture; mix until moistened.
Stir in carob chips (if using).
Pour or scoop batter into an oiled muffin pan.
Bake at 375°F for 18-20 minutes or until tops are firm to the touch.

Variations
* *Replace almond milk with coconut milk.*
* *Replace ½ cup rice flour with ½ cup tapioca flour.*
* *Replace 1 cup rice flour with ½ cup quinoa flour + ½ cup tapioca flour.*
* *Replace carob chips with dairy-free semi-sweet chocolate chips.*
* *Muffins can be frosted with Carob Frosting on page 306 or frosting from Almond Carob Cookies (use double the recipe) on page 276.*

Raspberry Muffins

(A sugar-free muffin with apple butter & raspberries)

$\frac{1}{2}$ cup unsalted butter, softened
$\frac{1}{2}$ cup apple butter
$\frac{1}{4}$ cup tahini
2 eggs
2 Tbsp. sugar-free raspberry jam
$\frac{3}{4}$ cup almond or soy milk
1 tsp. vanilla extract
2 cups brown rice flour.
1 Tbsp. baking powder
1 cup raspberries (fresh or frozen)

In a bowl, cream together butter, jam and tahini.
Beat in eggs.
Mix in jam, milk and vanilla until smooth.
In another bowl, combine flour and baking powder, and add to wet mixture; mix until moistened.
Stir in raspberries.
Pour or scoop batter into an oiled muffin pan.
Bake at 375°F for 18-20 minutes or until tops are firm to the touch.

Variations
* *Replace almond or soy milk with coconut milk.*
* *Replace $\frac{1}{2}$ cup rice flour with $\frac{1}{2}$ cup tapioca flour.*
* *Replace 1 cup rice flour with $\frac{1}{2}$ cup quinoa flour + $\frac{1}{2}$ cup tapioca flour.*
* *Replace raspberries and raspberry jam with any other kind of berries and berry jam.*
* *Muffins can be frosted with Carob Frosting on page 306 or frosting from Almond Carob Cookies (use double the recipe) on page 276.*

Pumpkin Muffins

(A wonderful flavoured pumpkin & spice muffin)

1/3 cup unsalted butter, softened
½ cup sucanat
1 egg
1 cup cooked mashed pumpkin
1 cup almond or soy milk
1 tsp. vanilla extract
2 cups brown rice flour
2 tsp. baking powder
½ tsp. baking soda
½ tsp. cinnamon
1/8 tsp. each ground cloves, ginger & nutmeg
pinch of allspice (optional)
¼ cup chopped pecans or walnuts (optional)
¼ cup raisins (optional)

In a bowl, cream together butter and sugar.
Beat in egg.
Mix in pumpkin, milk and vanilla until smooth.
In another bowl, combine flour, baking powder, baking soda and spices,
and add to wet mixture; mix until moistened.
Stir in nuts and/or raisins (if using).
Pour or scoop batter into an oiled muffin pan.
Bake at 375°F for 17-20 minutes or until tops are firm to the touch.

Variations
❖ *Replace almond or soy milk with coconut milk.*
❖ *Replace ½ cup rice flour with ½ cup tapioca flour.*
❖ *Replace 1 cup rice flour with ½ cup quinoa flour + ½ cup tapioca flour.*

Pumpkin Orange Muffins

(The mild tangy flavour of orange adds a little sunshine to this muffin)

$\frac{1}{4}$ cup macadamia, almond or walnut oil
$\frac{1}{2}$ almond or soy milk
$\frac{1}{2}$ cup fresh orange juice
1 egg
$\frac{3}{4}$ cup cooked mashed pumpkin
$\frac{1}{2}$ tsp. orange extract (optional)
2 cups brown rice flour
$\frac{1}{2}$ cup sucanat
1 Tbsp. baking powder
1 tsp. baking soda
1 tsp. grated orange peel
1 tsp. cinnamon
$\frac{1}{4}$ tsp. ginger & nutmeg
$\frac{1}{4}$ cup chopped nuts of choice

In a bowl, beat together oil, milk, orange juice and egg.
Mix in pumpkin and extract (if using) until smooth.
In another bowl, combine flour, sucanat, baking powder, baking soda, orange peel (if using) and spices, and add to wet mixture; mix until moistened.
Stir in nuts (if using).
Pour or scoop batter into an oiled muffin pan.
Bake at 375°F for 18-20 minutes or until tops are firm to the touch.

Variations
❖ *Replace almond or soy milk with coconut milk.*
❖ *Replace $\frac{1}{2}$ cup rice flour with $\frac{1}{2}$ cup tapioca flour.*
❖ *Replace 1 cup rice flour with $\frac{1}{2}$ cup quinoa flour + $\frac{1}{2}$ cup tapioca flour.*

Banana Cake

(A sugar-free cake, children of all ages will enjoy)

$\frac{1}{2}$ cup unsalted butter, softened
$\frac{1}{2}$ cup apple butter
1 egg
3 large bananas, mashed
$\frac{1}{4}$ cup almond or soy milk
$1\frac{3}{4}$ cups brown rice flour
2 tsp. baking powder
1 tsp. baking soda
$\frac{1}{2}$ tsp. cinnamon (optional)

In a bowl, cream together butter and apple butter.
Beat in egg.
Mix in bananas and milk until smooth.
In another bowl, combine flour, baking powder, baking soda and cinnamon (if using), and add to wet mixture; mix until moistened.
Pour batter into a small oiled cake pan.
Bake at 350°F for 30-40 minutes or until a toothpick inserted in centre of cake comes out clean.

Variations
- *Replace almond or soy milk with coconut milk.*
- *Replace $\frac{1}{2}$ cup rice flour with $\frac{1}{2}$ cup tapioca flour.*
- *Replace $\frac{3}{4}$ cup rice flour with $\frac{1}{2}$ cup quinoa flour + $\frac{1}{4}$ cup tapioca flour.*
- *Cake can be frosted with Carob Frosting on page 306 or frosting from Almond Carob Cookies (use double the recipe) on page 276.*

Lemon Cake

(A delicious zesty lemon cake with pecans)

½ cup unsalted butter, softened
1/3 cup sucanat
2 eggs
½ cup almond milk
1 tsp. lemon extract
1½ cups brown rice flour
¼ cup tapioca flour
2 tsp. baking powder
1 tsp. grated lemon peel
½ tsp. cardamom (optional)
½ cup chopped pecans
2 Tbsp. sucanat mixed in 3 Tbsp. fresh lemon juice

In a bowl, cream together butter and sucanat.
Beat in eggs.
Mix in milk and extract until smooth.
In another bowl, combine flours, baking powder, lemon peel and cardamom (if using), and add to wet mixture; mix until moistened.
Stir in pecans.
Pour batter into a small oiled cake pan.
Bake at 350°F for 30-40 minutes or until a toothpick inserted in centre of cake comes out clean.
Drizzle lemon juice mixture over cake as soon as it comes out of the oven.

Variation
* *Replace rice flour with 1¼ cups quinoa flour + ¼ cup more tapioca flour.*

Carob Marble Cake

(A sugar-free cake that is great for birthdays and all occasions)

$\frac{1}{4}$ cup unsalted butter, softened
$\frac{1}{2}$ cup apple butter
1 egg + 1 egg white
1 tsp. vanilla extract
1 cup plain soy or goat's milk yogurt
1$\frac{1}{4}$ cups brown rice flour
$\frac{1}{4}$ cup tapioca flour
2 tsp. baking powder
1 tsp. baking soda
$\frac{1}{2}$ tsp. cinnamon or cardamom

Marble:
1 Tbsp. apple butter
3 Tbsp. carob powder
3 Tbsp. almond milk

In a bowl, cream together butter and apple butter.
Beat in egg, egg white and vanilla until smooth.
In another bowl, combine flours, baking powder, baking soda and spice, and add to wet mixture alternating with yogurt; do not over mix.
Pour all but 1 cup of batter into a small oiled cake pan.
Stir together ingredients for marble along with reserved batter until smooth; pour over cake and draw or swirl a knife through to produce a marbled effect.
Bake at 350°F for 30-40 minutes or until a toothpick inserted in centre of cake comes out clean.

• Frost cake with Carob Frosting on page 306 or frosting from Almond Carob Cookies (use double the recipe) on page 276.

Variations
❖ *Replace $\frac{3}{4}$ cup rice flour with $\frac{1}{2}$ cup quinoa flour + $\frac{1}{4}$ cup more tapioca flour.*
❖ *Replace $\frac{1}{4}$ cup rice flour with $\frac{1}{4}$ cup amaranth flour.*
❖ *Replace $\frac{1}{2}$ tsp. vanilla extract with $\frac{1}{2}$ tsp. peppermint extract.*

Carob Carrot Cake

(A sugar-free cake that all will love; not as rich as standard carrot cake)

$\frac{1}{4}$ cup unsalted butter
$\frac{1}{4}$ cup unsweetened carob chips
$\frac{1}{4}$ cup almond or rice milk
2 eggs
$\frac{1}{4}$ cup apple butter
1 tsp. vanilla extract
4 medium carrots, finely shredded
$1\frac{1}{4}$ cups brown rice flour
2 tsp. baking powder
1 tsp. baking soda
$\frac{1}{4}$ tsp. cinnamon & nutmeg
$\frac{1}{4}$ cup chopped nuts of choice
$\frac{1}{4}$ cup raisins (optional)

In a saucepan, melt butter, carob chips and milk over medium-low heat until combined, stirring constantly.
In a bowl, beat together eggs, apple butter and vanilla.
Mix in carob mixture until smooth.
Stir in carrots.
In another bowl, combine flour, baking powder, baking soda and spices, and add to wet mixture; mix until moistened.
Stir in nuts and raisins (if using).
Pour batter into a small oiled cake pan.
Bake at 350°F for 30-40 minutes or until a toothpick inserted in centre of cake comes out clean.

Variations
❖ *Replace $\frac{1}{4}$ cup rice flour with $\frac{1}{4}$ cup tapioca flour.*
❖ *Cake can be frosted with Carob Frosting on page 306 or frosting from Almond Carob Cookies (use double the recipe) on page 276.*

Pumpkin Cheese Cake

1 unbaked Rice Crisp Pie Crust (see page 268)

Bottom filling:

  4 oz. (½ cup) rice cream cheese

  ½ cup goat's milk yogurt cheese (see page 148) or ½ cup regular tofu

  1 egg

  ¼ cup sucanat or 3 Tbsp. honey, brown rice syrup or maple syrup

  1 tsp vanilla extract

Top filling:

  ¼ cup raw cashew or macadamia nuts

  ¾ cup hot water

  1 cup cooked mashed pumpkin

  1/3 cup sucanat

  1 tsp. cinnamon

  ¼ tsp. ginger & nutmeg

Press mixture for pie crust into bottom of a lightly oiled 8" square pan or pie plate; chill.

To prepare bottom filling:

  In a food processor, combine all ingredients until smooth.

  Spread evenly over prepared crust.

To prepare top filling:

  In a blender, grind nuts to a powder.

  Add hot water and blend until smooth.

  Add remaining ingredients and blend until smooth.

  Pour evenly over cheese mixture.

Bake at 350°F for 50-60 minutes or until cake is set in the middle.

Variations

❖ *Replace egg with 1 Tbsp. ground flax seeds mixed in 3 Tbsp. water.*

❖ *Replace rice cream cheese with soy or goat's milk cream cheese.*

❖ *Replace goat's milk yogurt cheese with soy yogurt cheese.*

Carob Cheese Cake

(An awesome tasting cheese cake made with yogurt cheese or tofu)

1 unbaked Rice Crisp Pie Crust (see page 268)
Filling:
   8 oz. (1 cup) rice cream cheese
   8 oz. (1 cup) goat's milk yogurt cheese (see page 148)
      Or
   8 oz. (1 cup) regular tofu
   1 egg
   1/3 cup sucanat
   1 tsp vanilla extract
   $\frac{1}{4}$ cup carob powder
   $\frac{1}{4}$ cup sweetened carob chips

Press mixture for pie crust into bottom of a lightly oiled 8" square pan or pie plate; chill.
To prepare filling:
   In a food processor, combine all ingredients, except carob chips, until smooth.
   Add carob chips and process (pulse) just to mix in.
   Spread evenly over prepared crust.
Bake at 350°F for 45-50 minutes or until cake is set in the middle.

Variations
* *Replace egg with 1 Tbsp. ground flax seeds mixed in 3 Tbsp. water.*
* *Replace rice cream cheese with soy or goat's milk cream cheese.*
* *Replace sucanat with $\frac{1}{4}$ cup maple syrup or honey.*
* *For **Chocolate Cheesecake**: replace carob chips with dairy-free semi-sweet chocolate chips and carob powder with organic (caffeine-free) cocoa powder.*
* *Replace $\frac{1}{2}$ tsp. vanilla extract with $\frac{1}{2}$ tsp. peppermint extract.*

Rice Crisp Squares

(A healthy version of rice crispy squares that still taste great)

¾ cup nut butter of choice
½ cup brown rice syrup
¼ cup honey
1 tsp. vanilla extract (optional)
4 cups rice crisp cereal
1 cup chopped mixed nuts
1 cup unsweetened shredded coconut
      Or
1 cup chopped mixed dried fruit

In a saucepan, heat nut butter, rice syrup and honey over low heat;
stir until well combined.
Stir in vanilla (if using).
In a bowl, stir together remaining ingredients.
Pour liquid mixture over cereal mix; stir until well blended.
Press mixture into a 9"x13" pan.
Cool in the refrigerator.
Cut into bars.

Variations
❖ *Add ¼-½ cup unsweetened carob chips.*
❖ *Replace ½ tsp. vanilla extract with ½ tsp. extract of choice.*

Jam Squares

(A lovely tasting fruit square that is very low in sugar)

Crust:
½ cup unsalted butter, softened
¼ cup apple butter
1 egg
½ tsp. vanilla extract
1 Tbsp. almond milk
1 cup brown rice flour
1 tsp. baking powder
½ cup sugar-free jam of choice

In a bowl, cream together butter and apple butter.
Beat in egg, vanilla and milk until smooth.
In another bowl, combine flour and baking powder, and add to wet mixture; mix well.
Press mixture into an 8" or 9" square cake pan.
Cover crust with ½ cup, or more, jam of choice; spread to even out.

Topping:
1 egg
2 Tbsp. melted unsalted butter or almond oil
½ tsp. vanilla extract
2 Tbsp. brown rice syrup or honey
2 cups unsweetened shredded coconut

In a bowl, beat together egg, butter or oil, vanilla and sweetener until smooth.
Stir in coconut.
Spread mixture evenly over crust.
Bake at 350°F for 30-40 minutes, until top is golden and set.

Peanut Butter & Papaya Bars

(A sugar-free fruit bar good for day trips & outings)

¼ cup unsalted butter, softened
2/3 cup mashed papaya (1 small)
1/3 cup apple butter
1/3 cup peanut butter
1/3 cup almond milk
1 tsp. vanilla extract
1 Tbsp. ground flax seed mixed in 3 Tbsp. water
1½ cups quinoa flour
1 Tbsp. baking powder
½ cup carob chips
1/3 cup diced mixed dried fruit of choice
¼ cup chopped nuts of choice

In a bowl, cream together butter, papaya, apple butter and peanut butter until smooth.
Mix in milk, vanilla and flax mixture until smooth.
In another bowl, combine flour and baking powder, and add to wet mixture; mix well.
Stir in carob chips, dried fruit and nuts of choice.
Press mixture into an oiled 8" or 9" square cake pan.
Bake at 350°F for 30-40 minutes or until a toothpick inserted in center of cake comes out clean.

Variations
❖ *Replace quinoa flour with rice flour.*
❖ *Replace ½ cup of quinoa flour with ¼ cup amaranth flour + ¼ cup tapioca flour.*
❖ *Replace carob chips with dairy-free semi-sweet chocolate chips.*
❖ *Replace peanut butter with any other nut butter.*
❖ *Replace ½ tsp. vanilla extract with ½ tsp. extract of choice.*

Fruit Berry Crisp

(A pleasant fruit dessert that is good served hot or cold)

Fruit mix:
  2 cups peeled, cored & chopped apples
  1 cup blueberries
  1 cup raspberries
  2 cups cranberries
  2 Tbsp. brown rice flour
  1 tsp. cinnamon

In a bowl, stir together all ingredients.
Place fruit mix into an oiled baking dish.

Topping:
  $\frac{1}{2}$ cup rice flakes
  $\frac{1}{2}$ cup brown rice flour
  $\frac{1}{4}$ cup ground almonds
  1/3 cup sucanat
  $\frac{1}{4}$ cup chopped pecans (optional)
  $\frac{1}{4}$ cup unsalted butter

In a bowl, stir together all ingredients, except butter.
With fingers, rub in butter until crumbly.
Sprinkle over fruit mixture.
Bake at 350°F, uncovered, for 45 minutes, until bubbly and golden.

Variations
❖ *Replace rice flakes and flour with quinoa flakes and flour.*
❖ *Replace, or add, cinnamon with any spice or spice combination;*
   cardamom, ginger, orange peel, nutmeg, etc.
❖ *Replace sucanat with $\frac{1}{4}$ cup honey, brown rice syrup or maple syrup*
   and add $\frac{1}{4}$ cup more ground almonds.
❖ *Replace ground nuts and pecans with nuts of choice.*

Fudge

(A delicious & nutritious form of fudge; can be sugar-free)

$\frac{1}{2}$ cup almond butter
$\frac{1}{2}$ cup macadamia nut butter
1/3 cup honey, brown rice syrup or apple butter
$\frac{1}{4}$ cup sugar-free jam of choice
1/3 cup ground almonds
1/3 cup ground hazelnuts
1/3 cup ground pumpkin seeds
$\frac{3}{4}$ cup ground sesame seeds
$\frac{1}{4}$ cup carob powder
$\frac{1}{2}$ cup unsweetened shredded coconut or diced dried fruit mix

In a food processor, combine nut butters, sweetener and jam until smooth.
Add ground nuts, seeds and carob powder, and process until combined.
Add coconut or fruit and process (pulse) just until mixed in.
Scoop out mixture and press into 2-8" square or 1-9"x13" lightly oiled pan. (1-8" pan will also work; fudge will just be thick.)

• This freezes well; always keep refrigerated.
• Use raw nuts and seeds; not roasted.

Variations
❖ *Replace any amount of either nut butter with an equal amount of any other nut or seed butter.*
❖ *Replace any amount of any ground nuts or seeds with an equal amount of any other kind.*
❖ *Add $\frac{1}{4}$ cup carob chips; add with coconut or dried fruit.*
❖ *Replace carob powder with organic (caffeine-free) cocoa powder.*

Mixed Fruit Crepes

(A sugar-free rich tasting dessert)

2-3 Tbsp. ghee or unsalted butter
1 apple; peeled, cored & chopped
1 pear; peeled, cored & chopped
2 bananas, sliced
$\frac{1}{4}$-$\frac{1}{2}$ cup blueberries
$\frac{1}{4}$ cup chopped nuts of choice (optional)
2 tsp. sugar-free jam
$\frac{1}{2}$-1 tsp. cinnamon (optional)
4 dessert crepes (see page 257)

In a skillet, melt ghee or butter over medium-low heat.
Add all ingredients and stir gently to coat with ghee; cook for 3
minutes or until fruit is tender.
Divide fruit mix evenly over crepes and roll like a wrap.

- Serve as is, or top with carob syrup, carob topping, fruit berry sauce
  or lemon yogurt sauce.
- Makes 2-4 servings.

Variations
❖ *Use any other fruit to make interesting combinations: peaches, any
  berry, kiwi, mango, papaya, etc.*
❖ *Stir in $\frac{1}{4}$-$\frac{1}{2}$ cup yogurt before adding to crepes.*
❖ *Add any other spice: cardamom, cloves, ginger, orange peel,
  nutmeg, etc.*

Syrups, Toppings, Puddings & Ice Milks

Carob Syrup   304
Carob Nut Topping   305
Carob Frosting   306
Lemon Yogurt Sauce   307
Fruit Berry Sauce   308
Apple Berry Sauce   309
Apple Blueberry Butter   310
Rice Pudding   311
Millet Pudding   312
Banana Pudding   313
Pumpkin Pudding   314
Vanilla Pudding   315
Carob Pudding   316
Ice Milks   317
Creamscicle Ice Milk   318
Carob Mint Ice Milk   318
Carob Banana Ice Milk   319
Lemon Banana Ice Milk   319
Raspberry Mango Ice Milk   320
Berry Deluxe Ice Milk   320
Coconut Peach Ice Milk with Almonds   321

Carob Syrup

(A fast & easy to prepare delicious syrup with many uses)

1 cup almond milk
$\frac{1}{4}$ cup honey or brown rice syrup
$\frac{1}{4}$ cup carob powder
2 tsp. tapioca flour
$\frac{1}{2}$ tsp. vanilla extract (optional)

In a saucepan, whisk or stir together all ingredients, except vanilla, until smooth.
Bring mixture to a simmer and stir until slightly thickened.
Remove from heat and stir in vanilla (if using).

- Serve hot or chilled.
- Use as syrup for pancakes, dessert crepes, fruit and other desserts, or add to nut and seed milks or breakfast cereals.
- Cover and refrigerate for up to 2 weeks.

Variations
❖ *For thicker syrup: add $\frac{1}{2}$-1 tsp. more tapioca flour.*
❖ *For **Carob Mint Syrup**: replace $\frac{1}{2}$-1 tsp. vanilla extract with $\frac{1}{2}$ tsp. peppermint extract.*
❖ *For **Chocolate Syrup**: replace carob powder with organic (caffeine-free) cocoa powder.*

Carob Nut Topping

(A rich tasting topping that goes well with desserts of all kinds)

1 cup almond milk
¼ cup macadamia nut butter
3-4 Tbsp. honey or brown rice syrup
1/3 cup carob powder
1 Tbsp. ghee or unsalted butter
1 tsp. vanilla extract

In a blender, combine milk, nut butter, sweetener and carob until smooth.
Transfer to a saucepan and bring to a boil over medium heat.
Let boil for 5 minutes without stirring.
Remove from heat; stir in ghee or butter and vanilla.

- Serve hot or chilled.
- Use as topping for pancakes, dessert crepes, fruit and other desserts.
- Cover and refrigerate for up to 2 weeks.
- Topping thickens when chilled; reheat to thin.

Variations
- ❖ *Replace macadamia nut butter with hazelnut or almond butter.*
- ❖ *For thicker topping: add 1-1½ tsp. tapioca flour; add to milk mixture.*
- ❖ *For **Carob Mint Topping**: replace ½-1 tsp. vanilla extract with ½ tsp. peppermint extract.*
- ❖ *For **Chocolate Topping**: replace carob powder with organic (caffeine-free) cocoa powder.*

Carob Frosting

(An easy to make frosting for cakes or muffins)

$\frac{1}{4}$ cup unsalted butter
$\frac{1}{4}$ cup nut or seed milk
$\frac{1}{4}$ cup carob powder
$\frac{1}{4}$ cup almond butter
3 Tbsp. honey or brown rice syrup
$\frac{1}{2}$ tsp. vanilla

In a bowl, cream together all ingredients until smooth.

- Use to frost cakes and muffins.
- Cover and refrigerate for up to 2 weeks or freeze.
- Topping thickens when chilled.

Variations
- ❖ *Replace almond butter with hazelnut or macadamia nut butter.*
- ❖ *For **Carob Mint Frosting**: replace vanilla extract with peppermint extract.*
- ❖ *For **Chocolate Frosting**: replace carob powder with organic (caffeine-free) cocoa powder.*

Lemon Yogurt Sauce

(A refreshing light sauce)

1 cup yogurt cheese (see page 148)
2-3 Tbsp. honey, brown rice syrup, maple syrup or sucanat
1-2 Tbsp. fresh lemon juice
½ tsp. lemon extract (optional)
1 tsp. grated lemon peel
½ tsp. cardamom (optional)

In a bowl, cream together all ingredients until smooth.

• Serve over dessert crepes, pancakes, ices, etc.
• Makes about 1 cup.
• Cover and refrigerate for up to 2 days.

Variation
❖ *For **Orange Yogurt Sauce**: replace lemon juice, extract and peel with orange juice, extract and peel*

Fruit Berry Sauce

(A nice mixed fruit sauce, low in sugar)

2½ cups mixed berries
½ cup water
2 Tbsp. honey or sucanat (optional)
2 tsp. tapioca flour
½-1 tsp. almond extract (optional)

In a blender, combine 1½ cups berries, water, sweetener (if using) and tapioca flour until smooth.
Transfer to a saucepan and cook over medium heat, stirring constantly until thickened.
Stir in reserved berries and simmer for 1-2 minutes.
Stir in extract (if using).

• Serve over dessert crepes, pancakes, ices, etc.
• Makes about 1¼-1½ cups.
• Cover and refrigerate for up to 5 days.

Variation
❖ *Replace extract with extract of choice.*

Apple Berry Sauce

(Classic apple sauce with a berry twist)

3 lbs. apples; peeled, cored & chopped
1 cup blueberries or raspberries
$\frac{1}{2}$ tsp. cinnamon
$\frac{1}{4}$ tsp. ground ginger
$\frac{1}{4}$ cup sugar-free fruit juice of choice

Place all ingredients in a Dutch oven or large saucepan, cover and heat on high for 1-2 minutes.
Lower heat and simmer for 30-45 minutes or until apples are soft.
Cool slightly and mash in the pan or, process in a blender or food processor until smooth.

- Store in covered glass jars, in the refrigerator for up to 3 weeks or freeze.
- Makes about 5 cups.
- Stainless steel cookware works best.

Variations
- ❖ *Keep $\frac{1}{2}$ of the apples unpeeled. This adds fibre and nutrients to the sauce. Wash apples well and remove any blemishes.*
- ❖ *Replace berries with any other kind of berry: blackberries, cranberries or strawberries.*

Apple Blueberry Butter

(Apple butter with a blueberry twist)

5 lbs. apples; peeled, cored & chopped
1 cup blueberries
2 Tbsp. lemon juice

In a blender or food processor, combine ingredients in small batches until smooth; add a little water or apple juice, if necessary, to help process.
Transfer mixture to a Dutch oven, and bring to medium-high heat, uncovered.
When mixture starts to bubble, reduce heat to medium and cook, uncovered, for $1\frac{1}{2}$-$2\frac{1}{2}$ hours, or until butter is at preferred thickness and there is no liquid run off when spooned in a mound.

- *Note:* If there is too much splattering during cooking time, pot can be partially covered or, use a lid with an air vent. Also, the less liquid used to help process ingredients, the faster the ingredients will cook down; a food processor will eliminate the need for any liquid. (Water needs to evaporate in order for ingredients to condense.)
- Use butter as a sweetener in dessert recipes, as a spread for breads, flatbreads, as a topping for pancakes, etc.
- Store in covered glass jars, in the refrigerator for up to 4 weeks or freeze.
- Makes about $3\frac{1}{2}$-4 cups.
- Stainless steel cookware works best.

Variations
- ❖ *For a spiced butter add any of the following spices: cinnamon, nutmeg or ground ginger.*
- ❖ *For a sweetened butter add honey or brown rice syrup.*

Rice Pudding

4 cups cooked sweet brown rice
2 apples, peeled, cored & chopped
½ cup raisins
¼ cup chopped pecans
¼ cup unsweetened shredded coconut (optional)
1 cup almond milk
½ cup sugar-free fruit juice of choice
½ cup brown rice syrup or honey
¼ cup tapioca flour
1 tsp. guar gum
1 tsp. cinnamon
¼ tsp. nutmeg
1 tsp. grated orange or lemon peel (optional)
1 tsp. vanilla or almond extract (optional)

In a bowl, stir together rice , apples, raisins, pecans and coconut (if using).
In a blender, combine remaining ingredients until smooth.
Pour liquid mixture over rice mixture and stir to combine.
Pour mixture into an oiled baking dish and spread evenly.
Bake at 350°F, uncovered, for 35-45 minutes, until hot and bubbly.

• Serve warm or cold with milk and/or yogurt of choice.
• Makes about 7 cups.

Variations
❖ *Replace apples with any other fresh fruit, such as: 1 large mango, 1 papaya, 2 pears, 3 peaches, etc.*
❖ *Replace raisins with any other kind of dried fruit.*
❖ *Replace almond milk with coconut milk or milk of choice.*
❖ *Replace 1-2 cups rice with cooked millet or quinoa.*

Millet Pudding

1/3 cup almonds, cashews or macadamia nuts
1½ cups hot water
1½ cups water
¼ carob powder
1 Tbsp. tapioca flour
¼ cup brown rice syrup or honey
1/3 cup millet
2 bananas, sliced
1 tsp. vanilla extract (optional)
1 tsp. guar gum

In a blender, grind nuts to a powder; add hot water and blend until smooth. Transfer to a saucepan.
In blender, combine water, carob powder, tapioca flour and sweetener until smooth.
Stir into prepared saucepan with millet and bring to a boil.
Reduce heat and simmer, covered, for 20 minutes.
Add bananas and cook 5 minutes.
Transfer to blender or food processor; add vanilla (if using) and guar gum, and process until smooth.
Pour mixture into a bowl or individual sized serving bowls; chill and let set in the refrigerator.

• Makes 3-3½ cups.

Variations
❖ *Replace bananas with any other fresh fruit, such as: 1 large mango, 1 papaya, 3-4 peaches, 1 cup or more (or mix) berries of choice, etc.*
❖ *Pudding can also be poured into piecrust of choice.*
❖ *Replace carob powder with organic (caffeine-free) cocoa powder.*

Banana Pudding

(A tasty easy to make pudding)

1 cup almond milk
2 large bananas
$\frac{1}{4}$ cup brown rice syrup or honey
$\frac{1}{2}$ tsp. cinnamon or cardamom (optional)
2 Tbsp. tapioca flour & $\frac{1}{2}$ tsp. guar gum mixed in 3 Tbsp. water
1 tsp. vanilla extract

In a blender, combine milk and bananas until smooth. Add more milk or banana to make 2$\frac{1}{2}$ cups.
Add sweetener and spice (if using), and blend until smooth.
Transfer to a saucepan, and bring to a boil over medium-high heat, stirring occasionally.
Reduce heat to medium and cook for 3 minutes, stirring constantly.
Add tapioca mixture and vanilla and stir until thickened, approximately 5-10 minutes.
Pour mixture into a bowl or individual sized serving bowls; chill and let set in the refrigerator.

• Makes about 2$\frac{1}{2}$ cups.

Variations
❖ *Add $\frac{1}{4}$ cup unsweetened shredded coconut; stir into mixture in saucepan before heating.*
❖ *Add 2 Tbsp. carob powder to blender mix.*
❖ *For other fruit flavoured puddings: replace 1 or both bananas with any other fresh fruit, such as: mango, papaya, peaches, berries of choice, etc. (Make sure to have 2$\frac{1}{2}$ cups mixture when combined with milk.)*
❖ *Replace vanilla with extract of choice.*
❖ *Pudding can also be poured into piecrust of choice.*

Pumpkin Pudding

(A lightly sweetened fall harvest pudding)

1 cup almond or cashew milk
$1\frac{1}{2}$ cups cooked mashed pumpkin
$\frac{1}{4}$ cup honey
$\frac{1}{2}$ tsp. cinnamon
$\frac{1}{4}$ tsp. ginger & nutmeg
2 Tbsp. tapioca flour & $\frac{1}{2}$ tsp. guar gum mixed in 3 Tbsp. water
1 tsp. vanilla extract

In a blender, combine milk, pumpkin, honey and spices until smooth.
Transfer to a saucepan, and bring to a boil over medium-high heat, stirring occasionally.
Reduce heat to medium and cook for 3 minutes, stirring constantly.
Add tapioca mixture and vanilla and stir until thickened, approximately 5-10 minutes.
Pour mixture into a bowl or individual sized serving bowls; chill and let set in the refrigerator.

• Makes about $2\frac{1}{2}$ cups.

Variations
❖ *Replace honey with maple syrup.*
❖ *Replace vanilla with almond or orange extract.*
❖ *Pudding can also be poured into piecrust of choice.*

Vanilla Pudding

(An easy to make delicious creamy pudding)

2½ cups cashew or macadamia nut milk
1/3 cup sucanat
¼ cup tapioca flour
1 Tbsp. lecithin granules
2-3 tsp. guar gum
2 tsp. almond or walnut oil
1 Tbsp. ground flax seeds (optional)
2 tsp. vanilla extract

Combine all ingredients, except vanilla, in a blender until smooth.
Transfer to a saucepan and bring to medium heat, stirring constantly.
Mixture will start to thicken right away but continue to cook until it
starts to boil, stirring constantly.
Remove from heat and stir in vanilla.
Pour mixture into a bowl or individual sized serving bowls; chill and let
set in the refrigerator.

• Makes about 2½ cups.

Variations
❖ *Replace 1 cup nut milk with 1 cup coconut milk.*
❖ *Add ¼-½ cup unsweetened shredded coconut; stir into saucepan*
   after egg mix is added.
❖ *Replace vanilla with almond or orange extract.*
❖ *Pudding can also be poured into piecrust of choice.*

Carob Pudding

(A pudding that is mmm mmm good)

2 cups almond milk
1/3 cup sucanat
¼ cup millet or tapioca flour
¼ cup carob powder
2 Tbsp. ghee or unsalted butter
1 tsp. vanilla

In a saucepan, stir together milk, sucanat, flour and carob powder until well combined.
While stirring, cook over medium heat until thickened, approximately 10 minutes.
Remove from heat and stir in ghee or butter and vanilla.
Pour mixture into a bowl or individual sized serving bowls; chill and let set in the refrigerator.

• Makes about 2½ cups.

Variations
❖ *Replace 1 cup almond milk with 1 cup coconut milk.*
❖ *Add ¼-½ cup unsweetened shredded coconut; stir into saucepan with milk, etc. before cooking.*
❖ *Replace vanilla with almond or orange extract.*
❖ *For **Chocolate Pudding**: replace carob powder with organic (caffeine-free) cocoa powder.*
❖ *Pudding can also be poured into piecrust of choice.*

Ice Milks

All ice milk recipes call for a nut milk or coconut milk. All milks can be substituted with other nut, seed, rice or soy milks. If using seed milks: substitute $\frac{1}{2}$ of the milk with nut, rice or soy milk; or, add a little more sweetener, because straight seed milks tend to be slightly bitter when used alone in 'sweet' recipes. If using purchased milks that are sweetened, adjust sweetener in recipes. Lecithin granules are optional for each recipe, but they act as an emulsifier and will produce a creamier ice milk.

Preparation:
Combine all ingredients in a blender or food processor until smooth. Add more milk if mixture is too thick.

Freezing instructions:
Pour mixture into a metal pan or bowl and freeze until nearly solid. Remove from freezer and beat with an electric mixture or process in a food processor until smooth; refreeze and enjoy.
                    Or
Pour mixture into ice cube trays and freeze until solid. Feed frozen cubes through a juicer with a homogenizing attachment and enjoy or refreeze.
Before second freezing, chopped nuts, carob chips or diced dried fruit can be added.

Serving instructions:
Remove from freezer and allow mixture to soften in the refrigerator, about 30 or more minutes before serving.
Serve ice milks as is, or in bowls with fresh fruit, along with dessert crepes or pies, over pancakes, etc.

Creamscicle Ice Milk

(Make lots, because this one won't last long)

1 ugli (unique) fruit, sectioned
1 small papaya
½ cup almond milk
2-3 Tbsp. honey
1 tsp. vanilla
1 Tbsp. lecithin granules (optional)

Variation
❖ *Replace ½ tsp. vanilla extract with ½ tsp. orange extract.*

Carob Mint Ice Milk

(A nice refreshing treat for a hot summer day)

2 cups cashew or macadamia nut milk
1/3 cup carob powder
¼ cup honey or brown rice syrup
½-1 tsp. peppermint extract
1 Tbsp. ground flaxseeds
½ tsp. vanilla extract (optional)
2 Tbsp. lecithin granules (optional)

Variations
❖ *Add ¼ cup carob chips and/or chopped nuts to second freezing.*
❖ *For **Chocolate Mint Ice Milk**: replace carob powder with organic (caffeine-free) cocoa powder.*

Carob Banana Ice Milk

(A frozen sensation)

3 bananas
1½ cups almond milk
¼ cup carob powder
3-4 Tbsp. honey or brown rice syrup
1 tsp. vanilla
1 Tbsp. lecithin granules (optional)

Variations
* ❖ *Add ¼ cup carob chips and/or chopped nuts to second freezing.*
* ❖ *Replace ¾ cup almond milk with ¾ cup coconut milk.*
* ❖ *For **Chocolate Banana Ice Milk**: replace carob powder with organic (caffeine-free) cocoa powder.*

Lemon Banana Ice Milk

(A tropical treat)

1½ cups cashew or almond milk
3 small bananas
2 Tbsp. fresh lemon juice
1 tsp. lemon extract
pinch or 2 of cinnamon, nutmeg & cardamom
3-4 Tbsp. maple syrup or honey
1 Tbsp. lecithin granules (optional)

Variations
* ❖ *Add 1/3 chopped pecans to second freezing.*
* ❖ *Replace ¾ cup almond milk with ¾ cup coconut milk.*

Raspberry Mango Ice Milk

(An exotic combination)

1 cup raspberries
1 mango
1½ cups almond milk
3-4 Tbsp. honey or brown rice syrup
½ tsp. vanilla extract (optional)
1 Tbsp. lecithin granules (optional)

Berry Deluxe Ice Milk

(A pleasing mix of berries)

2 cups almond milk
½ cup blackberries
½ cup blueberries
½ cup raspberries
½ cup strawberries
3-4 Tbsp. sugar-free cherry jam
1 tsp. vanilla extract
2 Tbsp. lecithin granules (optional)

Variations
* *Add 1/3 chopped nuts and/or dried cherries to second freezing.*
* *Add 3 Tbsp. carob powder.*
* *Replace ½ cup almond milk with ½ cup coconut milk.*

Coconut Peach Ice Milk with Almonds

(A tropical island sensation)

1 cup coconut milk
$\frac{1}{2}$ cup almond milk
$1\frac{1}{2}$ cups mashed peaches (about 4-5)
3-4 Tbsp. maple or brown rice syrup
$\frac{1}{2}$ tsp. vanilla extract
$\frac{1}{2}$ tsp. almond extract
$\frac{1}{2}$ Tbsp. ground flax seeds
2 Tbsp. lecithin granules (optional)

Add 1/3 cup or more chopped almonds to second freezing.

Index

A

Almond butter, 12
Almond Carob Cookies, 276
Almond cheese, 7
Almond milk, 9, 10, 12
Almond oil, 4, 5
Almonds
  Sugar Toasted, 169
  Toasted with Green Beans, 109
Amaranth, 12, 21, 23
Amaranth Banana 'Risotto', 22
Amaranth Pancakes, 43
Amazake, 6
Apple Berry Sauce, 309
Apple Blueberry Butter, 310
Apple cider vinegar, 12
Applesauce Cookies, 280
Arrowroot flour, 12
Arugula, Spinach Salad with
  Raspberries, 102

B

Baked Chili Pasta, 225
Baked Rice Noodles with Pesto, 211
Baking Powder, Gluten-Free, 28
Basic Crepes, 256
Basic Curry Sauce, 154
Basic Egg-Free Pancakes, 43
Basic Tomato Sauce, 159
Barbecue Baked Beans, 233
Barbecue Sauce, 159
Banana

Cake, 290
Cherry Muffins, 286
Rice Flake Muffins, 284
Pudding, 313
Barley Malt, 6
Basmati rice, 16
Beans
  Baked Chili Pasta, 225
  Black Bean Tostadas, 234.
  Barbecue Baked Beans, 233
  Bean Burritos, 262
  Chili, 221
  Chili Pasta, 224
  Chili & Rice Wraps, 255
  Dried, 207, 208-209
  How to cook, 209
  Mixed Bean & Vegetable Salad, 243
  Rice Noodles with Bean Sauce, 220
  Rice Paper Chili Tacos, 250
  Three Bean Chili, 222
  Toasted Cumin & Navy Bean Chili,
   223
  Turkey Burrito Crepes, 262
  Vegetarian Burritos, 262
  Vegetarian Chili, 222
  Vegetarian Chili Pasta, 225
  Veggie Patties, 237
Beet, Creamy Salad, 103
Beet Salad Plus, 103
Belgium Endive Salad, 101
Berry Deluxe Ice Milk, 320
Black Bean Tostadas, 234
Breads, 25-37
  Baking Tips, 25-27
  Brown Rice; with eggs, 29
  Brown Rice; with flax seed, 34

Brown Rice; with gelatin; 37
Millet Rice; with eggs; 30
Multi Grain; with eggs, 32
Multi Grain; with flax seed, 36
Small Loaf Brown Rice; with eggs,
  33
Tapioca Millet; with eggs, 31
Tapioca Millet; with flax seed, 35
Tapioca Rice; with eggs, 31
Tapioca Rice; with flax seed, 35
Breakfast Crepes, 51
  Mexican, 51
Broccoli
  Lemon Salad, 95
  Lentil Soup, 61
  Sour Sauté, 111
Broccoli & Cauliflower Casserole, 118
Broccoli & Cauliflower Pie, 127
Broccoli & English Cucumber Salad, 96
Brown Rice, 16, 23, 206, 207
  Balls, 227
  Bread; with eggs, 29
  Bread; with flax seed, 34
  Bread; with gelatin, 37
  Pasta Primavera, 214
  Small Loaf Bread; with eggs, 33
Brown rice syrup, 6, 12
Buckwheat flour, 12
Butter, 3
Butter, nut & seed, 12
Butternut Squash & Sweet Potato
  Fries, 112
Butyric fatty acid; in butter, 3

C

Cabbage, Tangy Orange Salad, 106
Cakes, 290- 295
  Banana, 290

Carob Carrot, 293
Carob Cheese, 295
Carob Marble, 292
Chocolate Cheese, 295
Lemon, 291
Pumpkin Cheese, 294
Caprylic acid; in coconut, 5
Carob, 12-13
  Banana Ice Milk, 319
  Banana Muffins, 285
  Carrot Cake, 293
  Cheese Cake, 295
  Chip Cookies #1, 273
  Chip Cookies #2, 274
  Frosting, 306
  Marble Cake, 292
  Mint Frosting, 306
  Mint Ice Milk, 318
  Mint Syrup, 304
  Mint Topping, 305
  Nut Topping, 305
  Pudding, 316
  Syrup, 304
Carrot & Tahini Salad, 99
Carrot Lemon Soup, 66
Carrot Salad with Orange Ginger
  Dressing, 99
Casein, 7
Cashew milk, 9
Cauliflower
  Broccoli Casserole, 118
  Broccoli Pie, 127
  Celery Soup, 65
  Roasted Garlic Soup, 63
Cauliflower & Leek Pie with Saffron,
  128
Cajun Fish with Orange Salsa, 200
Cajun Spice, 168
Celery & Cauliflower Soup, 64
Celery & Leek Soup, 64

Celtic sea salt, 2, 13
Cereal Grains, Tips For, 20
Chapattis, 39
Cheese Scones, 48
Cheese & Dairy substitutes, 7, 13
Cheese Tea Biscuits, 49
Cherry Cookies, 277
Chicken
    Coconut Soup, 77
    Lemon Garlic with Basil & Rice
        Noodles, 218
    Roasted Cajun with Vegetables, 182
Chicken & Dumpling Soup, 78
Chicken & Spinach Crepes, 178
Chicken & Vegetables in Rosemary
    Tomato Sauce, 177
Chicken & Vegetables in Rosemary
    Yogurt Sauce, 177
Chicken Curry Stew, 86
Chicken Pot Pie, 180
Chicken Ragu, 193
Chicken Tandoori Wraps, 260
Chicken/Turkey Stock, 57
Chicken with Creamed Spinach, 178
Chicken Vegetable & Rice Noodle
    Casserole, 219
Chickpea Flour, 13
Chili, 221
    Three Bean Chili, 222
    Toasted Cumin & Navy Bean, 223
    Vegetarian, 222
Chili & Rice Wraps, 255
Chili Pasta, 224
    Baked, 225
    Vegetarian, 225
Chocolate Banana Ice Milk, 319
Chocolate Cheese Cake, 295
Chocolate Chip Cookies, 273
Chocolate Frosting, 306
Chocolate Mint Ice Milk, 318

Chocolate Pudding, 316
Chocolate Syrup, 304
Chocolate Topping, 305
Cinnamon Tea Biscuits, 49
Citrus Fish Fillets with Star Anise,
    202
Clarified butter, 4
Coconut
    Nut Butter Sauce, 151, 179
    Tomato Soup, 69
Coconut butter/oil, 4-5
Coconut Chicken Soup, 77
Coconut milk, 9, 11
Coconut Peach Ice Milk with Almonds,
    321
Coleslaw, 106
Conjugated Linoleic Acid (CLA); in
    butter, 3
Cooked Creamy Cereals, 23
Cooked Whole Breakfast Grains, 21
Cookies, 273-283
    Almond Carob, 276
    Applesauce, 280
    Carob Chip #1, 273
    Carob Chip #2, 274
    Cherry, 277
    Chocolate Chip, 273
    Double Carob, 275
    Double Chocolate, 275
    Hazelnut Almond, 276
    Lemon, 278
    Lemon Pecan, 279
    Orange, 278
    Rice Bran, 282
    Rice Crisp, 281
    Rolled Rice, 283
Cornish Hens, Curried, 195
Cream of tartar, 13
Creamscicle Ice Milk, 318
Creamy Beet Salad, 103

Creamy Cucumber Dressing, 141
Creamy Curry Sauce, 154
Creamy Lemon Garlic Sauce, 155
Creamy Pesto, 162
Creamy Pesto with Rosemary, 162
Creamy Salad Dressing, 141
Crepe Crisps, 171
Crepes, 256-265
    Basic, 256-257
    Bean Burritos, 262
    Breakfast, 51
    Chicken, 258
    Chicken & Spinach, 178
    Chicken Tandoori Wraps, 260
    Curried Lamb Wraps, 261
    Curried Vegetable Wraps, 261
    Dessert, 257
    Grilled Vegetable, 263
    Herb Chicken, 259
    Herb Vegetable, 259
    Mexican Breakfast, 51
    Mixed Fruit, 301
    Turkey Burritos, 262
    Turkey Club, 265
    Vegetable, 259
    Vegetable Korma, 264
    Vegetarian burritos, 262
Crispy Rice Noodles, 169
Crusted Quiche, 50
Crust-less Quiche, 50
Cucumber
    Broccoli Salad, 96
    Creamy dressing, 141
    Mango Salad, 97
Cucumber & Tomato Salad, 98
Cucumber & Tomato Salsa, 164
Curried Cornish Hens, 195
Curried Lamb Wraps, 261
Curried Lentils, 235

Curried Squash & Sweet Potato Soup, 68
Curried Vegetarian Wraps, 261
Curry Marinade, 146, 204
Curry Meatballs, 188

D

Date sugar, 6
Desserts, Tips, 272
Dips, 148-150
    Hazelnut Butter, 150
    Onion & Yogurt Cheese, 148
    Roasted Garlic, 148
    Roasted Red Pepper, 149
Double Carob Cookies, 275
Double Chocolate Cookies, 275
Dressings; see Salad Dressings
Dried fruit, 8
Duck
    Orange Ginger Roasted, 197
    Roasted Garlic Breasts, 196
    Roasted Mushroom Soup, 84
Dumpling
    Chicken Soup, 78
    Vegetable Soup, 78
Dumplings
    Rosemary, 78, 133
    Spinach, 132

E

Egg substitute, 13
Emu, meat, 13
Extracts, 7

F

Fats & Oils, 4
Fennel
  How to roast, 167
  in Roasted Vegetable Sauce, 156
  Roasted, with Tomato Sauce, 122
  Roasted, Tarragon Turkey with
    Tomatoes, 185
Fish, 198-204
  Cajun with Orange Salsa, 200
  Citrus Fillets with Star Anise, 202
  Fillets with Roasted Vegetable
    Sauce, 199
  Fillets with Tomatoes, Fennel &
    Saffron, 198
  Grilled Curried Steaks, 204
  Roast Salmon with Asian Sauce, 201
  Steaks with Teriyaki, 203
  Tips, 174-175
Flakes
  Quinoa, 13
  Rice, 13
  Soy, 13
Flatbread Crisps, 170
Flatbreads, 38-40
  Chickpea, 39
  Millet, 39
  Millet & Hempseed, 40
  Quinoa, 39
  Quinoa & Hempseed, 40
  Rice, 38
  Rice & Hempseed, 40
Flax seed oil, 4-5, 14
Flaxseeds, 13
French Leek Soup, 70
Fresh Tomato Sauce, 161
Fried Zucchini Lasagna, 126
Frostings, 306
  Carob, 306
  Carob Mint, 306

Chocolate, 306
Fructose, 6
Fruit Berry Crisp, 299
Fruit Berry Sauce, 308
Fudge, 300

G

Garam Masala, 14, 168
Garden Vegetable Soup, 73
Garlic Caesar Dressing, 142
Garlic French Dressing, 140
Garlic Lemon Sauce, 155
Garlic, roasted;
  Caesar Dressing, 142
  Cauliflower Soup, 63
  Dip, 148
  Duck Breasts, 199
  How to roast, 167
  Leek Soup, 62
  Squash Gratin, 121
  Tomato Sauce, 160
  Turkey Soup, 81
  Winter Salsa, 166
  Vegetable Sauce, 156
Gelatin, in bread, 27
Ghee, 4-5
Gluten-Free Baking Powder, 28
Goat's milk cheese, 7, 14
Goat's milk yogurt, 7, 14
Grains, Breakfast Cereal, 20-24
Grains, Tips, 206-207
Granola, 46
Green Beans & Toasted Almonds, 109
Grilled Curried Fish Steaks, 204
Grilled Rosemary Venison with
  Roasted Vegetable Sauce, 191
Grilled Vegetable Lasagna, 124
Grilled Vegetable Salad, 107

327

Grilled Veggie Wraps, 263
Grilling Marinade, 116, 146
Guar gum, 14

H

Hazelnut Almond Cookies, 276
Hazelnut Butter dip, 150
Hempseed oil, 4, 5, 14
Hemp seeds, 14
   Flour, 14
Herb Chicken Crepes, 259
Herb Dressing, 137
Herb Meatballs, 193
Herbs & Spices, 2
Herb Tea Biscuits, 49
Herb Vegetable Crepes, 259
Herb Vegetable Pie, 131
Honey, 6
Honey & Garlic Grilled Lamb Chops,
   189
Honey leaf, 6
Hot & Sour Soup, 75

I

Ice Milks, 317-321
   Berry Deluxe, 320
   Carob Banana, 319
   Carob Mint, 318
   Chocolate Banana, 318
   Chocolate Mint, 319
   Coconut peach with Almonds, 321
   Creamscicle, 318
   Instructions, 317
   Lemon Banana, 319
   Raspberry Mango, 320
Irradiation: in food, 1, 2, 10

Island Millet, 232
Italian Dressing, 239

J

Jam Squares, 297
Just Greens Soup, 59

K

Kelp, 2, 15

L

Lauric fatty acid; in butter, 3
   in coconut, 5
Lamb & Sweet Potato Curry, 190
Lamb & Vegetable Soup, 82
Lamb Chops, Honey & Garlic, 189
Lasagna
   Fried Zucchini, 126
   Grilled Vegetable, 124
   Mexican, 215
   Sweet & Red Potato, 216
Lecithin Granules, 15
   in bread, 27, 29, 34
Leek
   Celery Soup, 64
   Cauliflower Pie with Saffron, 128
   French Soup, 70
   Roasted Garlic Soup, 62
Leeks, Sweet & Sour, 110
Legumes, Tips, 206-207
Lemon Banana Ice Milk, 319
Lemon Broccoli Salad, 95
Lemon Cake, 291
Lemon Cookies, 278
Lemon Dill Dressing, 137

Lemon Dill Meatballs, 187
Lemon Garlic Chicken with Basil & Rice
  Noodles, 218
Lemon Garlic Sauce, 155
Lemon Garlic Spaghetti squash, 115
Lemon Ginger Dressing, 138
Lemon/Lime Ginger Marinade, 145
Lemon Pecan Cookies, 279
Lemon Yogurt Sauce, 307
Lentil & Broccoli Soup, 61
Lentils, 15, 207, 208
  Curried, 235
  Sweet & Sour, 236
Lentil, Vegetable Soup, 71
Liquid Aminos, 7, 15

M

Macadamia nut butter, 15
Macadamia nut oil, 4, 5, 15
Macaroni & Cheese Bake, 210
Mango & English Cucumber Salad, 97
Maple Sugar, 6
Maple Syrup, 6
Marinades
  Curry, 146
  Grilling, 147
  Honey & Garlic, 189
  Lemon/Lime Ginger, 145
  Orange Teriyaki, 145
  Tandoori, 146, 153
  Teriyaki, 145, 203
  Rosemary, 191
Meatballs
  Curry, 188
  Herb, 187
  Lemon Dill, 187
  Turkey Vegetable Stew, 89
Meat

Basic Stock, 57
  Tips, 174-175
Meatloaf
  Rice, 228
  Sweet Potato, 192
Meat Tomato Sauce, 160
Mexican Breakfast Crepes, 51
Mexican Lasagna, 215
Milk substitutes, 9-11
  How to make, 9
Millet, 15, 21, 23, 208
  Creamy, with Cherries, 24
  Flatbreads, 39
  Hempseed, flatbreads, 40
  Island, 232
  Rice Bread; with eggs, 30
  Tapioca Bread; with eggs, 30
  Tapioca Bread; with flax seed, 35
Millet & Saffron Risotto, 230
Millet & Tomato Risotto, 229
Millet Pudding, 312
Millet Stuffing, 238
Millet Vegetable Risotto, 231
Mint Pesto, 105
Miso, 15
  in soup, 54
Mixed Bean & Vegetable Salad, 243
Mixed Fruit Crepes, 301
Mixed Vegetable & Pesto Salad with
  Mint, 105
Mixed Vegetable Bake, 120
Molasses, 6
Muffins, 284-289
  Banana Cherry, 286
  Banana Rice Flake, 284
  Carob Banana. 285
  Pumpkin, 288
  Pumpkin Orange, 289
  Quinoa Banana, 284
  Raspberry, 287

Multi Grain Bread; with eggs, 32
Multi Grain Bread; with flax seed, 36
Mushroom Gravy, 163
Mushroom, Roasted Duck Soup, 84

N

Nut Butter & Coconut Sauce, 151, 179
Nut Milks, 9-11
  How to make, 9
Nuts, 10, 11
  in Bread, 27

O

Okra & Tomato Soup, 60
Olive oil, 4, 5
Onion & Yogurt Cheese Dip, 148
Orange Cookies, 278
Orange Ginger Dressing, 143
  with Cabbage Salad, 106
  with Carrot Salad, 99
Orange Ginger Roasted Duck, 197
Orange Salsa, 200
Orange Teriyaki Marinade, 145
Orange Yogurt Sauce, 307

P

Pancakes, 41-45
  Amaranth, 44
  Breakfast, 43
  Egg-Free, 43
  Pumpkin, 45
  Rice flatbreads, 41
  Sweet Potato, 45
Papaya Salsa, 165

Pasta
  Baked Rice Noodles with Pesto, 211
  Brown Rice Primavera, 214
  Chicken Vegetable & Rice Noodle
    Casserole, 219
  Chili Pasta, 224
  Lemon Garlic Chicken with Basil &
    Rice Noodles, 218
  Macaroni & Cheese Bake, 210
  Mexican Lasagna, 215
  Rice Noodles with Bean Sauce, 220
  Roasted Vegetables & Rice Noodles,
    213
  Spaghetti Pie, 217
  Spaghetti Salad 'Asian Style' 240
  Spaghetti Salad 'Italian Style' 239
  Sweet & Red Potato Lasagna, 216
  Tips, 206
  Turkey & Roasted Vegetable
    Casserole, 226
Peanut Butter & Papaya Bars, 298
Pear, Radicchio Salad, 100
Pesto
  Baked Rice Noodles, 211
  Creamy, 162
  Creamy with Rosemary, 162
  Mint, 105
  Mixed Vegetable Salad with Mint,
    105
Pie Crusts, 266-269
  Potato, 266
  Rice & Almond, 269
  Rice & Hazelnut, 269
  Rice Crisp, 268
  Rice Flour, 267
  Sweet Potato, 266
Pies
  Chicken, 180
  Spaghetti, 217
  Vegetable Pot, 181

Pies, Vegetable, 127-131
  Broccoli & Cauliflower, 127
  Cauliflower & Leek with Saffron, 128
  Curry Vegetable, 130
  Herb Vegetable, 131
  Pot Pie, 181
  Spinach, 129
Potassium Broth, 58
Potato; also see sweet
Potato Pie Crust, 266
Potatoes
  Roasted Pesto, 113
  Sweet & Red, Lasagna, 216
  Sweet & Red Scalloped with Saffron, 113
Poultry, Tips, 174-175
Primavera Tomato Sauce, 160
Puddings, 311-316
  Banana, 313
  Carob, 316
  Chocolate, 316
  Millet, 312
  Pumpkin, 314
  Rice, 311
  Vanilla, 315
Pumpkin & Squash Soup, 67
  with Sage & Apples, 67
Pumpkin Cheese Cake, 294
Pumpkin Muffins, 288
Pumpkin Orange Muffins, 289
Pumpkin Pancakes, 45
Pumpkin Pudding, 314
Pumpkin seed
  butter, 15, 16
  milk, 9
  oil, 4,5, 16
Pumpkin, Turkey Vegetable Soup, 79

Q

Quiche, Crusted, 50
  Crust-less, 50
Quick & Creamy Tomato Curry Sauce, 161
Quick & Creamy Tomato Sauce, 161
Quinoa, 16, 20, 21, 23, 206, 208
Quinoa Banana Muffins, 284
Quinoa, Flatbreads, 39
Quinoa flakes, 13, 23
Quinoa & Hempseed Flatbreads, 40
Quinoa Salad, 242

R

Rabbit Ragu, 194
Rabbit Vegetable with Saffron Soup, 83
Radicchio & Pear Salad, 100
Raspberry Banana Muffins, 287
Raspberry Dressing, 144
Raspberry Mango Ice Milk, 320
Raspberry, Spinach Salad, 102
Red pepper, roasted;
  Dip, 149
  How to roast, 167
  Tomato sauce, 160
  Vegetable sauce, 156
Rice, 19, see also brown rice, wild rice
  Basmati, 16
  Brown, 16, 206, 207
  Sweet Brown, 16, 23
  Wild, 16, 206, 207
Rice & Almond Pie Crust, 269
Rice & Hazelnut Pie Crust, 269
Rice & Hempseed Flatbreads, 40
Rice Bran Cookies, 282

Rice breads;
  Brown, with eggs, 29
  Brown, with flax seed, 34
  Brown, with gelatin, 37
  Millet, with eggs, 30
  Small Loaf Brown, 33
  Tapioca, with eggs, 31
  Tapioca, with flax seed, 35
Rice Cheese, 7
Rice Crisp Cookies, 281
Rice Crisp Pie Crust, 268
Rice Crisp Squares, 296
Rice Crispy Noodles, 169
Rice flakes, 13, 21
Rice Flatbreads, 38
Rice Flour Pie Crust, 267
Rice Meatloaf, 228
Rice milk, 11
Rice Noodles with Bean Sauce, 220
Rice Pancake Flatbreads, 41
Rice paper, wraps, 246
  Bean Burritos, 262
  Chicken Tandoori, 260
  Chili & Rice, 255
  Chili Tacos, 250
  Curried Lamb, 261
  Curried Vegetarian, 261
  Enchiladas, 254
  Grilled Veggie, 263
  Rolled Squash Surprise, 253
  Samosas, 248
  Spring Rolls, 249
  Turkey Burritos, 262
  Vegetarian Burritos, 262
  Vegetarian Enchiladas, 254
  Vegetarian Manicotti, 251
Rice, pasta, 15
Rice Pudding, 311
Roasted Cajun Chicken & Vegetables,
  182

Roasted Duck & Mushroom Soup, 84
Roasted Fennel with Tomato Sauce,
  124
Roasted Garlic & Cauliflower Soup, 63
Roasted Garlic & Leek Soup, 62
Roasted Garlic & Turkey Soup, 81
Roasted Garlic Caesar Dressing, 142
Roasted Garlic Duck Breasts, 196
Roasted Garlic Squash Gratin, 121
Roasted Garlic Tomato Sauce, 160
Roasted Garlic Winter Salsa, 166
Roasted Pesto Potatoes, 113
Roasted Red Pepper Dip, 149
Roasted Red Pepper Tomato Sauce,
  160
Roasted Root Vegetables, 114
Roasted Tofu with Asian Sauce, 201
Roasted Vegetables & Rice Noodles,
213
Roasted Vegetable Sauce, 156
  with Fish fillets, 199
  with Grilled Rosemary Venison, 191
  with Tofu, 199
Roasted Vegetable, Turkey Casserole,
  226
  Tofu Casserole, 226
Roast Salmon with Asian Sauce, 201
Rolled, rice, 16, 23
  soy, 16, 23
Rolled Rice Cookies, 283
Rolled Squash Surprise, 253
Rosemary Dumplings, 78
Rosemary Marinade, 191

S

Safflower, threads, 16
Saffron
  Rabbit Vegetable Soup, 83

Cauliflower & Leek Pie, 128
Fish Fillets with Tomatoes & Fennel,
   198
Millet Risotto, 230
Scalloped Sweet & Red Potatoes,
   117
Tofu with Tomatoes & Fennel, 198
Turkey Stew, 87
Saffron, threads, 16
Salads & Vegetables, Tips, 93
Salad Dressings 137-144
  Asian, 238
  Creamy, 141
  Creamy Cucumber, 141
  Garlic Caesar, 142
  Garlic French, 140
  Herb, 137
  Italian, 239
  Lemon Dill, 137
  Lemon Ginger, 138
  Orange Ginger, 143
  Raspberry, 144
  Roasted Garlic Caesar, 142
  Tahini, 99
  Thousand Island, 139
  Tips for, 136
  Toasted Cumin, 243
Salads, Vegetable, 95-107
Salads, 95-107, 239-243
  Beet Plus, 103
  Belgium Endive, 101
  Broccoli & English Cucumber, 96
  Carrot & Tahini, 99
  Carrot with Orange Ginger Dressing,
   99
  Creamy Beet, 103
  Cucumber & Tomato, 98
  Grilled Vegetable, 107
  Lemon Broccoli, 95
  Mango & English Cucumber, 97

Mixed Bean & Vegetable, 243
Mixed Vegetable & Pesto with Mint,
   105
Quinoa, 242
Radicchio & Pear, 100
Spaghetti, 'Asian Style', 240
Spaghetti, 'Italian Style', 239
Spinach & Arugula with Raspberries,
   102
Sweet Potato, 104
Sweet Potato with Tarragon
   Vinaigrette, 104
Wild Rice & Vegetable, 241
Salmon, Roast with Asian Sauce, 201
Salsa
  Cucumber & Tomato, 164
  Orange, 200
  Papaya, 165
  Roasted Garlic Winter, 166
Salt & Pepper, 2
Sauces, 151-163
  Apple Berry, 309
  Asian, 201
  Barbecue, 158
  Basic Curry, 154
  Basic Tomato, 159
  Creamy Curry, 154
  Creamy Lemon Garlic, 155
  Creamy Pesto, 162
  Fresh Tomato, 161
  Fruit Berry, 308
  Lemon Garlic, 155
  Lemon Yogurt, 307
  Mushroom Gravy, 163
  Nut Butter & Coconut, 151
  Orange Yogurt, 307
  Quick & Creamy Tomato, 161
  Quick & Creamy Tomato Curry, 161
  Roasted Garlic Tomato, 160
  Roasted Red Pepper Tomato, 160

Roasted Vegetable, 156
  Sweet & sour, 157
  Tahini, 152
  Tandoori, 153
Scalloped Sweet & Red Potatoes with
  Saffron, 117
Scones, 47
  Cheese, 48
Sea salt, 2, 17
Seed milks, 9-11
  how to make, 9
Seeds, 10, 11
  in bread, 27
Sesame oil, 4, 5
Sesame seed milk, 9, 17
Sloppy Joes, 186
Small Loaf Brown Rice Bread, 33
Sorghum, 6
Soups, 59-84
  Carrot Lemon, 66
  Celery & Cauliflower, 65
  Celery & Leek, 64
  Chicken & Dumpling, 78
  Coconut, Chicken, 77
  Curried Squash & Sweet Potato, 68
  French Leek, 70
  Garden Vegetable, 73
  Hot & Sour, 75
  Just Greens, 59
  Lamb & Vegetable, 82
  Lentil & Broccoli, 61
  Okra & Tomato, 60
  Pumpkin & Squash, 67
  with Sage & Apples, 67
  Rabbit Vegetable with Saffron, 83
  Roasted Duck & Mushroom, 84
  Roasted Garlic & Cauliflower, 63
  Roasted Garlic & Leek, 62
  Roasted Garlic & Turkey, 81
  Tips for, 54

Tomato Coconut, 69
Turkey Chowder, 76
Turkey Noodle, 80
Turkey Vegetable & Pumpkin, 79
Vegetable & Dumpling, 78
Vegetable & Wild Rice, 74
Vegetable Curry, 72
Vegetable Lentil, 71
Soup, stocks, 55-57
  chicken/turkey, 57
  meat, 57
  vegetable, 56
Sour Broccoli Sauté, 111
Soy cheese, 7
  flakes, 13, 23
  milk, 11
  sauce, 7
  yogurt, 7
Spaghetti Pie, 217
Spaghetti Salad 'Asian Style', 240
Spaghetti Salad 'Italian Style', 239
Spiced Turkey & Vegetable Stew, 88
Spinach
  Chicken Crepes, 178
  Creamed with Chicken, 178
Spinach Dumplings, 132
Spinach Pie, 129
Spinach & Arugula Salad with
  Raspberries, 102
Split peas, 208
Squash, baking, 115
  Butternut & Sweet Potato Fries, 112
  Curried Sweet Potato Soup, 68
  Curried Sweet Potato Soup with
    Sage & Apples, 68
  Lemon Garlic Spaghetti, 115
  Pumpkin Soup, 67
  Pumpkin Soup with sage & Apples,
    67
  Roasted Garlic Gratin, 121

Rolled, Surprise, 253
   Spaghetti & Turkey Parmigiana, 183
Stevia, 6
Stews, 85-90
   Chicken Curry, 86
   Spiced Turkey & Vegetable, 88
   Tips for, 54
   Turkey Meatball & Vegetable, 89
   Turkey Saffron, 87
   Vegetable Curry, 86
   Venison, 90
   Winter Vegetable, 85
Stocks, soup, 55-57
   Chicken/Turkey, 57
   Meat, basic, 57
   Vegetable, basic, 56
Sucanat, 6, 17
Sugar, raw, 6
Sugar Toasted Almonds, 169
Sweet & Red Potato Lasagna, 216
Sweet & Sour Leeks, 110
Sweet & Sour Lentils, 236
Sweet & Sour Sauce, 157
Sweet brown rice, 16, 23
Sweeteners, 6
Sweet Potato
   Butternut Squash Fries, 112
   Lamb Curry, 190
   Scalloped Red Potatoes with
     Saffron, 117
   Tofu Curry, 190
Sweet Potato & Rutabaga Bake, 119
Sweet Potato Casserole, 212
Sweet Potato Meatloaf, 190
Sweet Potato Pancakes, 45
Sweet Potato Pie Crust, 266
Sweet Potato Salad, 104
   with Tarragon Vinaigrette, 104
Sweets, Tips for, 272
Syrups, 304

Carob, 304
Carob Mint, 304
Chocolate, 304

T

Tandoori Sauce, 153
Tangy Orange Cabbage Salad, 106
Tahini, 17
   Carrot Salad, 99
   Dressing, 99
   Sauce, 152
Tamari, 7
Tandoori Marinade, 146, 153
Tandoori Sauce, 153
Tapioca flour, 17, 28
Tapioca
   Millet Bread; with eggs, 31
   Millet Bread; with flax seed, 35
   Rice Bread; with eggs, 31
   Rice bread; with flax seed, 35
Tarragon Turkey with Roasted Fennel
   & Tomatoes, 185
Tea Biscuits
   Cheese, 49
   Cinnamon, 49
   Herb, 49
Teriyaki Marinade, 145
   with Fish Steaks, 203
Teriyaki Tofu, 203
Thousand Island Dressing, 139
Three Bean Chili, 222
Toasted Cumin & Navy Bean Chili, 223
Tofu, 17
Tofu & Roasted Vegetable Casserole,
   226
Tofu & Sweet Potato Curry, 190
Tofu, Roasted with Asian Sauce, 201
Tofu Sloppy Joes, 186

Tofu, Teriyaki, 203
Tofu Tomato Sauce, 160
Tofu with Roasted Vegetable Sauce, 199
Tofu with Tomatoes, Fennel & Saffron, 198
Tomato Coconut Soup, 69
Tomato
  Cucumber Salad, 98
  Cucumber Salsa, 164
Tomato Sauce, Basic, 159
  Fresh, 161
  Meat, 160
  Primavera, 160
  Quick & Creamy, 161
    Curry, 161
  Roasted Garlic, 160
  Roasted Red Pepper, 160
  Tofu, 160
Toppings, 305
  Carob Nut, 305
  Carob Mint, 305
  Chocolate, 305
Turkey
  Chili, 221
  Chili Pasta, 224
  Roasted Garlic Soup, 81
  Spiced Vegetable Stew, 88
  Tarragon, with Roasted Fennel & Tomatoes, 185
Turkey & Roasted Vegetable Casserole, 226
Turkey & Spaghetti Squash Parmigiana, 183
Turkey Biryani, 184
Turkey Burrito Crepes, 262
Turkey Chowder, 76
Turkey Club Crepes, 265
Turkey Meatball & Vegetable Stew, 89

Turkey Noodle Soup, 80
Turkey Saffron Stew, 87
Turkey Strips, 176
Turkey Vegetable & Pumpkin Soup, 79
Turkey with Nut Butter & Coconut Sauce, 179

V

Vanilla Pudding, 315
Vegetable & Dumpling Soup, 78
Vegetable & Wild Rice Soup, 74
Vegetable, Basic Stock, 56
Vegetable Crepes, 259
Vegetable Curry Pie, 130
Vegetable Curry Soup, 72
Vegetable Curry Stew, 86
Vegetable dishes, 109-131
  Broccoli & Cauliflower Casserole, 118
  Broccoli & Cauliflower Pie, 127
  Butternut Squash & Sweet Potato Fries, 112
  Cauliflower & Leek Pie with Saffron, 128
  Fried Zucchini Lasagna, 126
  Green Beans & Toasted Almonds, 109
  Grilled Vegetable Lasagna, 124
  Herb Vegetable Pie, 131
  Lemon Garlic Spaghetti Squash, 115
  Mixed Vegetable Bake, 120
  Roasted Garlic Squash Gratin, 118
  Roasted Fennel with Tomato Sauce, 121
  Roasted Pesto Potatoes, 113
  Roasted Root Vegetables, 114
  Scalloped Sweet & Red Potatoes with Saffron, 117
  Sour Broccoli Sauté, 111

Spinach Pie, 129
Sweet & Sour Leeks, 110
Sweet Potato & Rutabaga Bake, 119
Vegetable Curry Pie, 130
Vegetable Gratin, 123
Vegetable Pakora, 116
Vegetable Korma Crepes, 264
Vegetable Lentil Soup, 71
Vegetable Manicotti Wraps, 251
Vegetable Pakora, 116
Vegetable Pot Pie, 181
Vegetarian Burritos, 262
Vegetarian Chili, 222
Vegetarian Chili Pasta, 225
Vegetarian Chili Tacos, 250
Vegetarian Enchiladas, 254
Vegetarian Spring Rolls, 249
Veggie Patties, 237
Venison
    Grilled with Rosemary & Roasted
    Vegetable Sauce, 191
Venison Stew, 90

How to make, 148
Onion Dip, 148
Roasted Garlic Dip, 148
Roasted Red Pepper Dip, 149

Z

Zucchini, Fried Lasagna, 126

W

Walnut oil, 4, 15
Wild rice, 16, 206, 207
Wild Rice & Vegetable Salad, 241
Wild Rice, Vegetable Soup, 74
Wine, 8
Winter Vegetable Stew, 85
Wraps
    Rice paper, 246-265
    Crepes, 256-265

Y

Yogurt cheese, 148

ISBN 155395019-4